HITLER

and the Final Solution

HAMISH HAMILTON

LONDON

First published in Great Britain 1985
by Hamish Hamilton Ltd
Garden House 57-59 Long Acre
London WC2E 9JZ

Originally published as *Hitler und die
Endlösung: "Es ist der Führers Wunsch
..."* ©1982 by Gerald Fleming

ISBN 0-241-11388-1

Printed in the United States
of America
1 2 3 4 5 6 7 8 9

HITLER

and the Final Solution

Contents

v

Contents

Introduction

Gerald Fleming's *Hitler and the Final Solution* is an unconventional and important book. It is unconventional in its structure; although it follows a broad chronological pattern, each of the twenty-three chapters takes a new, unexpected direction, and at each step the landscape of death is presented from an angle the readers could not have prepared themselves for. Some of the most important material reappears in various places, like the recurrent theme of a nightmare. Such a structure, more akin to literary than historical discourse, is puzzling at first, but it gives the book its full impact.

The initial impetus for writing *Hitler and the Final Solution* seems to have come from British historian David Irving's thesis that Hitler was not aware of the extermination of the Jews of Europe, at least until 1943.[1] According to Irving, this extermination was planned and implemented in great part by Heinrich Himmler and the SS without Hitler's knowledge. If it were to be proven, this thesis would substantially change our image of Nazism. Irving's revisionist claim was controverted long before Fleming's book, but Fleming settles the case once and for all. Fleming has gathered and analyzed a vast amount of evidence concerning

1. David Irving, *Hitler's War* (London, 1977).

Hitler's knowledge of and involvement in the Final Solution; and he is the first to have done so on such a scale.

In his research Gerald Fleming used most of the published sources, from well-known documents presented during the Nuremberg trials to seldom-quoted information from trials of the sixties and the seventies. He combed Western archives and gained access to Soviet archives in Riga—a rare feat. This investigation brought to light unexpected details. Finally, the primary sources were augmented and interpreted through painstaking written inquiries that reached little-known, although well-informed, participants in the events. Every historian is something of a detective; Gerald Fleming has proven himself a master in that line.

Of course, some critics may find fault with using as evidence testimonies given thirty-five or more years after the events. How would anybody recall the exact terms of an order, a discussion, or a speech after so many years? To this possible argument I see two obvious answers. First, the events were so unusual that those in any way involved would doubtless remember them with much greater precision than they would more recent, but ordinary, events. Second, the testimonies tally with the documents; they bolster the author's demonstration but are not the basis of it.

Hitler and the Final Solution is important not only as a documentary achievement, but also as a timely resource in the growing debate among historians of Nazism. The debate opposes two interpretations of the Nazi system, which may apply to the interpretation of Nazi policies toward the Jews and of the Final Solution in particular. It is an important debate, and in my opinion, Fleming's book will play a major role in the arguments for or against each position. Let me try to show the significance of the debate and the meaning of Fleming's work in that context.

From the end of the sixties on, the traditional interpretation of National Socialism has been increasingly challenged. Recently the term "intentionalist" was appended to the traditional school, the term "functionalist" to the new wave.[2] The debate, limited for a long time to German historians, is now spreading. Although theoretical issues are central, the arguments on both sides are not devoid of moral undertones: the functionalists, for instance, have been accused of banalizing National Socialism; the intentionalists, of concentrating all responsibility on Adolf Hitler.

For the intentionalists, there is a direct relation between Hitler's ideology and Nazi policies; there were initial aims and once the Nazis came to power, steps were taken systematically to implement those aims. And the absolute centrality of Adolf Hitler within the system appears so obvious to the intentionalists that, according to Hildebrand, "one should not speak of National Socialism, but of Hitlerism."[3]

The functionalists, on the other hand, feel that there is no necessary relationship between the ideological dogmas of Nazism and the policies of the Third Reich; that decisions are functionally linked to one another and do not follow a preestablished plan; that the constant interaction and the constant pressures exercised by multiple agencies within

2. The terms were coined by Tim Mason in his "Intention and Explanation: A Current Controversy about the Interpretation of National-Socialism," in *Der Führerstaat: Mythos und Realität*, ed. Gerhard Hirschfeld and Lothar Kettenacker (Stuttgart, 1981). These labels are useful to clarify the issues, but one should remain aware of their normalizing effect and not forget the nature of the events beneath such abstractions. See my own *Reflections of Nazism: An Essay on Kitsch and Death* (New York, 1984) on the normalizing effect of historical discourse concerning the Final Solution.

3. For a detailed presentation of Klaus Hildebrand's position, see his "Monokratie oder Polykratie? Hitlers Herrschaft und das Dritte Reich," in *Der Führerstaat: Mythos und Realität*, ed. Hirschfeld and Kettenacker, 75ff.

the system necessarily limit the role of the central decision-maker; and that his decisions take the aspect of a planned policy with clear aims only through the artifices of propaganda or, for the historian, in retrospect.

The difference between these two groups is manifest in their contradictory interpretations of the genesis and implementation of Nazi policies toward the Jews. For the intentionalists, there is a straight line from Hitler's anti-Semitic ideology of the twenties (as expressed in his early speeches, his dialogue with Dietrich Eckart, and *Mein Kampf*) to the policies of the Third Reich and all the way to the Final Solution:

> Whether or not it is possible to establish a link between the gas war of the First World War and the gas chambers of the Second World War, it is sure that Hitler's anti-Semitism, as it is presented in *Mein Kampf*, was determined by war. It was born from the war, it needed warlike methods, and it came to its ultimate realization in wartime. It was therefore logical that this anti-Semitism should find in the next war, which, in any case, was foreseen from the very beginning, its bloody culmination.[4]

We find this clear link between Hitler's early anti-Semitic ideology and his later anti-Semitic practice posited in the writings of Helmut Krausnick, Ernst Nolte, Eberhard Jäckel, Karl Dietrich Bracher, Klaus Hildebrand, and Andreas Hillgruber, to mention only German historians.[5] In this and every other respect Gerald Fleming would be considered a straight intentionalist, an ultra-intentionalist in fact. At the very beginning of his study, the relation between

4. Eberhard Jäckel, *Hitlers Weltanschauung*, 2d ed. (Stuttgart, 1981), 71–72.

5. Most non-German historians of Nazi anti-Semitism may be considered intentionalists, with the clear exception of Karl A. Schleunes; his *Twisted Road to Auschwitz: Nazi Policy Towards the German Jews, 1933–1939* (Urbana, Ill., 1970) is perhaps the first comprehensive functionalist presentation of Nazi policies during the thirties toward the Jews.

Hitler's early anti-Semitic ideology and the ultimate extermination orders is stressed in no uncertain terms:

> The line that leads from these early manifestations to
> the liquidation orders that Hitler personally issued during
> the war—the actual target of this investigation—is a di-
> rect one. A sample taken from Hitler's utterances over the
> years reveals this striking continuity: Hitler's remark to
> his childhood friend, August Kubizek, as the two passed
> the small synagogue in the Bethlehemstrasse in Linz,
> "That does not belong here in Linz"; Hitler's unshakable
> conviction that "the Jews had continued to perform ritual
> murders" up to the most recent past; the Führer's state-
> ment on 21 October 1941, at noon in the Führer's Head-
> quarters, preserved in a memorandum signed by Martin
> Bormann: "When we finally stamp out this plague, we
> shall have accomplished for mankind a deed whose sig-
> nificance our men out there on the battlefield cannot even
> imagine yet"; and Hitler's assertion four days later, in the
> presence of Himmler and Heydrich: "It is good that we
> are preceded by an aura of terror for our plans to extermi-
> nate Jewry." This unbroken continuity of explicit utter-
> ances was reflected in a more or less tacit continuity of
> deeds. Hitler's anti-Semitism in his Linz years (1904–
> 1907) was followed by his introduction into the Viennese
> "Antisemitenbund" (Anti-Semite Association) in April
> 1908. Much later, but still to be ranged along the same
> continuum, were the first shootings of German Jews in
> Fort IX in Kovno on 25 November 1941 and in the Rumbuli
> Forest outside Riga on 30 November 1941 at 8:15 A.M.
> (pp. 2–3 below)

Few historians, even among the staunchest intentionalists, would accept such an extreme linear thesis. But
even if the intermediary stages between Hitler's early anti-
Semitism and his final policies toward the Jews were numerous and complex, Fleming's position is helpful on one
essential point: it reminds us of the implacable aspect of
Hitler's anti-Semitism, of its deep and early roots, as well as

of its obsessional character. To deny that it was a factor in the later extermination policies needs more explanation than to declare it a major impetus.

To prove their point, the intentionalists can show the clear and rapid succession of stages in Nazi anti-Jewish policies (as well as in other fields, foreign policy being perhaps the most telling example): "The National Socialist program called for the disenfranchisement of all Jews; anti-Semitic activities were part of its early history. Once in power, the Nazis began the systematic organization of the persecution of Jews. No tactical considerations were allowed to interfere substantially with instituting the boycott of Jews, expelling them from public life, making them subject to special laws, and finally annihilating them."[6]

In addition to viewing a continuity between Hitler's ideology and his policies and pointing to a quick succession of stages, the intentionalists sometimes assume technical planning. For instance, the euthanasia program at the beginning of the war could represent a technical preparation for the Final Solution; in any case, killing by gas on a small scale certainly led to the idea of mass extermination by gas: "The method that was later used for the mass extermination of Jews by gas was then tried from the very beginning of 1940, during the extermination of people interned in psychiatric institutions, within the framework of the action called 'T4.'"[7] Here too Gerald Fleming takes an extreme position:

> A straight path leads from the built-in gas chambers of the euthanasia institutes in Brandenburg, Bensburg, Grafeneck, Hartheim, Hadamar, Sonnenstein, and Eichberg to the extermination camp in Sobibor, under SS-Major Christian Wirth, formerly of the euthanasia institute

6. Karl Dietrich Bracher, *The German Dictatorship* (London, 1979), 252.
7. Ino Arndt and Wolfgang Scheffler, "Organisierter Massenmord an Juden in Nationalsozialistischen Vernichtungslagern," *Vierteljahrshefte für Zeitgeschichte*, 24 (1976): 112.

in Brandenburg. In the euthanasia institutes German victims—chiefly mental patients—were "quickly and quietly" eliminated with carbon-monoxide gas; and already in June 1940 the practice of pilfering gold-filled teeth from the corpses of the Jewish victims among them had begun. At Sobibor, identical liquidation procedures, along with the same despoliation of Jewish corpses, were the order of the day. (p. 24 below)

Strangely enough, although Gerald Fleming deals with every minute aspect of Hitler's intervention in Jewish matters during the summer and autumn of 1941, he does not deal directly with the problem at the heart of the present debate: was a general order to exterminate the Jews given by Hitler, and if so, under what form did he give it and when? For intentionalist historians, such an order was probably given in the spring of 1941, on the eve of the attack on the Soviet Union. This was the time when the order was issued to shoot the Red Army Commissars, when the Einsatzgruppen were instructed to exterminate the Jews in occupied Soviet territory, and when a "certain final solution of the Jewish problem" was mentioned in the Reich Main Security Office's statement forbidding further Jewish emigration from Belgium and France.[8] Or, it could have been given in the early summer of 1941, after the beginning of the German attack on Russia, when Göring instructed Heydrich to prepare the "total solution of the Jewish problem in all the territories under German control."[9]

No historian today would believe that such an order was given in writing. In its oral form it could have been either a clear instruction passed on to Göring or to Himmler, or, more probably, a broad hint that everybody understood

8.   Helmut Krausnick et al., *Anatomy of the SS State*, trans. Richard Barry et al. (London and New York, 1968), 60, 67.
9.   Raul Hilberg, *The Destruction of the European Jews* (Chicago, 1961), 262.

(Fleming, as we shall see later, shows how Hitler tried to avoid having his name directly linked to orders concerning the extermination process). In any case, for intentionalist historians, a signal must have come from Hitler to set the Final Solution in motion.

For the functionalists, many of the basic tenets of the intentionalist position are improbable. Let us recall, first of all, the common denominator of all functionalist interpretations: the Nazi system was in great part chaotic, and major decisions were often the result of the most diverse pressures, without any imperative central planning, forecasting, or clear orders from the top indicating the aim and the means of a given policy.

Two major studies, that of Karl Schleunes and that of Uwe Dietrich Adam (both of which deal mostly with the thirties, although Adam's includes the first two years of the war), represent some of the basic functionalist positions on the anti-Jewish policies.[10] In the words of Karl Schleunes, "during the first years of the Third Reich, nobody within the Nazi movement, starting with the Führer himself, could define what the solution to the Jewish problem could be. . . . It is only in the widest sense that the anti-Semitic premises of National Socialism help us to explain the course taken by the great variety of measures concerning the Jews."[11]

Uwe Dietrich Adam pushes the functionalist thesis one step further. After following in detail the anti-Jewish measures of the thirties in which, according to him, no clear direction is to be found until 1938—when the SS took over and furthered a systematic emigration policy—Adam reaches a first general conclusion: "One cannot speak of a coordinated and planned policy towards the Jews . . . a global plan con-

10. Schleunes, *Twisted Road*; Uwe Dietrich Adam, *Judenpolitik im Dritten Reich* (Düsseldorf, 1972).
11. Schleunes, *Twisted Road*, 257–58.

cerning the nature, content and scope of the persecution of the Jews never existed; it is even highly probable that the mass extermination was not an aim that Hitler had set a priori and that he tried to achieve."[12]

In Adam's view of the crucial events of 1941, the extermination of the Jews in occupied Soviet territory was not necessarily part of a global extermination plan; it was only between September and December of that year, following the situation created by deporting Jews from the Reich to the ghettos of the East on the one hand and the stalling of the German offensive in Russia on the other, that Hitler decided to replace the "territorial solution" of the Jewish problem with global extermination.[13]

Martin Broszat adopts Adam's general description of the 1941 events, but he in turn takes the argument one step further: whereas Adam believed that Hitler had ordered the global extermination of European Jews some time in the fall of 1941, Martin Broszat believes that such an order probably never existed. The Final Solution was the result of a series of local initiatives aimed at solving local problems (the chaotic situation in the ghettos); it only gradually became an overall action:

> It thus seems that the liquidation of the Jews began not solely as the result of an ostensible will for extermination but also as a "way out" of a blind alley into which the Nazis had manoeuvered themselves. The practice of liquidation, once initiated and established, gained predominance and evolved in the end into a comprehensive "programme."
>
> This interpretation cannot be verified with absolute certainty but in the light of circumstances, which cannot be discussed here in detail, it seems more plausible than

12. Adam, *Judenpolitik*, 357.
13. Ibid., 303–13.

the assumption that there was a general secret order for the extermination of the Jews in the summer of 1941.

In a footnote to the above lines Broszat adds: "It appears to me that there was no overall order concerning the extermination of the Jews and that the programme of extermination developed through individual actions and then reached gradually its institutional and factual character in the spring of 1942 after the construction of the extermination camps in Poland."[14]

In Martin Broszat's demonstration, Hitler's anti-Jewish ideology is stressed, but its direct relation to policies is questioned. For Hans Mommsen likewise ideology loses all concrete significance, and the ultimate outcome of Nazi policies toward the Jews, as of Nazi policies in general, can best be explained by "cumulative radicalization," a process resulting from the constant competition between various Nazi agencies, and representing the overall fight for power positions within the system:

> In each individual case the common denominator of the competing power blocs was not a midstream compromise, but whatever in any given circumstances was the most radical solution, previously considered as beyond the realms of possibility. To avoid surrendering its overall authority on the Jewish question, the Ministry of the Interior consented to drastic discriminatory measures which once and for all showed that the "rule of law" had been nothing but a painstakingly maintained facade. To prevent Jewish property from falling into the hands of the Gau organizations as a result of wild-cat "aryanization,"

14. Martin Broszat, "Hitler und die Genesis der 'Endlösung': auf Anlass der Thesen von David Irving," *Vierteljahrshefte für Zeitgeschichte* 25 (1977). The English translation used here is from *Yad Vashem Studies* 13 (1979): 93, 93n. Some of Martin Broszat's arguments have been neatly countered in Christopher R. Browning's "Zur Genesis der Endlösung: Eine Antwort an Martin Broszat," *Vierteljahrshefte für Zeitgeschichte* 29 (1981): 97–109. We shall deal with some of them further on.

Goering, following the November Pogrom (of which he, like Heydrich, disapproved), gave orders for aryanization by the state; the departments involved hastily busied themselves with supporting legislation, even if only to retain their share of responsibility. The impossible situation created by the material and social dispossession of the Jews caused individual Gauleiters to resort to deportations, regardless of consequences, a move bitterly resisted by the departments concerned. However, the result was not the replacement of deportation by a politically "acceptable" solution, but, on the contrary, the systematic mass murder of the Jews, which no one had previously imagined possible—the most radical solution, and incidentally one which coincided with Hitler's own wishes.[15]

More recently Hans Mommsen has presented the functionalist position in its most extreme form: there is no direct Hitler-instruction for destroying the Jews, Hitler's declarations concerning their annihilation are mere propaganda ("even the talks with Marshal Antonescu and Admiral Horthy"—in which Hitler mentions annihilation of the Jews—"have to be considered as typical metaphors of Hitler's propaganda"), and the Wannsee Conference itself is not about an extermination program ("the annihilation program still appeared to be quite vague and Heydrich's remarks could be interpreted differently, although he mentioned the necessity of a late extinction of those deported who might survive the annihilation process through work").[16] It is obvious why Gerald Fleming's book has an essential place in the current debate.

15. Hans Mommsen, "National-Socialism: Continuity and Change," in *Fascism: A Reader's Guide*, ed. Walter Laqueur (London, 1979), 179.

16. Hans Mommsen, "The Holocaust" (Lecture given at the International Conference on the Historiography of the Holocaust, Yad Vashem, Jerusalem, 27 March 1983, Mimeograph). In his article "Die Realisierung des Utopischen: Die 'Endlösung' der Judenfrage im Dritten Reich,' *Geschichte und Gesellschaft* 9, no. 3 (1983): 381–417, Hans Mommsen has presented a more nuanced interpretation of the Wannsee conference. See below, p. xxiii.

II

It may be tempting to state that each approach has its merits and to seek a synthesis between the two positions. In fact functionalism, which stresses the dynamics of a system instead of the central role of a leader, fits better in many ways within the mainstream of modern historiography. The image it offers of Nazism is more "normal," easier to explain: any group can stumble haphazardly, from step to step, into the most extreme criminal behavior. Responsibility remains, obviously; but it is more diluted, more nebulous, because of the very automatism of the process, its outcome unforeseeable, and because of the absence of real premeditation as well. Intentionalism, on the other hand, asserts that the course of action was in some way planned. This latter view gives Hitler a predominant role, but it also implies much greater awareness at various levels; whereas functionalism, pushed to its logical conclusion, gets very close to denying that Hitler had accurate knowledge of the Final Solution. It leaves most of the operation to subordinate agencies—in a nutshell, to police terror.

These considerations are not to be dismissed lightly. But for the historian the only valid test is that of documentary evidence. It appears, in my opinion, that in scanning available evidence—and Fleming's study has been of major importance in bringing a great deal of it together—historians may tend to be more convinced by the traditional, intentionalist position, at least insofar as anti-Jewish policies and the Final Solution are concerned. Let me state my own point of view: In the matters with which Hitler was obsessed, those forming the core of his system—conquest of the *Lebensraum*, as well as the all-embracing fight against the Jews—his intervention is clearly seen at crucial stages. In other fields, the functionalist position could easily be proven. The problem of interference between the other fields and the major elements of Hitler's system remains open.

Let us now concentrate entirely on key issues relating to the Final Solution itself. The main problem is to verify Hitler's orders for and personal involvement in the extermination process versus the thesis of a more or less haphazard development—one initiated at a local level and systematized only later, chiefly within the SS and without any overall extermination order ever having been given, at least by Hitler. The latter argument is made possible by the fact that no written Hitler-order about the Final Solution has ever been found; but one may assume that it would never have been given in writing. Since, in one way or another, the extermination process reached its full-scale form in the second half of 1941 and the first weeks of 1942, we shall systematically review the various interpretations relating to that period.

In his study of the genesis of the Final Solution, Martin Broszat points out that none of Hitler's main aides, when interrogated after the war, had any recollection of an oral order for the overall extermination of the Jews; moreover, Broszat shows that entries from Goebbels's unpublished diaries, when referring to the Jewish problem during the summer and fall of 1941, often allude to evacuation to camps on Russian territory but do not mention any extermination order. Finally, still in terms of documentary evidence, Broszat quotes the controversy between Himmler and SS-Brigadeführer Dr. Friedrich Übelhör, who was in charge of the Lodz Ghetto. Übelhör strongly objected, at the beginning of October 1941, to deportations from the Reich to Lodz, because the ghetto was already overcrowded; this controversy would be meaningless if extermination had been decided upon.[17]

17.　For these various arguments, see Broszat, "Hitler und die Genesis der 'Endlösung,'" 746ff.

American historian Christopher R. Browning pointedly answered that Himmler and Heydrich, the main architects of the Final Solution, were dead when the interrogation started and that Göring, the principal defendant at Nuremberg, was fighting for his life and would certainly not have admitted that he had forwarded a global extermination order. And the Goebbels diaries were a poor source at best, as Goebbels since November 1938 was notoriously kept out of Jewish affairs by Göring, Himmler, and Heydrich. On the other hand, Browning points to a whole series of references to the preparation of the Final Solution during the summer and fall of 1941 that gives an unmistakable sense of mass annihilation. He also points to the fact, strangely omitted by Broszat, that after the war Auschwitz commandant Rudolf Höss and Adolf Eichmann both referred to the planning during that period for overall extermination. Finally, Browning indicates that what Broszat describes as "vague" Nazi plans for dealing with the Jews in the summer and fall of 1941 (forced labor whereby many would die; then possibly "helping" the others to die) in fact represents an extermination program. [18]

But let us turn now to the sequence of events. Until the fall of 1941, Soviet Jews are the only ones systematically exterminated; Uwe Adam and Martin Broszat do not find a necessary link between those exterminations and an overall Final Solution through mass killing. In the fall of 1941, however, deportations from the Reich start, mostly to Lodz, Kovno, Minsk, and Riga. Some of the deportees sent to Riga and Lodz are exterminated on the spot, along with local Jews, near Riga and in the Chelmno (Kulmhof) extermination camp near Lodz. It would seem that we are now confronted with stages of an overall plan, as the extermination process includes Jews transported from Germany to the kill-

18. Browning, "Zur Genesis der Endlösung," 98ff.

ing sites. But in Broszat's view these killings are still initiated to solve local problems (the deportations from the Reich add to the overcrowding of the ghettos and the Jews cannot be sent further east, as the Wehrmacht's advance in Russia is slowing down). In fact, according to Broszat, the very chaotic aspect of the deportations from the Reich, owing to Hitler's sudden wish to see the Reich cleared of Jews as soon as possible, seems to preclude any systematic planning of an extermination process.

Gerald Fleming brings important evidence to show that the Riga exterminations are not a local improvisation: the Reichskommissar Ostland, Hinrich Lohse, is advised by Himmler through SS-General Friedrich Jeckeln that the exterminations are on order from Himmler and in accordance with a "wish" of the Führer (see p. 75 below: "Tell Lohse it is my order, which is also the Führer's wish"). Clearly then, this is no local initiative but, for all purposes, a Hitler-initiative.

For the genesis of the Chelmno exterminations the evidence is more complex. Martin Broszat reminds us that the idea of exterminating some of the Lodz ghetto Jews in order to solve the problems of overcrowding was already discussed among local SS officers and with the Reich Main Security Office as early as July 1941, when no general plan for the Final Solution could yet have existed.[19] Would not the extermination in the fall be the result of the same type of consideration, developed at a lower echelon?

Here again, Fleming brings us new evidence. In March 1944, Wartheland Gauleiter Arthur Greiser (in whose domain Lodz and Chelmno were included) proudly reports to his Führer that practically all of the Wartheland Jews have been exterminated (mostly in Chelmno). On 21 November 1942, Greiser informed Himmler that when he had met with

19.   Broszat, "Hitler and die Genesis der 'Endlösung,'" 749n. Dr. Friedrich Übelhör's protests against sending deportees from the Reich to Lodz ties in with this reasoning.

Hitler he was told, as far as the Jews were concerned, to act according to his own judgment. Greiser had had two meetings with Hitler, 1 October and 11 November 1942. (See p. 22 below.)

Greiser's report to Hitler in 1944 clearly means that Hitler's words of October or November 1942 had been understood. Yet Greiser had started the exterminations in Chelmno a year before those meetings. If Greiser had received the same kind of order as that given to Lohse in the fall of 1941, Hitler's directive, a year later, would not make sense. Therefore, information about the overall planning could not have been passed on automatically to those responsible for various killing operations. Although for the Chelmno exterminations "Sonderkommando Lange" (a special task force that used gassing vans, as it had for the euthanasia killings) was sent from Berlin, Greiser was possibly unaware that this was part of an overall action—until he got the hint from Hitler a year later.

If one moves from the single operations to the general context, the whole picture becomes much clearer. In the fall of 1941, the Einsatzgruppen had exterminated nearly one million Jews in the Soviet Union, and Jews from the Reich were being killed in Riga and Chelmno; all emigration of Jews from occupied Europe was forbidden (order of 23 October 1941); construction of the Belzec extermination camp in the Generalgouvernement had begun; and the first killing experiments with Zyklon-B gas had taken place in Auschwitz. The groping phase that characterized the summer and early fall—and that gave the impression of the haphazardness Broszat uses as a key argument—was coming to an end: the various projects were falling into place within the general framework of the Final Solution.

In this context the meaning of the Wannsee Conference of 20 January 1942—at which Heydrich presented the outline for the Final Solution to the assembled representatives of various ministries and SS agencies—seems unmistakable. Nonetheless, Hans Mommsen states:

> The forthcoming "Wannsee Conference" is generally identified with the immediate starting of the overall European Genocide, although the "Initiatives" *(Aktionen)* mentioned by Heydrich in relation to the "evacuation of the Jews to the East" were presented as alternatives *(Ausweichmöglichkeiten)*, aimed at gathering practical experience "in view of the coming final solution of the Jewish Question." The liquidation of those Jews who were unable to work was mentioned implicitly and the later extermination of the "remainder" was mentioned explicitly. The fiction of compulsory labour *(Arbeitseinsatz)* created the psychological link between the emigration, then the reservation solution, and the holocaust itself; at the same time, the chimera of a territorial "final solution," which was now to be located beyond the Urals, was still held forth *(schimmerte noch durch)*.[20]

If the inclusion of the Jews in a compulsory labor program was fictitious—as indeed it was—then Heydrich's whole scheme was the overall plan for destruction of the European Jews. The setting up of the extermination camps in the Generalgouvernement during the following months dispels any doubt or vagueness about what was meant at Wannsee.

Moreover, what logic indicates, direct evidence confirms. At his trial in Jerusalem Adolf Eichmann—who was the technical organizer of the Wannsee Conference and who attended its meetings—when asked by the President of the Tribunal what the general sense of the discussion was, answered: "The discussion covered killing, elimination, and annihilation" (p. 92 below).

If we admit that the meaning of the Wannsee Conference is unmistakable, if we remember that Heydrich in

20. Mommsen, "Die Realisierung," p. 412.

his opening remarks refers not only to the order given him by Göring but also to Hitler's agreement to start evacuating the Jews to the East, it can mean only one thing: Hitler's agreement to the extermination plan. One can hardly imagine that Heydrich would present an extermination plan to a whole array of high-ranking civil servants if Hitler had meant a bona fide evacuation plan.

Since the conference was first set for 9 December 1941 (and finally postponed to 20 January 1942) and, moreover, since the preparation of the scheme presented by Heydrich must have taken several months, it is probable that Hitler's "agreement" was expressed sometime in the summer of 1941, at the latest. And Hitler's "agreement," like Hitler's "wish," means in fact Hitler's "order," without the necessity of a formal decree.

Moreover, references have been made to Hitler's explicit instructions regarding the exterminations. When Otto Bradfisch, head of the Einsatzkommando 8 operating in the Minsk region, asks Himmler in August 1941 who bears the responsibility for the executions, Himmler answers that "these orders . . . come from Hitler as the supreme Führer of the German government, and . . . they [have] the force of law" (p. 51 below). A year later, SS-General Gottlob Berger suggests, in the name of the Ministry for the Occupied Eastern Territories, devising a more precise definition of the term "Jew." Himmler rejects the very idea of further definition, which would entail only limitations, and adds: "The occupied East will be freed of Jews (*judenfrei*). The Führer has laid upon my shoulders the execution of this very difficult order. Moreover, no one can relieve me of this responsibility. I have therefore forbidden any further meddling in the matter."[21]

During the first half of 1944 Himmler refers to the

21. P. 112 below. See also Krausnick et al., *SS State*, 69.

very hard Führer-order concerning the Final Solution in no less than four different speeches, three of which were delivered before large audiences of senior Wehrmacht officers (26 January, 5 and 24 May, and 21 June 1944).[22] And there are still other available references to Hitler's orders, which Fleming does not cite. For instance, according to the testimony of SS-Judge Konrad Morgen, when Christian Wirth's special sections were dispatched to the Generalgouvernement to help Globocnik in the extermination process, "Himmler is supposed to have asked of each of them to swear an oath of silence and to have told them: 'I have to expect of you superhuman acts of inhumanity. But, it is the Führer's will.'"[23]

At the end of December 1941, Bernhard Lösener, the Adviser on Jewish Affairs at the Ministry of the Interior, tells State Secretary Wilhelm Stuckart, that because of the exterminations of the Jews in the Riga region, news of which had reached him, he cannot remain in his position. Stuckart answers: "Don't you realize that all of this is being done on orders from the highest level?"[24] And in May 1942, the Head of the Reich Main Security Office and newly appointed Protector of Bohemia and Moravia, Reinhard Heydrich, and several intelligence officers meet in Prague. In the course of a very heated discussion of the exterminations, Heydrich declares that the Reich Main Security Office was not responsible for the killings; they are being executed on personal order from the Führer (see p. 60 below).

Fleming shows that not only are there many references to Hitler's orders, there is also much evidence con-

22. See pp. 52–54 below. As was already mentioned in the case of Heydrich at the Wannsee Conference, one cannot imagine that Himmler would have referred to a nonexistent Führer-order, especially before such audiences.

23. Krausnick et al., *SS State*, 97.

24. Bernhard Lösener, "Als Rassereferent im Reichsministerium des Innern," *Vierteljahrshefte für Zeitgeschichte*, 9 (1961): 311. See also below, pp. 106–7.

cerning the Führer's interest in the process of extermination. On 1 August 1941, Gestapo Chief Heinrich Müller sends the following order to the heads of the four Einsatzgruppen: "The Führer is to be kept informed continually from here about the work of the Einsatzgruppen in the East" (p. 45 below). In December 1942, report number 51 is sent by Himmler to Hitler. It deals with the Einsatzgruppen-actions in Soviet territory for the period August through November 1942, and it mentions "363,211 Jews executed" (according to a note by Hitler's adjutant Pfeiffer, the report was submitted to Hitler on 31 December) (see below, p. 129). During the same month, Himmler notes down, after a meeting with Hitler: "3. Jews . . . to get rid of: Jews in France 600 – 700,000, to get rid of" (p. 8 n. 24 below). In fact, as far as statistics are concerned, Himmler will be better informed at the end of December, when the SS Inspector for Statistics, Richard Korherr, will have prepared for him a complete and precise report on the course of the Final Solution. In April 1943 the report, updated to 31 March of the same year and condensed to 6½ pages, is ready for the Führer. The report, typed on the special "Führer-typewriter" (a typewriter with extra-large letters), is submitted to Hitler a few days before 19 April 1943.[25] According to Eichmann's testimony, when the report was sent back to the Reich Main Security Office, it bore the mention: "The Führer has taken note: destroy.— H. H." (i.e., Heinrich Himmler; see p. 138 below).

Here we must turn to the strange contradictions of Nazi camouflage of the Final Solution. Richard Korherr is asked to eliminate the word *Sonderbehandlung* (special treatment), which appeared on his report; Rudolf Brandt, Himmler's personal assistant, writes to Korherr:

25. For the text of both Korherr reports and the related correspondence, see *The Holocaust and the Neo-Nazi Mythomania*, ed. Serge Klarsfeld (New York, 1978).

He [Himmler] has requested that "special treatment of the Jews" be mentioned nowhere in the document. Page 9, point 4, should read as follows: "Transport of Jews from the eastern provinces to the Russian East: passed through camps in the Generalgouvernement, . . . through the camps in the Warthegau. . . ." No other wording may be used. I am returning the copy of the report, with the Reichsführer SS's initials, and with the request that page 9 be altered accordingly and then resubmitted.[26]

One wonders about the inconsistency of the camouflage measures; on the one hand, even the code word *Sonderbehandlung* is eliminated from the report sent to Hitler;[27] on the other hand, Himmler refers several times to Hitler's orders when he speaks of the total elimination of the Jews. Or, to sharpen the paradox: in a document sent to Hitler himself, no reference to the Final Solution is allowed; but in speeches held before wide audiences (and not only to SS officers, but to regular officers of the Wehrmacht), Himmler openly refers to Hitler's order.

This paradox is reflected in Fleming's book. The author puts great emphasis on showing how carefully Hitler avoided having his name directly linked to the Final Solution, but clearly Fleming is successful in uncovering many references to Hitler's interventions in the extermination process. The formula "the Führer's wish" was understood by everybody concerned to mean a Führer-order. Therefore, it seems that one has to limit the argument to its core issue: Hitler's name never appears on any document referring to

26. Below, p. 137; and ibid.
27. It may well be that the explanation, in this case, is supplied by an instruction issued somewhat later, on 11 July 1943, by the head of the Party Chancellery, Martin Bormann, whereby, in agreement with the Führer, the "Final Solution" was in no way to be mentioned in any documents relating to the Jewish question; mention was only to be made of Jews being sent to work. See Joseph Walk, ed., *Das Sonderrecht für die Juden im NS-Staat* (Heidelberg, 1981), 400.

the overall extermination of the Jews, and any document dealing with the Final Solution as a whole and submitted to Hitler was to bear no mention of a killing process. For that reason we have no direct proof of an initial Hitler-order and, for that very reason too, the Korherr report had to be expurgated. But in fact, even this interpretation is insufficient if we take into account that in April 1943, Hitler more or less admitted the extermination of the Jews in his talks with the Romanian Chief of State Antonescu and the Hungarian Regent, Admiral Horthy, and that, in his political testament, written at the eve of his death on 29 April 1945, he boasted about it quite emphatically.

There is, finally, indirect evidence of Hitler's attention to the extermination process. For instance, Odilo Globocnik, the Higher SS and Police Leader in charge of the four extermination camps set up in the Generalgouvernement during 1942, visited the Reich Chancellery in autumn of the same year; a note by Himmler referring to a conference with Hitler on 7 October 1942 bears the following mention: "Conditions Gen. Gouv. Globus" (Globocnik bore the nickname "Globus") (below, p. 63). The subject of the conference thereby becomes obvious.

On 13 April 1943, the proposal to raise Christian Wirth (Globocnik's right-hand man and specialist in killing by gas—first the mentally ill and later the Jews) to the rank of SS Sturmbannführer is submitted to the Main Personnel Office of the SS; the file bears the mention that since the beginning of the war Wirth has been "serving in a special mission for the Führer" (below, p. 25).

That Hitler could have been unaware of the Final Solution up to 1943, as suggested by David Irving, goes against all evidence; that he gave an oral order sometime in the spring or summer of 1941 for the overall extermination of the Jews of Europe is highly probable, but cannot be proven with absolute certainty on the basis of existing documents. We have seen, however, that he was kept constantly informed of the extermination process and made ad hoc interventions in it. In essence, the known evidence indicates a clear Hitler-intention of mass extermination, in whatever form the intention was expressed and transmitted to those directly in charge of planning and execution—Himmler, Heydrich, and the various SS agencies.

This intention does not mean that from the very beginning of his political career Hitler concretely planned the extermination of the Jews of Europe, nor does it mean that such a plan existed in 1933, 1938, or even 1940. Indeed, Hitler's declarations did not always tally with the actual policies that the Reich's agencies were pursuing; when, for instance, he spoke to Czech Foreign Minister František Chvalkovsky, on 21 January 1939, of "destroying" the Jews, or when he declared to the Reichstag, on 30 January 1939, that a new war would mean the annihilation of the Jews of Europe, Heydrich's services were still organizing Jewish emigration in a systematic way. Examples like these allow historians to deny any link between Hitler's declarations and the evolution of Nazi policies. Yet from all the evidence, it seems that one should argue just the opposite. Destruction was the constant leitmotif. As long as there was no concrete possibility of realizing this destruction, Hitler allowed various policies to develop; but once the appropriate moment arrived, the constant theme became policy.[28]

But even between 1933 and 1941—when, because of internal and external circumstances, Nazi policy toward the Jews followed a "twisted road" indeed—one thing is clear enough: the persecution grows increasingly severe, and each step leaves the door open for further, still worse measures. There is no stopping on the way and certainly no turning back. Moreover, when one carefully reads the evidence, Hitler's presence is felt at every stage: from his talk with

28. For the same interpretation, see for instance Hilberg, *European Jews*, 257.

Goebbels on 28 March 1933 about the projected boycott of Jewish business, to his decisions in April of the same year regarding the fate of Jewish civil servants and lawyers, to his decision about the biological separation of Jews from Aryans (the Nuremberg Laws) in September 1935, to his orders concerning Jewish civil servants in Austria after the Anschluss in March 1938, to his probable conference with Goebbels a few hours before the onset of the pogrom of 9 November 1938 (the *Kristallnacht,* "night of the broken glass"), to his designating Göring—and Himmler and Heydrich as well—to coordinate Jewish affairs from November 1938 on, to his instigating the expulsion of the Jews from Baden and the Palatinate into France in October 1940, and finally to his "agreeing" to the "evacuation to the East" sometime in 1941.

The destruction theme is always there. In reference to an article in a provincial newspaper in which the editor asked for special signs to distinguish Jewish firms, Hitler declares, in a secret address on 29 April 1937, to the party Kreisleiters (district leaders):

> From whom is he demanding this? Who can give the necessary orders? Only I can give them. The editor, in the name of his readers, is asking me to act. First, I should tell you that long before this editor had any inkling about the Jewish problem, I had made myself an expert in the subject. Secondly, this problem has been under consideration for two or three years, and will, of course, be settled one way or another in due course. My point is then this: the final aim of our policy is crystal clear to all of us. All that concerns me is never to take a step that I might later have to retrace and never to take a step that could damage us in any way. You must understand that I always go as far as I dare and never further. It is vital to have a sixth sense that tells you, broadly, what you can do and what you cannot do. Even in a struggle with an adversary it is not my way to issue a direct challenge to a trial of strength. I do not say "Come on and fight, because I want a fight." Instead I shout at him (and I shout louder and louder): "I mean to

destroy you." And then I use my intelligence to help me to manoeuvre him into a tight corner, so that he cannot strike back, and then I deliver the fatal blow.[29]

In quoting those lines, Helmut Krausnick writes that "nothing perhaps betrays Hitler's innermost feelings about his Jewish policy and its dreadful consequences as clearly as did this text." Other quotes of Hitler concerning the Jews have the same sadistic tone, but, in some ways, this text is indeed of major significance: Hitler insists on the fact that he alone can decide about measures against the Jews, even relatively minor measures, like the marking of Jewish firms. He stresses the fact that *he*—and nobody else—calculates every step in this "fight"; he speaks of maneuvering in such a way that the enemy be paralyzed; and he asserts that "the final aim of our policy is crystal clear to all of us." There is no way of assessing the exact meaning of the last words; but a moment later he reaches the theme of destruction, of extermination.

The Reichstag declaration of 30 January 1939 did not reflect the emigration policies followed at that time, but it was an announcement of what would happen to the Jews in case of war. It may have been purely rhetorical at the moment, but later on, when the Final Solution was already being implemented, Hitler came back to that speech, more or less repeating the same sentences on three different subsequent occasions and stressing thereby, quite openly, that the fatal turning point had come: once again he had been a

---

29. Krausnick et al., *SS State*, 34. (For the full text of this speech, see *Es spricht der Führer: Sieben exemplarische Hitler-Reden*, ed. Hildegarde von Kotze and Helmut Krausnick [Gütersloh, 1966]). The translation does not fully convey the brutality of the last lines: "Ich sage nicht 'Kampf,' weil ich kämpfen will, sondern ich sage: 'Ich will dich vernichten!' Und jetzt Klugheit hilf mir, dich so in die Ecke hineinzumanövrieren dass du zu keinem Stoss kommst und dann kriegst du den Stoss ins Herz hinein. Das ist es!"

prophet, he declared, and once again he had been laughed at; but many of those who had laughed stopped laughing and soon, maybe, none of them would laugh anymore.

On 26 January 1944, Himmler spoke to several hundred high-ranking Wehrmacht officers at the municipal theater in Posen; nobody in the assembly, one may safely assume, thought the Reichsführer's words inconsequential. Himmler said:

> When the Führer gave me the order to carry out the total solution of the Jewish question, I at first hesitated, uncertain whether I could demand of my worthy SS-men the execution of such a horrid assignment. . . . But this was ultimately a matter of a Führer-order, and therefore I could have no misgivings. In the meantime, the assignment has been carried out, and there is no longer a Jewish question. (p. 53 below)

On the limited level of the analysis of Nazi policies, an answer to the debate between the various groups appears to be possible. On the level of global interpretation, however, the real difficulties remain. The historian who is not encumbered with ideological or conceptual blinkers easily recognizes that it is Nazi anti-Semitism and the anti-Jewish policy of the Third Reich that gives Nazism its *sui generis* character. By virtue of this fact, inquiries into the nature of Nazism take on a new dimension that renders it unclassifiable. "Fascism" fails as a sufficient concept, and so does "totalitarianism." Marxist or Freudian interpretations are inadequate. Nazi anti-Semitism poses an essential difficulty to analysis, which the ever-increasing number of studies on Nazism attempt to evade: with a page or two recalling the "racial madness" of Hitler, they avoid shaking the usual interpretations. Yet if one admits that the Jewish problem was at the center, was the very essence of the system, many of these studies lose their coherence, and historiography is confronted with an anomaly that defies the normal interpretive categories.

At most one can mention the emergence, unique to date, of a messianic faith and an apocalyptic vision of history at the heart of the political, bureaucratic, and technological system of an advanced industrial society. Yet here again, the image is false, since there was no mass movement with respect to the Jews, nor even a crusade by a fanatic sect. A bureaucracy occupied center stage, indifferent to the destruction but pushed by its leader, who was moved by the most intense of convictions.

The historian's paralysis comes from the simultaneity and the interaction of entirely heterogeneous phenomena: messianic fanaticism and bureaucratic structures, pathological impulses and administrative decrees, archaic attitudes and advanced industrial society.

We know in detail what occurred, we know the sequence of events and their probable interaction, but the profound dynamics of the phenomenon escapes us. And what likewise escapes us is the almost immediate disintegration of the German political, institutional, and legal structures, as well as of the moral forces that by their very nature ought to have been important obstacles to the Nazis in Germany, in the other European countries, and in the entire Western world.

Saul Friedländer

Author's Preface ·

To regard the destructive tendencies of National Socialism "as nothing more than the reaction" to the Stalinist terror and its heavy toll of victims would, according to the German historian Ernst Nolte in his article on the "negative vitality of the Third Reich," be "a crude simplification."[1] The destructive tendencies of National Socialism, Nolte writes, had "specific, historical roots that reach far back into the past." These roots were:

1. The "lessons in annihilation" provided by the "earliest exponents of the right" in reaction to the political aspirations and programs of the French Revolution and Terror; and the concomitant appearance, even then, of such pejorative labels as "vermin" and "lice."

2. The general program of "annihilation as therapy," conceived by the most radical proponents of Malthusianism as a remedy to rampant overpopulation; and the specific suggestion that "surplus children be eliminated painlessly by gassing them."

3. "The translation of Napoleon's military strategy of total annihilation into Prussian practice; from that

---

1. Ernst Nolte, "Die negative Lebendigkeit des Dritten Reiches: eine Frage aus dem Blickwinkel des Jahres 1980," *Frankfurter Allgemeine Zeitung*, 24 July 1980, p. 6.

point, the Clausewitzian restraints could easily be stripped away, and in fact were during the Second World War, at the very latest."

Classic examples of this will to annihilate are found in the early modern era: witness the ruthless victimization of infidels and heretics as a result of the Spanish Inquisition and the repeal of the Edict of Nantes. In our own day, the memory of such tendencies is still fresh. They are manifest in the racial hatred underlying the confrontation between the Armenians and the Turks, as well as in the ideologically and fanatically motivated hatred of the Pol Pot/Heng Samrin regime in Cambodia, which erected a new social order at the price of enforced collectivization, the elimination of currency and the free-market economy, and the destruction of urban life.

The "Final Solution of the European Jewish question" willed and ordered by Adolf Hitler, however, distinguishes itself from all previous recorded tides of human destruction through its unprecedented, systematic, and wholesale murder of five million Jews, a race whose existence Hitler ultimately regarded as an insufferable provocation.

This book was written in an effort to come to grips with the issues surrounding this "quasi-industrial" mass extermination: How could our age produce it and, more specifically, how can we establish the links between the "Führer's wish" and its execution at different administrative levels? If I have succeeded in contributing to a clearer understanding of these controversial questions, if the following pages serve to awaken particularly the younger generations to the dangers inherent in "the beast in man" and to a distrust for demagogues and zealots of whatever political leaning, then this book shall have served its purpose.

March 1982   Gerald Fleming

1

The Growth of an
Obsession

During the Aschaffenburg Hitler Congress held on 1 and 2 July 1978, the writer David Irving asked Professor Eberhard Jäckel, "When, in your view, did Hitler become an anti-Semite?" Irving's own opinion was that Hitler had veered into a radically anti-Semitic position, carried by the momentum of his own propaganda, during August of 1920[1]—not, in other words, during his Vienna period (from his mother's death in Linz on 21 December 1907 to April 1913). Jäckel replied that the issue was a very controversial one indeed. He suggested that here, as elsewhere, one had to allow for gradual and fluid distinctions, such as those that apply to Hitler's complex roles as dictator and demagogue, or as statesman and propagandist. In Jäckel's opinion a letter written by Hitler in September 1919 seemed to betray the first signs of a conversion to virulent anti-Semitism as opposed to the less radical position he had held in Vienna.[2]

---

1. As reported by Guido Knopp, ed., *Hitler heute* (Aschaffenburg, 1979), 57–58.
2. Jäckel refers to Hitler's letter to Adolf Gemlich, dated 16 September 1919. Gemlich, who was with Hitler a member of the "Aufklärungskommando" (Enlightenment commando) in Munich, had requested information on "the Jewish peril." Cf. Ernst Deuerlein, "Dokumentation: Hitlers Eintritt in die Politik und die Reichswehr," *Vierteljahrshistorische Zeitschrift 7* (1959): 177–227.

In this present study, however, we shall begin by focusing on the earliest attestable symptoms in the biographical record of Hitler's personal anti-Semitism, his congenital hatred for the Jews. For the line that leads from these early manifestations to the liquidation orders that Hitler personally issued during the war—the actual target of this investigation—is a direct one. A sample taken from Hitler's utterances over the years reveals this striking continuity: Hitler's remark to his childhood friend, August Kubizek, as the two passed the small synagogue in the Bethlehemstrasse in Linz, "That does not belong here in Linz";[3] Hitler's unshakable conviction that "the Jews had continued to perform ritual murders" up to the most recent past;[4] the Führer's statement on 21 October 1941, at noon in the Führer's Headquarters, preserved in a memorandum signed by Martin Bormann: "When we finally stamp out this plague, we shall have accomplished for mankind a deed whose significance our men out there on the battlefield cannot even imagine yet";[5] and Hitler's assertion four days later, in the presence of Himmler and Heydrich: "It is good that we are preceded by an aura of terror for our plans to exterminate Jewry."[6] This unbroken continuity of explicit utterances was reflected in a more or less tacit continuity of deeds. Hitler's anti-Semitism in his Linz years (1904–1907) was followed by his introduction into the Viennese "Antisemitenbund" (Anti-Semite Association) in April 1908. Much later, but still to be ranged along the same continuum, were the first shootings of German Jews in Fort IX in Kovno on 25 Novem-

---

3. August Kubizek, *Adolf Hitler, mein Jugendfreund* (Graz, 1975), 94.
4. Dietrich Eckart, *Der Bolschewismus von Moses bis Lenin: Zwiegespräch zwischen Adolf Hitler und mir* (Munich, 1924), 20–21.
5. *Adolf Hitler, Monologe im Führerhauptquartier: 1941–1944*, ed. Werner Jochmann (Hamburg, 1980), 99, 421.
6. Ibid., 106.

ber 1941[7] and in the Rumbuli Forest outside Riga[8] on 30 November 1941 at 8:15 A.M. And in the following year report number 51, addressed "to the Führer, re: campaign against gangs," inventories 362,211 Jews executed for the period from 1 September to 1 December 1942. This report from the Reichsführer-SS Heinrich Himmler was submitted to Hitler on 31 December 1942 by Hitler's personal adjutant, Hauptsturmführer Pfeiffer, as indicated in Pfeiffer's hand on page one of the report.[9]

Hitler's objection at fifteen or sixteen to the synagogue in Linz raises the question whether the young Hitler might have been influenced by remarks at home or by his classmates, and perhaps also his teachers, at the Realschule in Linz, and had thereby learned to understand the word "Jew" in an increasingly pejorative sense. Hitler had the following to say about his attitude in Linz to the Jewish problem: "It is difficult if not impossible for me to say today when the word 'Jew' first gave me pause for serious reflection. I cannot recall ever having even heard the word in my father's house while he was still alive. I believe that the old gentleman would have regarded as culturally backward a particular emphasis given to this word. . . . At school I found no reason to question the picture I received from home, either. . . . It was not until I was fourteen or fifteen that I came across the word 'Jew' more frequently, partly in connection with political discussions."

According to Hitler's childhood friend, August Kubizek, nicknamed "Gustl" by Hitler (the two youths were

---

7.   Einsatzkommando 3, geheime Reichssache, 1 December 1941, FG 76, p. 5, Institut für Zeitgeschichte.

8.   Riga Trial, 23 February 1973, (50) 9/72, pp. 74–75, StA Hamburg.

9.   Under point 2 of the report, headed "Reports to the Führer, re: campaign against gangs, report number 51," we read: "Gang accomplices and suspects: (a) arrested: 16,553; (b) executed: 14,251; (c) Jews executed: 363,211" (NS 19/291, Bundesarchiv, Koblenz). (See plates.)

very close from 1904 to 1908, chiefly because of their mutual love of Wagner's music), Hitler "touched up" the portrait of his father in *Mein Kampf* to give it a more "liberal tint." The customs inspector Alois Hitler was, again according to Kubizek, a regular at the local worthies' lunch table in his Leonding pub, where many believed in the ideas of the anti-Semitic politician August Georg von Schönerer. Clearly, even Hitler's father had wanted "nothing to do with the Jews." Hitler's account of his schooldays in Linz further conceals the fact that certain teachers at the Realschule in Linz were unequivocal anti-Semites and had "openly professed their anti-Semitism," and that Hitler himself was, already in 1904 at the tender age of fifteen, "a pronounced anti-Semite."[10] According to Werner Maser, schoolmates of Hitler from his Linz period independently concur on the fact that as early as his schooldays of 1904–1905, Hitler was a "biological anti-Semite," and that this biological anti-Semitism of the young Hitler can be traced back to a programmatic pamphlet of the "Alldeutsche Verband" (Pan-German League), published in 1904, which Hitler had read and which he had openly talked about during recesses at the Realschule in Linz. This pamphlet, they allege, was studded with references to biological anti-Semitism.[11] In the 1890s the Alldeutsche Verband had indeed issued warnings against the "Jewish peril," demanding that rigorous restrictions be imposed on the "Jewish press"—which included the *Berliner Tageblatt* and the *Frankfurter Zeitung*—and advocating that the Jews be treated as "foreigners."[12] Yet in the registered publications of the Alldeutsche Verband from the years 1891–1901, there is no trace of a discussion of biologi-

---

10. Kubizek, *Mein Jugendfreund*, 94.
11. Werner Maser quoted in Knopp, *Hitler heute*, 60.
12. Robert Waite, *The Psychopathic God: Adolf Hitler* (New York, 1977), 286. Cf. Fritz Fischer, *War of Illusions: German Policies from 1911–1914* (New York, 1975), 283–84.

cal anti-Semitism.[13] Since, according to Kubizek's fully credible recollection, Adolf Hitler went off to Vienna already "a pronounced anti-Semite," we cannot rule out the possibility that he had been influenced by individual teachers at the Realschule in Linz.

Walter C. Langer, on the other hand, has maintained that Adolf Hitler could not possibly have been an anti-Semite in his Linz period.[14] As evidence, Langer points to the fact that Hitler offered tokens of gratitude to the Jewish physician of the Hitler family, Dr. Eduard Bloch, who cared for Hitler's mother, Klara, until she succumbed to breast cancer in Linz on 21 December 1907. Moreover, at the end of November 1940, Hitler exceptionally allowed Bloch to emigrate to the United States.[15] In view of Kubizek's convincing demonstration, these gestures seem irrelevant. Langer's argument, however, does raise an important issue that bears on Hitler's anti-Semitism, a hatred which, nourished on various sources, incubated and intensified as the years passed. Throughout his life Hitler was repeatedly indebted for the personal assistance he received or the kind-

13. Hauptleitung des Alldeutschen Verbandes, *Zwanzig Jahre alldeutsche Arbeit und Kämpfe* (1910), 10–13. Cf. statement by Heinrich Class: "Jews are barred from all public offices, whether these are salaried offices or honorary offices without pay. . . . They enjoy neither voting eligibility nor the occasion to exercise the right to vote. . . . Newspapers staffed by Jews are to be designated as such. . . . By way of compensation for the protection Jews enjoy as foreign nationals, they pay double the tax Germans pay" (*Wenn ich der Kaiser wär'*, 2d ed. [Leipzig, 1912], 71 [F 4529*, Deutsche Staatsbibliothek, Berlin]). As Edgar Hartwig points out, "A final diffusion of anti-Semitism was part of the program put together by the Verband in 1912 in response to the deepening political crisis" (*Alldeutscher Verband (ADV): 1891–1939* [Leipzig, 1968], 13).

14. Walter C. Langer, *The Mind of Adolf Hitler: The Secret Wartime Report* (New York, 1972), originally prepared in 1943 for the OSS as "The Hitler Source-Book." Cf. Waite, *The Psychopathic God*, 237–38.

15. Dr. Eduard Bloch, "My Patient Adolf Hitler," *Collier's Magazine*, 15 and 22 March 1941.

ness he was shown by Jews, as a few examples will illustrate. From Vienna the young Hitler sent Dr. Bloch two postcards with grateful words, one of which Hitler had embellished by hand.[16] He was on perfectly good terms with his Jewish landlady in Vienna, Frau Zakreys, a "little old and shrivelled woman" who cheaply let the rear apartment of Stumpergasse 29 to Hitler and his friend Kubizek until November 1908. Nor were Jewish art dealers in Vienna niggardly when it came to buying Hitler's rather mediocre watercolors. During the war the Romanian dictator Antonescu, who, like Hitler, suffered from a chronic stomach ailment, sent Hitler his Jewish cook, Fräulein Kunde; when the Reichsführer SS expressed reservations, the Führer allowed her family to "Aryanize." However, Hitler proved less responsive to the support of Hugo Gutmann, the adjutant of his regiment during World War I. Although Gutmann had nominated Hitler for the Iron Cross First Class on several occasions, in the Führer's Headquarters on 11 November 1941 Hitler had nothing but base lies to say about his former well-wisher.[17] Or perhaps Hitler's spitefulness, twenty-three years after the event, was in fact his particular response to the great lengths that this officer—a Jewish officer—had gone to on his behalf. Could it be, then, that all his personal interactions with Jews contributed over the years not to a weakening, but rather to an intensification, of Hitler's irrational, fanatical anti-Semitism?

But to return to the earliest traceable anti-Semitic influences, we should recall what was noted in passing above: that the friendship between Hitler and his childhood companion Kubizek was cemented by their mutual passion

16. Both postcards were confiscated by the Linz Gestapo fourteen days after the annexation of Austria (*Collier's Magazine*, 22 March 1941, p. 70).

17. *Adolf Hitler, Monologe im Führerhauptquartier, 1941–1944*, ed. Jochmann (1980), 132.

for the music of Richard Wagner. Wagner's tracts and essays were readily available in lending libraries in Linz,[18] and the sixteen- or seventeen-year-old Hitler absorbed the works and life of Wagner with systematic diligence. Today it seems clear that the genius of this artist, unfortunately for the German people, contributed to the creation of a political monster, for the collected works of Wagner exerted a decisive influence on Hitler's development and consequently on National Socialism. To quote Hitler's own words, "Whoever wishes to comprehend National Socialism must first know Richard Wagner."[19] And with good reason. In his *Bayreuther Blätter* Wagner gave expression to a synoptic view of history and of the world, to a *Weltanschauung* that was founded on a racial theory. Transmitted through the writings and pamphlets of Georg von Lanz-Liebenfels and Theodor Fritsch,[20] which Hitler read and reread in his first years in Vienna,[21] the substance of Wagner's thought found its way into the heart of the National-Socialist *Weltanschauung*—the National Socialist racial doctrine.

18. E.g., "Das Judentum in der Musik," an essay published in 1850 with the signature, "K. Freigedank," and again in 1869 as a pamphlet.

19. Hermann Rauschning, *The Voice of Destruction* (New York, 1940), 230.

20. Georg von Lanz-Liebenfels (1872–1954) left the order of the Holy Cross in 1900 to establish his own secret society, the "New Temple," which heralded the coming of a racist "New Order." Lanz-Liebenfels was the author of the "Ostara" pamphlets, which Hitler read in Vienna in 1908 and 1909 ("Ostara Bände 1905–1915," Österreichische Nationalbibliothek, 442920-B.Per.; esp. "Ostara" nos. 25 and 26 [1908]).

Theodor Fritsch (1852–1934) became well known through his widely read *Handbuch der Judenfrage* (Handbook of the Jewish question), which by 1907 had already had twenty-six printings. This book Hitler also read in Vienna.

21. In "Ostara" no. 256 (1913) we read: "The primordial socialistic Bolshevist race of men has renounced their patronage of us. Good, we will renounce in return beneficence and humanitarianism toward them. They want a class war; they shall have a race war—a race war begun by us and finished by the castration knife."

This racial doctrine rested on the following axioms: (1) The fundamental inequality of mankind, determined by genetic traits; (2) the existence of different human types (races); (3) the existence of an irrevocably inferior race, a kind of anti-race: the Jews. From these postulates the Nazis deduced that the best and purest race (the Aryan-Germanic race) has a preordained title to rule and to prevail; and that therefore, the races of inferior status—the less significant, culturally impoverished races—exist to serve the master race. Finally, at the bottom end of the scale, the anti-race (the Jewish race) represents "worthless life" (*unwertes Leben*).

Like Hitler, Wagner looked forward to a time when there would be "no more Jews." Like Hitler, he yearned for "the emancipation from the yoke of Judaism" and spoke urgently of "this war of liberation."[22] Whether Wagner would have assented to the nucleus of Hitler's *Weltanschauung*—to the "elimination,"[23] "ridding,"[24] "evacuation,"[25] "reduction,"[26] (read: "extermination") of the Jews—is another question.

22. *Richard Wagner's Prose Works*, trans. William Ashton Ellis (1894; reprint, St. Clair Shores, Michigan, 1972), 3:82; Richard Wagner, *Ausgewählte Schriften*, ed. Julius Kapp (Leipzig, 1914), 230.

23. Per Hitler's second address on 22 August 1939: "Our objective is the elimination of the vital capacities" (of the Polish opponent); and the guidelines of the head of the Wehrmacht Operational Staff, Gen. Alfred Jodl, following a briefing with Hitler on 3 March 1941: "that the Jewish-Bolshevist intelligentsia must be eliminated."

24. Under point 3 of notes from a Führer-briefing on 10 December 1942, "Jews ... to get rid of" (*abschaffen*), we read: "Jews in France, 600-700,000 to get rid of" (Handwritten Memo by the RFSS Himmler, NS 79/275 Bundesarchiv).

25. Point 5 of Himmler's briefing with the Führer on 19 June 1943, at Obersalzberg, reads: "Responding to my briefing on the Jewish question, the Führer declared that the evacuation of the Jews ... must be radically implemented and endured." With handwritten signature: "H. Himmler" (NS 19 (neu)/1447, p. 125, Bundesarchiv).

26. At the end of March 1943, Gauleiter Greiser (Wartheland) appeared at the Kulmhof (Chelmno) extermination camp and addressed the entire SS-Sonderkommando Bothmann and the Wachkommando in the castle courtyard, thanking them in the name of the Führer for the job they

Feeling himself to be misunderstood and thwarted by his surroundings, the young Hitler lost himself in Wagner's world. There he could find consolation, understanding, and the welcome affirmation of his personal prejudices—an affirmation he later repeatedly sought and would later also admit had provided the major impetus for his reading. It is no accident that Hitler was especially fond of quoting from act 2, scene 3 of the *Meistersinger:*

> Und doch's will halt nicht gehen:—
> Ich fühl's und kann's nicht verstehen,—
> kann's nicht behalten, doch auch nicht vergessen:
> und fass ich es ganz, kann ich's nicht ermessen!—
>
> And yet, it just won't go—
> I feel it, and cannot understand it—
> I cannot hold on to it, nor yet forget it;
> and if I grasp it wholly, I cannot measure it!—

> (from the libretto accompanying Deutsche Grammophon recording 2740 149, English translation copyright 1974 by Peter Branscombe)

For Hitler in his Vienna years these lines were an ever-potent spell by which his hero Wagner had lashed out at his contemporaries' lack of understanding. Shortly before the war broke out in 1939, the Reich Chancellor revealed to Winifred Wagner in Bayreuth that it was the production of

---

had done there. In April 1944 the Kulmhof extermination camp was reerected by parts of this same Sonderkommando, for the purpose of the "reduction" and "removal" of all Jews from the Lodz ghetto: "The reduction will be carried out by SS-Hauptsturmführer Bothmann's Sonderkommando, which previously was active in the Gau" (Greiser to Pohl, 14 February 1944). At the end of April 1943, the entire SS Sonderkommando was ordered to appear in Berlin at the RSHA, where SS-Obergruppenführer Kaltenbrunner once more communicated the personal gratitude of the Führer to the assembled men (Minutes M. 8 Js 52/60, of 27 June 1960; Bundesarchiv ZStL, vol. 1, fol. 84; R. Brandt to Kaltenbrunner, 29 March 1943). On 7 March 1944, Greiser reported to Hitler that the Warthegau was now *judenrein* (Jew-free). There is proof that 152,477 Jews were killed in Kulmhof.

the *Rienzi* in Linz, when he was seventeen, which first incited him to become a politician. "That was the hour when it all began,"[27] by which Hitler meant that his experience of the Wagner opera had opened his eyes to his mission in life: to elevate his nation to greatness and power.

Hitler's definitive decision to pursue a political career came, according to him, when he discovered that he was a uniquely gifted public speaker.[28] In other words, Hitler saw, with increasing certainty, that he could convince the German masses of his entitlement to power and leadership. But the real mission that lay behind this claim to power was formulated in his maxim: "Indem ich mich des Juden erwehre, kämpfe ich für das Werk des Herrn" (By keeping the Jews at bay, I fight for the good Lord's way).[29] With this slogan Hitler, the anti-Semitic nationalist, sought to present himself as a new *Christus militans*. With his linguistic shrewdness he had wisely come up with a formula that the National Socialist propagandists would inevitably make use of. Its overtones of traditional Christian anti-Semitism were easy enough to link up with the Nazi brand of biological anti-Semitism; the move from the one form of anti-Semitism to the other constituted a big step, but nonetheless, no more than a step.

Hitler's frustration in his youth with a world that he felt misunderstood him reached crisis proportions when, as an art student at eighteen and nineteen, he failed the examination that would have gained him entry to the art academy of Vienna. His unsatisfactory portfolio was the official reason for his failure; but Hitler placed the blame for this great disappointment on the Jews. Many years later he recounted to friends that he had learned, after the exams were over,

27. Kubizek, *Mein Jugendfreund*, 118.
28. Hitler, *Mein Kampf*, 3d ed. (Munich, 1943), 225, 235.
29. Ibid., 84.

that four of the seven members of the examination committee were Jews; whereupon he had sent the director of the
academy a letter of protest that closed with the threat, "The
Jews will pay for this."[30] The incident was a total confabula-
tion. And yet, this retrospective explanation for his failure
of the entrance exams indicates the degree to which Hitler
was gripped by a pathological hatred for the Jews. The personal component of this hatred combined with Hitler's repeatedly articulated delusion of a global Jewish conspiracy
to serve as a safety valve that, ironically, protected him from
a future, subjectively insurmountable mental illness.

We have already alluded to clerical anti-Semitism,
which prevailed mainly in the Austro-Hungarian Empire.
This form of anti-Semitism must be regarded as a forerun-
ner of the biological-racialist anti-Semitism that the Nazis
were to perfect; it represents a long-standing, sinister tradition from which Adolf Hitler demonstrably was unable, and
indeed unwilling, to escape. In view of its significance, a
representative sample (taken from the Christmas issue of
1904) of the widely circulated *Korrespondenz-Blatt für den
katholischen Klerus Österreichs* is in order:[31]

> It pains me to attest to the fact that the Teutons to this
> very day have grown no wiser but remain the spineless
> creatures they always were. And the tragedy of the matter
> is that they have allowed a generally backward race of for-
> eigners to dictate how they should think. These failings
> are true especially of us Austrians. The Jews—for now—
> paint and draw patterns on the board, much like teachers
> in primary school, while we copy our ABC's without once
> asking whether the Jewish scribbler is the kind of author-
> ity a reasonable being ought blindly to follow. . . .

30. Michael Musmanno, *Ten Days to Die* (New York, 1950), 100; cf.
Waite, *The Psychopathic God*, 190.
31. In Gerhart Binder, *Geschichte im Zeitalter der Weltkriege* (Stuttgart,
1977), 434.

Because of this, the Jews have become positively impudent. They don't even feel it worth their while to behave in a more cautious, circumspect fashion and to be on the alert lest one day they overreach themselves. . . . The Jew whistles, the Germanic people dance. Ancient terminology is being uprooted, the Teutons bow to the edicts issued by the circuit courts of Jerusalem and Samaria. One always used to call it swindling when a lawyer made off with the money of his client. But since many Jews have made embezzlement their trade, swindlers are no longer considered scoundrels. . . .

If a Jew is unanimously found guilty of murder on three separate counts, the logic has it, he must be granted a reprieve. For naturally a Christian has no right to treat the descendents of the eldest nobility on earth—and that is what Jews are according to the Jewish Gospel—as ordinary human beings.[32]

32. The last paragraph quoted here alludes to "ritual murder" trials, a topic also discussed by Hitler and Dietrich Eckart in 1924; cf. Eckart, *Der Bolschewismus von Moses bis Lenin: Zwiegespräch zwischen Adolf Hitler und mir*, 20–21. Cf. also in this connection, *In der Stunde Null*, a position paper of the Freiburg "Bonhoeffer Circle" (Tübingen, 1979), paper 5, "Vorschläge für eine Lösung der Judenfrage in Deutschland" (proposals for a solution to the Jewish question in Germany): "(3) It is the task of Christianity to bring the Gospel to all races and peoples. This task also applies in the case of the Jewish people, whose critical failing is their refusal, up to the present day, to accept the revelation of God in Jesus Christ" (p. 147). Cf. further: Reichsführer SS to the Head of the Security Police and SD, 19 May 1943, Classified (NS 19 (neu)/1076, Bundesarchiv):

Dear Kaltenbrunner,

I have ordered a large number of copies of the book *Die jüdischen Ritualmorde* (Jewish Ritual Murders) and shall have it distributed all the way down to the Standartenführer. I will send you several hundred copies so that you can distribute them to your Einsatzkommandos, above all to those men who have to deal with the Jewish question.

In connection with this book, I am giving the following assignments:

1. Investigations into Jewish ritual murders are to be opened wherever Jews have not yet been evacuated. Such cases should be singled out and submitted to me. We must then begin instituting more proceedings in this direction.

2. The whole ritual murder question should be taken up by the competent authorities in Romania, Hungary, and Bulgaria. I

Twenty years after this article had appeared, Hitler, in conversation with Dietrich Eckhart, would hold forth on precisely the subject addressed in the paragraph above. The 1904 polemic, Hitler's discussion of ritual murder with Dietrich Eckhart in 1924, and the special "Ritual Murder" issue, in May 1934, of the sensationalistic anti-Semitic paper *Der Stürmer*, all lie along a single, unbroken, and fatal continuum.

In retrospect, we can say that Hitler's political career was directly shaped by two experiences, which in their combined impact dictated both his political goal and the means by which to achieve it. The first experience was his service on the front and the shock of defeat; the second was his growing awareness that he could mobilize the masses, that he could virtually "conquer" them with his powers of sug-

---

am considering publicizing these ritual murder cases in our press, to facilitate the removal of Jews from those countries.

These things can, of course, only be done with the consent of the Foreign Office.

3. Consider whether we would not be able to create an illegal, purely anti-Semitic broadcasting station for England and America, in cooperation with the Foreign Office. It would have to be fed material—the way *Der Stürmer* did in the *Kampfzeit* [the years of political confrontation in the streets prior to Hitler's taking over power]—that could be served to the English and the Americans. I believe that a sensational presentation is of the utmost importance here. I suggest that you contact SS-Gruppenführer Dr. Martin so that you can get hold of one or more staff members of *Der Stürmer*.

Moreover, we should at once employ people who pursue and control the judicial and police announcements on missing children in England, so that we can give brief news reports in our radio stations to the effect that in such and such a place a child was reported missing, and that it looks like a case of Jewish ritual murder.

All in all, I think that with a large-scale anti-Semitic propaganda campaign . . . on top of a very intense ritual murder propaganda campaign, we could activate anti-Semism [sic] in the world tremendously.

This was the level on which the second most powerful man in the Third Reich operated.

gestion. Of the two, the first in particular left an indelible imprint on Hitler for life. "A November 1918 shall never repeat itself in German history," Hitler vowed on 1 September 1939, the day on which World War II broke out. His experience of the short-lived November Revolution of 1918, which he regarded as a Jewish-Marxist plot against the German nation,[33] translated over time into the obsessive idea that Providence had elected him to perform an unprecedented feat in the history of the German people. In its radicalization, his hatred for the Jews thus acquired the dimensions of a destiny. Nearly five months after his Reichstag address of 1 September 1939, Hitler prophesied to Czechoslovak Foreign Minister František Chvalkovsky: "The Jews shall be annihilated in our land. They shall not have staged 9 November

33. Once the Weimar Republic had more or less achieved a measure of stability, the November Revolution of 1918 was represented in the political propaganda of the counterrevolutionary elements as predominantly the handiwork of Jews. This view was maintained most intransigently with regard to the short-lived Munich *Räterepublik* of March and April 1919. Among the revolutionaries of the *Räterepublik*, a few politicians of Jewish descent (Ernst Toller, Gustav Landauer, Erich Mühsam, Eugen Leviné) did step into the forefront as proponents of republican and communist (Leviné) ideas. Toller committed suicide in May 1939 in America. Landauer was killed by a Free Corps soldier during the collapse of the *Räterepublik*. Leviné was condemned and executed for high treason on 3 June 1919.

Kurt Eisner had numerous adversaries among Jews of a conservative or patriotic orientation. Jews stood on both sides in the short-lived revolution. Those in the camp of the radical revolutionaries and in the ranks of the democrats proportionately outnumbered the Jewish percentage of the general German population, but they hardly outnumbered the proportion of Jews of the German intellectual circles who had been politically activated by the war. Those Jews who played any kind of role in the revolution at all, major or minor, stood out more strongly in the public mind than the many non-Jewish functionaries of the Eisner government and the *Räte* movement. The memory of Eisner's Finance Minister Edgar Jaffé remained more vivid than that of the Minister of Transport von Frauendorfer. And until well into the Third Reich, the opposition continued to talk more about the heads of the *Räterepublic* Leviné, Toller, Mühsam, and Landauer, than about the Chairman of the Central Committee Ernst Niekisch, the Minister of War of the *Räterepublik* Fritz Sauber, its Foreign Minister Franz Lipp, or military commander Eglhofer.

1918 with impunity. That day shall be avenged!"[34]

As Kubizek reports, the *Rienzi* production in Linz provoked in Hitler his sense of mission. It was 9 November 1918, however, that gave him his true raison d'être: the unswerving conviction that the antichrist—Jewry—must be exterminated. From his speeches of 1919 and 1920 to his political testament of 29 April 1945, Hitler continuously held this goal up before the German nation. These key experiences prior to his political career thus formed the basis on which, in the early twenties, Hitler developed a strategy that would enable him to realize his goal.[35]

The plan entailed several steps. The first stage in Hitler's political conception was to "uncover the Jewish imperialist designs on world hegemony and parade them before the largest segments of our nation" (27 January 1921), to immunize the masses against the "Jewish-Marxist poison" of internationalism and class struggle. Already at this rudimentary stage the masses were to be roused and made ready for the day when they would put an end—by violence, if necessary—to the "Jewish dominion" that had afflicted the nation since 1918. "Hatred, burning hatred—this is what we want to pour into the souls of our millions of fellow Germans, until the flame of rage ignites in Germany and avenges the corrupters of our nation," wrote Hitler on 8 February 1921, in *Der Völkische Beobachter*. The second step in Hitler's strategy was to translate agitation into an effective mass movement. Propaganda and organizing would be crucial in the third step, which would establish the prerequisites for victory in the final phase of the struggle against the

34. Memorandum by Walther Hewel (personal staff of the Reich Foreign Minister), 21 January 1939. "Akten zur deutschen auswärtigen Politik," vol. 158, p. 170.
35. Albrecht Tyrell, "Wie Hitler der Führer wurde," paper delivered at Aschaffenburg Congress, 1 July 1978; cf. Knopp, *Hitler heute*, 27–28.

domestic political enemy. Step four would definitively grant domestic peace through the founding of a "genuinely National Socialist Grossdeutschland [German and Austrian nation]" to be headed by a national "government invested with power and authority." The military and economic power of Grossdeutschland would, in step five, assure the permanent establishment, for Führer and country, of Germany's proper place in the system of world powers. By "proper place," Hitler had nothing less in mind for his nation than a preeminent, superpower role in a restructured, new Europe. The open enemy of this new Europe, the eternal archenemy to whom the collective guilt for all evil was inexplicably attached, was of course "the Jew."[36]

---

36. Cf. on this Martin Gregor-Dellin, *Richard Wagner* (Munich, 1980); and *Frankfurter Allgemeine Zeitung*, 20 August 1980, p. 22: "Possession is evil, the Jew is possession; therefore the Jew is the cardinal source of evil. This hopeless identification of the Jew with all evil became an *idée fixe* for Wagner." Cf. Walther Hewel's notes, "Gespräch zwischen dem Führer und dem südafrikanischen Verteidigungs- und Wirtschaftsminister Pirow, 24 Nov. 1938": "As we see it, the Jews are a collective community. Whatever they do to us, the entire Jewish community does to us" (Hewel Ledger, AA serial 271, p. 293). On collective guilt see also Thomas S. Szasz, *Die Fabrikation des Wahnsinns* (Olten, 1974), 148, for a discussion of a painting from the seventeenth century, now kept in the royal gallery in Naples. The subject of the painting is the delivery of the city from the plague of 1656: led by priests, the citizens execute the instigators of the pestilence, viz. Jews, heretics, and witches, with unspeakable torments, while in heaven the Virgin Mary and St. Januarius implore Christ to sheathe his sword and put an end to the plague.

2   The Art of Dissembling

In 1922 Josef Hell asked Hitler, "What do you want to do to the Jews once you have full discretionary powers?"[1] Hitler, who until then had spoken calmly and with measured words, underwent a total transformation:

> His eyes no longer saw me but instead bore past me and off into empty space; his explanations grew increasingly voluble until he fell into a kind of paroxysm that ended with his shouting, as if to a whole public gathering: "Once I really am in power, my first and foremost task will be the annihilation of the Jews. As soon as I have the power to do so, I will have gallows built in rows—at the Marienplatz in Munich, for example—as many as traffic allows. Then the Jews will be hanged indiscriminately, and they will remain hanging until they stink; they will hang there as long as the principles of hygiene permit. As soon as they have been untied, the next batch will be strung up, and so on down the line, until the last Jew in Munich has been exterminated. Other cities will follow suit, precisely in this fashion, until all Germany has been completely cleansed of Jews."

Josef Hell adds: "Perhaps because he had worked himself into such a state of excitement, Hitler was more candid with

1. Josef Hell, "Aufzeichnung," 1922, ZS 640, p. 5, Institut für Zeitgeschichte. The retired Major Josef Hell was a journalist in the twenties and in the beginning of the thirties, during which time he also collaborated with Dr. Fritz Gerlich, the editor of the weekly newspaper *Der Gerade Weg*.

me in his subsequent remarks than perhaps he was with others. He, as it were, abruptly cast off the mask that I had taken for his true face."

Hitler's self-disclosure on this one occasion was not entirely unique. In September 1938 General Franz Halder reported to Hitler to be installed as Chief of Staff of the Army. Halder, who had been recommended for the position by Brauchitsch but only grudgingly approved by Hitler, recalls the following dialogue from his session with Hitler:

> Hitler : You should know first of all that you will never be able to discover my thoughts and intentions until I give them out as orders.
>
> Hadler : We soldiers are accustomed to forming our ideas collectively.
>
> Hitler (*laughing, with a disparaging gesture of the hand*) : No, in politics things are entirely different. You will never learn what is going on in my head. As for those who boast of being privy to my thoughts—to them I lie all the more.[2]

Ernst von Weizsäcker, Hitler's State Secretary for Foreign Affairs, also describes how immensely difficult it was to see through Hitler: "Only as time went on did I come to recognize his remarkable talent for dissimulation: agitation, moral indignation, sympathy, shock, sincerity, condolence, reverence—he had a posture for everything."[3] On that day in September 1938, Adolf Hitler consciously permitted the new Chief of Staff a glimpse of his true face—that is, he squarely stated that any attempt to penetrate prematurely into the Führer's thought processes, to gain insight into the status of ongoing decisions, was destined to fail miserably.

2. H. Countess Schall-Riaucour, *Aufstand und Gehorsam* (Wiesbaden, 1972), 44. On 8 February 1970, Halder personally confirmed to the author the content of this dialogue.
3. Schall-Riaucour, ibid. Also quoted in Ernst von Weizsäcker, *Erinnerungen* (Munich, 1950), 199 – 200.

Although no one can pierce Hitler's mind, it is absolutely essential to establish the centrality of this aspect of deceptiveness, his cunning and his lies, particularly with reference to the enactment of the Final Solution that Hitler conceived for the Jewish question, not to mention other orders for liquidation issued by Hitler during the war. Evidence of his deceptiveness may be found in his "wishes"— the only personal elucidations available to us—and in the authentic documents connected with them that were either a product of or a factor in the Final Solution – related events; as well as in dependable, verifiable accounts.

A handwritten memorandum by Field Marshal Wilhelm Keitel, dated 7 October 1945, is quite revealing in this respect.[4] It states that the Führer employed "semantic conventions" (*eine Sprachregelung*) to communicate with his closest political aids, a subject we shall explore in depth below. Although in his speeches Adolf Hitler repeatedly broadcast threats and prophecies of a Jewish annihilation,[5] throughout the design, preparation, and above all the execution of his long-harbored plan for annihilation, Hitler shrewdly calculated his own exculpation. By observing the agreed upon "semantic conventions"—that is, code language—in his spoken responses to Himmler's briefings on the Jewish question (responses that Himmler at least once committed to paper) and by deliberately misleading those in his midst, including some of his intimate collaborators, Hitler threw a mantle of secrecy over his undeniably personal responsibility for the Final Solution of the Jewish question.

That Hitler did not wish the outside world to connect his name with the liquidation actions in the extermina-

4. Wilhelm Keitel, handwritten notes, 7 October 1945, 54/46, vol. 7, Bundesarchiv-Militärarchiv.
5. E.g., Hitler's Reichstag address of 30 January 1939; further threats issued on 30 January 1941 in the Berlin Sportpalast, likewise on 30 January 1942 and 30 September 1942. There are further references to the annihilation of the Jews in the New Year's speech of 1 January 1943; and on 24 February 1943, at the anniversary celebration of the Party.

19

tion camps is confirmed in the seven sole attested references by Himmler to a "Führer-order." Already at the beginning of the euthanasia program Hitler had told Bouhler, "the Führer's Chancellery must under no circumstances be seen to be active in this matter"[6]—that very chancellery, in other words, whose branch "T4" was responsible both for the "mercy killing" program and, after the discontinuation of that program in the summer of 1941, for all phases of the operation "Reinhard." Department T4 of the Führer's Chancellery appointed not only the entire German personnel of the liquidation camps Belzec, Sobibor, and Treblinka, but also the inspector of "Einsatz Reinhard"—the code name given to the Sonderkommandos (special task forces) for these camps—Christian Wirth. The head of the Führer's Chancellery, Reichsleiter Bouhler, as well as other key functionaries in T4, visited the extermination camps on the eastern front that had been specially built for the Final Solution of the Jewish question. We will have occasion to discuss T4 at greater length below.

The code language agreed upon by Hitler and his most intimate political advisers originated in the widespread, systematic secrecy that cloaked the euthanasia program, and it remained instrumental in later schemes. For example, on 19 June 1943—eight days after he had issued the commands for the liquidation of every ghetto in Poland and Russia—Himmler held a briefing session at the Führer's mountain retreat on the Obersalzberg. Under point 5 of Himmler's dossier notes on this session, we read the following: "Responding to my briefing on the Jewish question, the Führer declared that the evacuation of the Jews, regardless of the disturbances it will provoke in the next three to four

6. Js 20/61, pp. 18, 22, 25, Generalstaatsanwalt Frankfurt am Main.

months, must be ruthlessly implemented and endured to the end." Now what was the actual meaning of the code word "evacuation" (*Evakuierung*)? The answer to this question can be found in a report of the State Police Bureau in Lodz on 9 June 1942: "With regard to the Jewry, the State Police directed its work toward organizing a Gaughetto, as per the instructions of the Gauleiter. Pursuant to said instructions, all Jews in the Gau who are unfit for labor shall be evacuated, and all those fit for labor shall be rounded up into the ghetto in Litzmannstadt [Lodz]."[7] Sonderkommando Lange, which earlier had been active in the Wartheland and had been called in to kill mental patients in Soldau, was assigned to carry out the "evacuation."

This Sonderkommando was ultimately under the jurisdiction of the Reich Main Security Office (*Reichssicherheitshauptamt*, or RSHA). The nature of its activities is evident in a communiqué sent on 18 October 1940 to SS-Gruppenführer Jakob Sporrenberg by Wilhelm Koppe, the Higher SS and Police Leader (*Höhere SS- und Polizeiführer*, or HSSPF) in the Reichsgau Wartheland: "The so-called Sonderkommando Lange, assigned to me for special tasks, was detached to Soldau in East Prussia from 21 May to 8 June 1940, as per agreement with the Reich Main Security Office. During this period, it successfully evacuated 1,558 mental patients from the Soldau transit camp."[8] From this communiqué and related correspondence it is irrefutably evident that the "evacuation" amounted to the killing of mental patients who had been transferred from East Prussian sanatoria to the Soldau concentration camp. And it has been proven that the Sonderkommando Lange, which had previ-

7. Gestapo Lodz 234/III, Archive of the Ministry of Justice, Warsaw.
8. Original documents in the Bundesarchiv, Koblenz; copy in the collection Zentrale Stelle für Landesjustizverwaltungen: vol. 9, fols. 806–7.

ously been at work in the extermination camp at Chelmno in the Warthegau, was at that time already using gassing vans for liquidation.[9]

On 7 March 1944, the above-mentioned Gauleiter Greiser, head of the new Reichsgau Wartheland, cabled to Hitler news of the elimination of the Jews in his Gau— "down to a very insignificant remnant."[10] Nearly 153,000 Jews had been murdered in the Warthegau liquidation camp at Chelmno, mainly by means of gassing vans. Prior to this, in a top secret state document (*geheime Reichssache*) dated 21 November 1942, Greiser had apprised his immediate superior in Final Solution–related matters, Reichsführer-SS Himmler, that the Führer "in our most recent discussion about the Jews has told me to proceed against them in whatever manner I judge best." And Greiser—who had met with Hitler on 1 October 1942 and again on 11 November 1942— did exactly that.

Within the framework of such semantic cunning and carefully contrived camouflage tactics coupled with the stringent observance of secrecy, we can readily understand why "the 'Final Solution' of the Jewish question was a 'masterpiece of concealment.'"[11] As late as 11 July 1943, in circular number 33/43, Reichsleiter Martin Bormann communicated the following "by order of the Führer": "In public discussion of the Jewish question any mention of a future total solution must be avoided. However, one may discuss the fact that all Jews are being interned and detailed to purposeful compulsory labor forces."[12] This circular communiqué was brought to the attention of all Reichsleiters and Gauleiters, as well as to all

9. Adalbert Rückerl, *NS-Vernichtungslager* (Munich, 1977), 259.
10. Document NO 5503, Institut für Zeitgeschichte.
11. Remark made after the war at Nuremberg by Gen. Alfred Jodl, former Chief of the OKW Operations Staff (Wehrmachtführungsstab).
12. 10 a Js 39/60, p. 239, Landgericht München II.

Higher SS and Police Leaders and SS Chiefs of Administrative Headquarters. The greater public was to believe that the deported Jews were serving in compulsory labor programs.

Hitler was on his guard, mistrustful and suspicious not only of his citizenry but of the Church as well. The euthanasia program had proved to be a "bad experience"; several prominent clerics had vociferously protested against the liquidations carried out in permanent, built-in gas chambers at institutions created expressly for the purpose. This public outcry caused Hitler to rescind, in August 1941, his euthanasia command of 1 September 1939 and to order the immediate stoppage of Action T4. On 28 August 1941, the action, which had taken ninety thousand lives, was discontinued. [13]

Characteristic of the code language used in the T4 Action is a memorandum dated 15 January 1943 and written by the director of the "euthanasia institute" in Brandenburg, Dr. Eberl: "The work of the Charitable Foundation for Institutional Care [Gemeinnützige Stiftung für Anstaltspflege] has been suspended since 24 August 1941. Since then, disinfections [Desinfektionen] have been conducted only on a very small scale." [14] According to statements by witnesses, the term "Desinfektion" stood for the "gassing process" and was reserved for internal communications." [15]

Likewise characteristic of the tight connection between the coordinating office "T4" (that is, Tiergartenstrasse 4, Berlin), controlled by the Führer's Chancellery, and the "Reinhard" extermination program (the liquidation of Polish Jews and of Jews deported from the occupied West) is the formula used continually by the inspector of the spe-

---

13. At least eighty thousand mental patients and ca. ten thousand concentration camp prisoners under "special treatment 14f13" (Js 20/61, p. 375), Generalstaatsanwalt Frankfurt am Main).

14. Ibid., p. 114.

15. Ibid., p. 115.

cial units of Action Reinhard, Christian Wirth: "Wir in der Stiftung" (we in the Foundation). T4, the extermination agency of the Führer's Chancellery, headed by Reichsleiter Bouhler, operated under the cover names (1) Die gemein-nützige Stiftung für Anstaltspflege (The Charitable Foundation for Institutional Care; known as *Stiftung*), (2) Die ge-meinnützige Kranken-Transport GmbH (The Charitable Corporation for the Transport of the Sick, abbreviated as *Ge-krat*), and (3) Die Reichsarbeitsgemeinschaft Heil- und Pfle-geanstalten (The Reich Work Cooperative for Institutional Care; or *RAG*). Without exception, the key functionaries of the Führer's Chancellery/T4 in Berlin appeared before the public under false names: SS-Oberführer Viktor Brack, as Jennerwein; Werner Blankenburg, as Brenner; Reinhold Vorberg, as Hintertal. Hitler had expressly commanded that the Führer's Chancellery not surface in public and that the link between the extermination organ T4 and the Chancel-lery be rigorously concealed.[16]

A straight path leads from the built-in gas chambers of the euthanasia institutes in Brandenburg, Bensburg, Grafeneck, Hartheim, Hadamar, Sonnenstein, and Eich-berg to the extermination camp in Sobibor, under SS-Major Christian Wirth, formerly of the euthanasia institute in Brandenburg. In the euthanasia institutes German vic-tims—chiefly mental patients—were "quickly and quietly" eliminated with carbon-monoxide gas; and already in June 1940 the practice of pilfering gold-filled teeth from the corpses of the Jewish victims among them had begun.[17] At Sobibor, identical liquidation procedures, along with the same despoliation of Jewish corpses, were the order of the day: in the period from March to June 1943 alone, 34,294

16. Ibid., p. 18.
17. Kalisch testimony, 25 January 1960, Js 20/61, p. 102.

Dutch Jews were liquidated with carbon-monoxide gas.[18] It is significant that the document transferring SA-Sturmführer (and Stuttgart Kriminalkommissar) Christian Wirth to the security service, dated 8 April 1938, bears the remark, "z.V. Führer" (at the disposal of the Führer);[19] just as the proposal to promote Wirth to the rank of Sturmbannführer, dated 13 April 1943, informs the Head of the SS Personnel Main Office that Wirth had been "serving in a special mission for the Führer" since the beginning of the war.[20] At the time of this nomination, Wirth was actively engaged at Sobibor—right at the time of the RSHA transports and the liquidation of the Dutch Jews—as the request for his promotion, made by SS-Obergruppenführer Bouhler (Head of the Führer's Chancellery) and SS-Gruppenführer Globocnik, establishes.[21] In subsequent pages the reader will be given ample opportunity to form a more exact picture of the astounding system of deception that was designed to veil and to shield the methods of the euthanasia program and their eventual application to the Final Solution in the East.

We now turn to the most precisely documented events to occur in the euthanasia institutes. It began with minutely detailed and freely invented medical histories which took the same course toward their supposed conclusions. The conclusions were supplied by the doctors who, after the killings, registered in the medical records a history of disease

18.   L. de Jong, *Gedeporteerde Joden* (Amsterdam, 1970), Table 9, p. 708. Of the 107,000 deported Dutch Jews, 5,200 repatriated (L. de Jong, Rijksinstituut voor Oorlogsdocumentatie, to author, 9 July 1980).
The assertion of David Irving (in *Hitler's War* [London and New York, 1977], xiv) that Hitler never ordered the liquidation of the European Jews, that these were ad hoc measures brought about by a dilemma, is a fiction.
19.   Berlin Document Center; photocopy in author's possession.
20.   Ibid.
21.   Recommendation for nomination to the SS Personnel Main Office, 13 April 1943, states: "Sobibor, where Wirth is currently at work" (Berlin Document Center).

that would justify a death by the assigned natural cause.

Fabricated causes of death and medical histories, however, were not, in and of themselves, enough. One had to justify somehow the immediate cremation of the corpses without the prior consent of the next of kin. Consequently, someone hit upon the idea that the local police authorities had ordered immediate cremation on the grounds of a hazard of epidemic. "Letters of condolence," forwarded to the nearest relatives, would read: "For purposes of avoiding the outbreak or the communication of an infectious disease the local police authorities, as per §22 of the ordinance concerning the combatting of communicable diseases, have ordered the immediate cremation of the corpse and the disinfection of any remaining effects." As every euthanasia institute had its own registry office and local police,[22] it was not hard to issue an order of this kind, although no reasonable grounds for fearing an epidemic existed. The only logistical concern was to make room for the new bodies as quickly as possible, and to guard against the risk of relatives learning the truth should they request an autopsy, which was not inconceivable. Just as the conclusions for the course of the fictitious disease were the product of official falsification, so were the death certificates official false documents. Only the fact of death was accurate.

The most astounding and utter fabrication within the realm of the cover-up of the euthanasia program, however, was the registry office of Cholm, near Lublin in the Generalgouvernement (a portion of occupied Poland). As five witnesses have attested, a subsection of T4 in the Columbushaus, on the Papestrasse in Berlin, under the name of "registry office of Cholm," post address Lublin, registered the deaths in a number of cases—mainly the deaths of Jews, in particular the ones killed in the Brandenburg euthanasia

22. Ks 2/63, p. 86, Generalstaatsanwalt Frankfurt am Main.

institute. The registry office was nonexistent. In order to make the falsification maximally credible, both the certificates of death and letters of condolence were written out in Berlin, delivered by courier to Lublin, and mailed from there. In this way, the documents bore the official postal stamp from Lublin.[23]

A nonexistent registry, documents with false reports of causes and circumstances of death, the pretense of an epidemic hazard as justification for the cremation of corpses, cover names for physicians and officials, fabricated medical histories, gas chambers disguised as tiled shower facilities with dummy shower nozzles, hypocritical demonstrations of sympathy and condolence, deceptive claims about the purpose of patient relocations and the registration forms: this is what actually constituted the euthanasia program, which was so readily termed a program of "mercy killing" (*Gnadentod*), and about which no one—least of all, the victims—was permitted to know for whom, when, and where "mercy" would be granted.

"When the ten-thousandth killing had occurred in Hadamar, the personnel of the institute made this the occasion for a party. Amid the gathering in one room of the institute, while drinks were being served, somebody donned the garb and acted the part of a priest. This was the joke with which the ten-thousandth death was celebrated."[24]

"The law of existence prescribes uninterrupted killing, so that the better may live," asserted Adolf Hitler on the afternoon of 10 October 1941.[25] We have already mentioned Hitler's plans for annihilation, as he disclosed them to Josef Hell in 1922. We have furthermore noted Hell's statement that in a moment of extreme excitation Hitler divulged his

23. Ibid., pp. 86–87.
24. Ibid., p. 44.
25. *Adolf Hitler, Monologe im Führerhauptquartier: 1941–1944*, ed. W. Jochmann (Hamburg, 1980), 76.

plans for destruction—to liquidate the Jews throughout Germany, once he was in power—and then "abruptly cast off the mask" and began to speak more candidly in his subsequent remarks than he was accustomed to do with others. What were these subsequent remarks that revealed Hitler's world of thought in all its stark reality, particularly with regard to the Jewish question? We read the following in Josef Hell's account:

> When I now broached the question of what the source of his so strongly felt hatred for the Jews was, and why he wanted to destroy this so undeniably intelligent race—a race to which the Germans and all other Aryans, if not the entire world, owed an incalculable debt in virtually all fields of art and knowledge, research and economics—Hitler suddenly calmed down and gave this unexpectedly sober and almost dispassionate explanation: "It is manifestly clear and has been proven in practice and by the facts of all revolutions that a *struggle for ideals*, for improvements of any kind whatsoever, absolutely must be supplemented with a struggle against some social class or caste. My object is to create first-rate revolutionary upheavals, regardless of what methods and means I have to use in the process. Earlier revolutions were directed either against the peasants, or the nobility and the clergy, or against dynasties and their network of vassals, but in no case has revolution succeeded without the presence of a lightning rod that could conduct and channel the odium of the general masses.
>
> "With this very thing in mind I scanned the revolutionary events of history and put the question to myself: against which racial element in Germany can I unleash my propaganda of hate with the greatest prospects of success? I had to find the right kind of victim, and especially one against whom the struggle would make sense, materially speaking. I can assure you that I examined every possible and thinkable solution to this problem, and, weighing every imaginable factor, I came to the conclusion that a campaign against the Jews would be as popular as it would be successful. There are few Germans who

have not been vexed with the behavior of Jews or else have not suffered losses through them in some way or other. Disproportionately to their small number they account for an immense share of the German national wealth, which can just as easily be put to profitable use for the state and the general public as could the holdings of the monasteries, bishops, and nobility.

"Once the hatred and the battle against the Jews have been really stirred up, their resistance will necessarily crumble in the shortest possible time. They are totally defenseless, and no one will stand up to protect them."[26]

Here we have evidence of Hitler's two kinds of anti-Semitism: the one a traditionally inspired and instinctively affirmed anti-Semitism that due to its racialistic/biological component took a particularly rigid form; and the other a flexible, goal-oriented anti-Semitism that was pragmatically superimposed on the first. Over the years, Hitler slowly and systematically accumulated the explanations and grounds for his amalgam of Jew hatred. Then, once in power, he refined from this manifold compound of perspectives what would prove to be, propagandistically and psychologically speaking, an effective, synthetic distillate of words and images that spelled and evoked hate. It was with this refined ideology that Hitler sought to work the German people, and later occupied Europe as well, into the desired frame of mind. Considering the intensity that this baiting campaign assumed, a certain impact within the German-speaking lands was inevitable. The question is whether Hitler succeeded in implanting in the Germans his personal and virulent will to annihilate the Jews.

Although, with one bold exception,[27] the Church did not publicly protest against the deportation of Jews from the

26. Josef Hell, "Aufzeichnung," 1922, ZS 640, p. 6, Institut für Zeitgeschichte.
27. Provost Bernhard Lichtenberg told his Gestapo interrogators in

Reich, Hitler was politically too shrewd to assume that the majority of Germans would, in the last analysis, share his unbounded hatred for the Jews and be willing to grant him carte blanche in the Final Solution. He felt that he understood his citizenry, and he considered it absolutely imperative that the "total solution" of the Jewish question be painstakingly masked—only thus could he indulge his destructive impulses. That millions of persons in the Reich suspected what was happening to the Jews at the time is, however, likely. That many at home knew what was occurring on the eastern front at "the Führer's wish" (a euphemism whose great import will be examined below) is certain; for not every soldier returning home on leave maintained total silence about things he had seen or heard, as we shall see.

Upon Provost Bernhard Lichtenberg's arrest in St. Hedwig and his subsequent detention in Berlin-Dahlen, Josef Goebbels had privately stated, "We'll make them all criminals." Such was in fact Hitler's tactic. The Führer intended to brand the Jews enemies of the state, which would then enable him to represent his policy of annihilation as a measure of "self-defense." Only in light of this pretense may we understand his statement: "After the treatment that the Jews have received from me, they simply must be my enemies; and especially in war, one is entitled to fight one's enemies. Hundreds of soldiers fall each day at the front, without having incurred any guilt whatsoever."[28] Hitler's

---

October 1941 that he wished to share the fate of the Jews who had been sent to the East. Theophil Wurm, Bishop of Württemberg, wrote an open letter of protest to a ministerial official on 28 January 1943 denouncing the "systematic murder of Jews and Poles," and he wrote further letters of protest to Gauleiter Wilhelm Murr on 8 February 1943, to the Reich Minister of the Interior on 14 March 1943, and to Hitler on 16 July 1943; this last letter was prudently withheld from submission by Dr. Lammers.

28. Dr. Otto Bräutigam to the author, 23 January 1978.

pretense is likewise significant with regard to his reaction, in October 1941, to complaints about the "deportation of Jews" that were submitted to him and to Hermann Göring by officers in the Department of War Administration at the Quartermaster General's office: "The Jewish question takes priority over all other matters."[29]

29. Ibid., 25 May 1978.

3

Hitler's Influence on

the Conduct of War

We have noted General Alfred Jodl's remark that in his view the Final Solution of the Jewish question was "a masterpiece of secrecy." Should Jodl possibly have been aware at an early date of his Commander in Chief's intentions? Before we delve deeper into this question, by considering the Führer-order received by Field Marshal Rommel on 9 June 1942, we will want to consult the head of the OKW (High Command of Combined Forces), Field Marshal Keitel. In a memorandum written in Keitel's hand and dated 16 February 1946, with the heading "The influence of the SS on the conduct of war," we read the following:

> It must have been in *March of '41—before* the Yugoslav revolution—when Hitler addressed the assembled generals in preparation for the attack on the Soviet Union planned for the middle of May 1941 (it was, in other words, eight weeks prior to the invasion and in connection with bringing up the troops by rail) when Hitler disclosed *for the first time* his views on the war—a war that was ideologically conditioned and that *deviated from the normal rules*—and on its methods. Already at this time, not at the last round of talks held in mid-June 1941, Hitler developed ideas that demonstrated to the generals the ruthlessness of war and the dangers presented by those segments of the population that had been infected with Bolshevist fanaticism, by the rule of the Commissars and

by the anticipated partisan resistance. He further directed at this meeting that draconian measures be used to fight these dangers. Hitler's disclosures were all the more serious and unforgettable since he himself indicated that he did not envisage any *agreement from the generals* but instead was expecting them to credit him with an accurate appraisal of the situation; for he alone—not the generals—understood the war he was conducting in Germany against communism and the global enemy that was a fanaticized product of communist ideology.

No one among the generals, including those who had long been involved in the plans for war, did or could envisage what *methods* would be implemented in this *war between soldiers*. Not a single word was spoken about the extermination of the population or of the *Jews*, or about mass executions or relocations into concentration camps. Not a word about setting up a regime of terror by the Gestapo. The discussion centered, rather, on the economic exploitation of the land, on the stockpiling of foodstuffs and raw materials. At the time no general even fleetingly imagined that—except for reasons of self-defense, for which all countermeasures would be admissible—he might ever be required to act in a way that would necessarily, or even intentionally, compromise the integrity and honor of the Wehrmacht. For these reasons, no general stepped forward to protest. Inwardly, however, many disputed the necessity of the war and had deep misgivings, especially about the orders that political activists, agents, and commissars be eliminated, that prisoner of war status be abolished, that the prisoners be turned over to the Gestapo (Security Service), and furthermore, that both civilians and military personnel be made subject to the wartime judicial machinery. While these were the most serious encroachments on the customary codes of the rules of war to date, they were, as a last resort, understandable and admissible, so long as the commanding officers and the commanders were to be entrusted with the *sole* responsibility for the *implementation* of such measures; that is to say, so long as non-soldiers would not be invested *with special powers* for this task. In any case, no higher commanding officer expressed to me his refusal to obey these instructions. Subsequently, when the time came to follow up the verbal commands with written directives, Hitler and I fell into serious dispute, particularly when he ordered the *intervention of the Reichsführer SS*. The preparation of "guidelines" for the "Barbarossa" order regarding the administration and utilization of territories that were to be occupied led to severe disagreements over the special powers granted to the Reichsführer SS. It dawned on me that here, *alongside* the Wehrmacht and the power that was to be wielded over the population solely by the Commander in Chief of the Army, a police force was being created whose executive authority (such as Hitler would later grant it) caused me to have very serious reservations. My counterproposals, which, so far as I know, received support from von Brauchitsch, got nowhere; Hitler's personally *revised* "guidelines" received the wording he had required, although none of us was aware of the actual consequences. My fears soon proved to be only too well founded. With this authorization, Hitler cleared the way for Himmler to become, *alongside* the Wehrmacht, a *key factor in the conduct of the war* in the East. The justification for this move was sought in the claim that the Soviet government had not ratified the "Haag Agreement" of 1907 or the Geneva accords and had intentionally set itself above the conventions of international law; their breach relieved us of our corresponding obligations. The SS, led by Himmler, began to enact its plans with utter lack of restraint, as witnessed by the Wehrmacht. The Wehrmacht (the OKW and the OKH) was deceiving itself by hiding beneath the wording of the orders, the claim that the SS (Himmler) was operating in *"its own capacity, responsible only to itself."* Both the SS and the Wehrmacht had to follow the orders of *the same supreme commander, Hitler;* this obviously could not leave the Wehrmacht unaffected. What forms and effects Himmler's authorization would take, no one foresaw or could foresee. The veil that Hitler himself had drawn over this aspect of the conduct of war blocked the army's perception, until deeds followed the authorizations and the events, if not in their full extent, then at least in their systematic relation, no longer remained hidden from the view of the commanders and commanding officers. Nor is the scandalousness of this development altered by Hitler's repeated insistence that he was deliberately dissociating the *Wehrmacht* from everything that would taint it in the eyes of the public and of the world, and in particular from any dishonorable breach of international law regarding the conduct of war. Such dirty work was the province of the *police*, he claimed.

To recapitulate briefly:

1) *Alongside* the Wehrmacht, which provided the legitimate defense of the Reich against both internal and external threats (as would an armed force in any state), a separate and fully autonomous element, invested with extraordinary powers, evolved out of the party Schutzstaffeln [defense squads]. This element was the SS. Once sanctioned, it held in its hands the virtual authority of the state, which is to say, it exercised decisive control on a sweeping scale—in politics, administration, law enforcement, and racial policy.

2) Even before warlike developments and acts of war, the SS, as Hitler's instrument, had become the veritable champion and standard-bearer of a power politics bent on conquest in Europe.

3) With the beginning of military actions, the SS entered into the plan. It worked as circumstances demanded, at first in concealment, or at least keeping a low profile. Its alleged function was to defend annexed or occupied territories against political opponents. In reality, the purpose of the SS was to "cleanse" said territories.

4) The path of conquest cut a straight line, beginning with the occupation of the Sudeten, across Poland and the western territories, and curved sharply into Russia. Occupations were routinely preceded by destabilizations, the staging of political unrest by means of the so-called liberation and Germanization actions and incidents. Upon reaching Russia, the goal was to depopulate the area and reappropriate it as a space for German settlements.

1) With the Barbarossa "guidelines" for the administration and exploitation of the occupied eastern territories, the Wehrmacht—albeit *contrary* to its intentions and in ignorance of the implications of its compliance—provided the means for all consequent developments and actions that took place under its cover, and in which it steadily became more and more deeply enmeshed.

2) Neither I nor my colleagues had any deeper insight into the repercussions of Himmler's authority; unlike the OKH [Army High Command], which had actually entered directly into agreements with Himmler's agencies without murmur or objection. In retrospect, the OKW cannot hide itself very well behind the OKH, and the reverse is even less possible; for the Commander in Chief of the Army had *competence to issue orders* and so was responsible for the consequences of his orders, while the OKW lacked all such authority.

3) The Commander in Chief did not have the executive power or authority to *issue* and *enforce* laws in the occupied East. This prerogative belonged strictly to Himmler and Heydrich, who held *de facto discretionary powers* over the life and death of the population and prisoners, including prisoners of war, in whose camps they exercised executive power.

4) The traditional training and perception of duties in the German officers' corps encouraged unquestioning obedience and the automatic transfer of responsibility onto superiors. In the East this system broke down and gave way to an ambivalent posture: the officers recognized the illegality of orders and methods, yet they shied away from resistance.

5) Insofar as we were concerned, the Führer Hitler irresponsibly *abused* his *authority* and his basic "Order No. 1," which read approximately as follows:

    1) *No one shall be informed* about classified matters that do not fall within the scope of his assignments.

    2) *No one* shall *learn more* than is necessary for the completion of his assignment.

    3) *No one* shall obtain information *earlier* than is necessary for his assigned duties.

4) *No one* shall be permitted to *transmit* classified assignments to their destinations *sooner,* or in greater detail, than is absolutely essential to the prosecution of any given objective.

6) [sic] If the entire complex of developments resulting from Himmler's authorization for the activities of the SS in the East had come to light *earlier* than it did, all senior generals would have protested *for the first time.* This is my belief. While these monstrosities were developing step by step, each one from its predecessor, in ignorance of the consequences, fate ran its tragic course—with all its fateful consequences.[1]

"Both the SS and the Wehrmacht were immediately subordinate to the same supreme commanding officer, Hitler," Keitel writes, and then adds that this could not possibly have left the Wehrmacht "unaffected." Not every Wehrmacht commander, however, was prepared to heed an order that violated international law and that had originated in Hitler's unbridled hatred for the Jews.

On 9 June 1942, the head of the panzer army in Africa, Field Marshal Erwin Rommel, received a top priority telegram. Its contents read:

Chefsache [top secret]. 9 June 1942. Per officer only.
1. To the Panzer Army in Africa
   via German General at High Command of the Italian Armed Forces, Rome

Inform: 2. OKH/GenQu
3. Gen. z.b.V. bei OKH
4. Ob.d.L./Gen.Qu
5. OKW/WR

According to current intelligence reports, numerous

---

1. Wilhelm Keitel, 16 February 1946. This copy was checked for accuracy against the handwritten notes by Maj. Ernst-Wilhelm Keitel (retd.), who gave the author a confirmation of its accuracy on 31 July 1980. Marked as in original.

German political refugees are to be found with the free French units in Africa.

The Führer has ordered that they be proceeded against with the utmost rigor. They should therefore be ruthlessly destroyed in battle. Captives should be summarily shot on orders of the nearest German officer, unless they are to be spared temporarily for intelligence purposes.

Further written communication of this order is forbidden. The commanders should be instructed by word of mouth.

OKW/WFSt/Qu (Verw.)
no. 55, 994/42.g/Kdos. Chefs.[2]

The Führer-order reproduced here was not carried out by Field Marshal Rommel. On this incident General Siegfried Westphal has the following to say in his *Erinnerungen* (recollections): "Bir el Hacheim was particularly courageously defended by the Free French First Brigade, and alongside it the Thirteenth Half-brigade of the Foreign Legion under General König. This stronghold was a key post. According to the OKW, König also had a Jewish battalion under his command. We received a radio signal from Hitler ordering that all captured Israelis be 'slaughtered in battle.' We destroyed this order, as we did not want to have anything to do with such methods."[3] The commando-order of 18 October 1942, signed by Hitler, was likewise destroyed with Rommel's approval.[4]

As head of the OKW operations staff and Hitler's strategic adviser, General Jodl not only accepted and relayed

2. Bundesarchiv-Militärarchiv, RW 4/659 (alt. III w 77) (see plates). On the same day, Himmler addressed the SS, which had assembled in the Mosaic Hall of the New Reich Chancellery for the state ceremony in honor of Reinhard Heydrich. He made an appeal for retaliation: "Ours is, however, the holy obligation to avenge his death, to take over his task, and to destroy with even greater determination the enemies of our nation, mercilessly and pitilessly."
3. Siegfried Westphal, *Erinnerungen* (Mainz, 1975), 162.
4. General Westphal to the author, 17 October 1978; cf. ibid., 181.

"Hitler's mistaken decisions," both against his better judgment and without consideration for the possible consequences; he had, "to an increasing extent, personally fallen under Hitler's pernicious influence."[5] In the guidelines that Jodl drew up after a briefing session with Hitler on 3 March 1941—essentially, a blueprint for the future administration of German-occupied Russian territories, which was to be handled by his department—we find the straight doctrinal assertion that the Jewish-Bolshevik intelligentsia must be eliminated, on the grounds that it had acted as an oppressor of the people. Similarly, Jodl had no fundamental reservations about the executions as directed in Hitler's commissar-order. In the OKW briefing agenda of 12 May 1941, point 1 states that high-ranking political officials and leaders (commissars) must be eliminated. Moreover, a handwritten marginal note by Jodl reads: "We can count on future reprisals against German pilots. Therefore, we shall do best to organize the whole action as if it were an act of reprisal."

We have known for several years how difficult it was at the Nuremberg trials for Field Marshal Keitel to bear the weight of his own crimes, especially in view of his performance as Hitler's all-too-willing instrument when he countersigned the orders from Hitler that led to the murder of prisoners of war and civilians in the occupied territories. The final months of Keitel's life, writes Robert M. W. Kempner, "were overshadowed by a particular tragedy."[6] Keitel wanted to confess his crimes before the world. There is no doubt that his confession would have made a crucial and weighty contribution toward the indictment of the Wehrmacht's conduct in the earlier stages of the war; but Göring, who even in Nuremberg was still a kind of superior

5. *Die Nachhut,* information organ for former members of the German Intelligence Service only, no. 4 (1968):17.
6. Robert M. W. Kempner, *Das Dritte Reich im Kreuzverhör* (Munich, 1969), 94.

for Keitel, forbade his intended confession.[7] As Hitler's immediate subordinate in the chain of command that was responsible for the "evacuation" of Jews to the East, Göring understandably had a vested interest in seeing Keitel's confession thwarted.[8] But in order to understand Keitel's behavior at Nuremberg and to do justice to that individual, we must briefly consider some aspects of German mentality.

Despite his feelings of culpability, Wilhelm Keitel did not, in the last analysis, wish to appear as a "traitor" in the eyes of his fellow defendants, nor did he wish to expose himself to the charge of having defected through his confession from the "community of fate." This "community," to which the most prominent Nuremberg accused all belonged, was an avatar in microcosm of the blood brotherhood between Führer and Volk that the dictator had longed for, an alliance in which disobedience, or even resistance, was unthinkable. Dieter Ehlers describes the German conception of dutiful obedience, the characteristic readiness to submit unquestioningly to hierarchical structure, as a formally conservative "inertia of a historical, centuries-old public ethic of reverential respect toward authority." He adds that the Führer-concept of the Third Reich was by no means an absolute novelty in Germany. "It was merely the culmination, albeit in a modified and fanaticized form, of the well-established historical tradition of unconditional obedience that had its beginnings in Prussian absolutism."[9] Yet there also existed in Prussian military history—from the Prince von Homburg, through Seydlitz, Ziethen, Yorck von Wartenburg, Blücher, Gneisenau, Wrangel, Moltke, and on

---

7. Ibid., 97.
8. On 20 January 1942, Heydrich stated "that he had been commissioned by Reich Marshal Göring on the Führer's instructions, and that in place of emigration the Führer had sanctioned the future evacuation of the Jews to the East" (Notes by Martin Luther, 21 August 1942, NG 2586 J).
9. Dieter Ehlers, *Technik und Moral einer Verschwörung* (Frankfurt, 1964), 56.

to the army commanders of the First World War—a tradition wherein "courage before the thrones of kings" and standing up for one's convictions were a matter of course. Hitler and his top functionaries knew full well that among a considerable number of senior Wehrmacht officers there existed this courageous attitude of mind and the morally and religiously instilled ethic closely bound up with it. They were equally aware of the fact that the Wehrmacht as a fighting machine was not the maximally ideologically fanaticized army that the leadership wanted it to be.[10]

Such, at least, were the assumptions behind Himmler's address to the Führer-corps of the SS Division "Das Reich"[11] on 19 June 1942. He took this occasion to explain why the SS, and not the Wehrmacht, was qualified to wage the race war in an appropriately ruthless fashion:

> The German soldier has in the past frequently operated under long-outmoded conceptions that once went unquestioned; these he carried with him to the battlefield in 1939. From the very moment the enemy was taken captive, this erroneous notion of what war is all about showed itself unmistakably. Thus, for instance, it was thought that one had to say that even a Jew was a human being and that as such, he could not be harmed. Or, in the case of a Jewess—even if she had been caught harboring partisans at the time—one couldn't touch her; she was, after all, a lady. The same held for this eastern campaign too, when the whole German nation took to the field, their heads filled with such absolute rubbish and overrefined, civilized decadence. We SS men were less encumbered, one might even say practically unencumbered, by such rubbish. After a decade of racial education we, the entire cadre of the SS, entered this war as unshakable champions of our Germanic people. The principle I enunciated in my speech at the state ceremony for

10. Cf. Martin Bormann, secret decree to all Gauleiters, 7 June 1941: "National Socialist and Christian perspectives are irreconcilable" (Bundesarchiv, Koblenz).

11. 10 a Js 39/60, pp. 312–13, StA München.

> SS-Obergruppenführer Heydrich, namely, that we ought to spare neither our own nor foreign blood if the nation so requires, was for us law. As the spirit that permeated many, many other laws, it was the sum of the ideological education in respect to foreigners that the entire SS, but in particular the Waffen SS, the SS-V.T. [black-uniformed SS], and the SS-T.V. [SS units mainly guarding concentration camps] received.

Thus, sections of the SS and the police became the executors of the Führer's "will" and "wish" that the "Jewish race in Europe be exterminated"—and the word "wish" plays a key role, as will be shown.

In the context of the Führer's "will" and "wish" and its subsequent execution, we shall select a number of significant moments from the past, some of which will be brought to light for the first time, including a number of documents and statements produced by Hitler that will make clear his leading and literally commanding role in the large-scale "actions" of the Final Solution. For, as Eberhard Jäckel has said, scholarship proceeded perhaps too hurriedly over this complex of issues when no written liquidation order from Hitler regarding the Final Solution could be found after the war in the surviving documentary evidence.[12]

12. Eberhard Jäckel, "Hitler und der Mord an den europäischen Juden," *Frankfurter Allgemeine Zeitung*, 25 August 1977, p. 17.

4

Four Key Commissions

In his capacity as chief administrator of the Four Year Plan,[1] on 24 January 1939, Göring assigned Reinhard Heydrich, the head of the Security Police, to bring "the Jewish question . . . to as favorable a solution as present circumstances permit," through emigration.[2] At this stage, the objective of the German Jewish policy was still, in general, to remove the Jews from Germany and from the already annexed territories. With this object in view, Göring created a central agency for Jewish emigration in 1939 and then turned it over to Heydrich.[3] In line with this policy, the Foreign Office proposed, after the fall of France in July 1940, that all Jews be removed not simply from the Reich and the annexed territories, but from Europe as a whole. It further recommended that "the island of Madagascar be requested as a resettlement area for the Jews from France."[4]

The Madagascar Plan had not yet been conceived when, in June 1940, Heydrich informed Joachim von Ribbentrop, the Reich Foreign Secretary, that more than 200,000 Jews had "emigrated from the Reich," but the "prob-

1. In the same year, Göring was named Chairman of the Ministerial Council for the Defense of the Reich.
2. IMT, vol. 26, PS 710, pp. 266–67.
3. Notes by Martin Luther, 21 August 1942, NG 2586 J.
4. Ibid.

lem as a whole"—namely, the fact that almost three and a quarter million Jews stood under German jurisdiction— could no longer be resolved *"through emigration"* (emphasis in the original). "A territorial Final Solution has thus become necessary," Heydrich wrote to von Ribbentrop;[5] while in a predated memorandum from the summer of 1940, in connection with the "treatment of foreign nationals in the East," Himmler wrote, "I hope to see the concept of Jew completely eradicated, through a large-scale deportation of the entire Jewish population to Africa, or else to some colony."[6] At the same time, "out of inner conviction," he still rejected "the physical extermination of a race through Bolshevik methods as un-Germanic and impracticable."

It was almost a year before the Jewish policy of the Third Reich took its fateful turn, in the summer of 1941. On 10–11 November 1941, the Higher SS and Police Leader Ostland, Friedrich Jeckeln, received precise liquidation instructions in the Prinz Albrechtstrasse headquarters from the Reichsführer-SS Himmler, in which we find—as transmitted by Jeckeln—the formula, "the Führer's wish" *(des Führers Wunsch).*[7] In place of emigration from Europe, the solution was now couched in terms of an "evacuation to the East." This formula stood for the physical liquidation, and the liquidation through labor, of the Jewish deportees.

On 2̣ May 1941, Walter Schellenberg, acting for Heydrich, notified the departments of the Security Police by

5. Heydrich to von Ribbentrop, 24 June 1940, Rijksinstituut voor Oorlogsdocumentatie.

6. 10 a Js 39/60, pp. 90–91. On 28 November 1940, Karl Wolff had informed Dr. Walter Gross of the Race Policy Bureau about this RFSS memorandum.

7. "Himmler said I should go over it with Lohse, and even if he was against it, the Riga ghetto was to be liquidated. Tell Lohse, it is my order, which is also the Führer's wish" (Shorthand note, interrogation transcripts from Jeckeln's arrest, 14 December 1945 [Major Zwetajew, interrogator; Sergeant Suur, interpreter], p. 2, Historical State Archive, Riga). Of the 28,564 German Jews deported to Riga and Kovno, 3 percent survived.

circular that "in view of the undoubtedly imminent Final Solution of the Jewish question," the emigration of Jews from France and Belgium was to be forbidden.[8] This decree was issued two months after Hitler had addressed the assembled generals and disclosed his views on the conduct of the war in the East that "deviated from the normal rules." On 1 October, Heydrich's Adviser on Jewish Affairs in the Reich Main Security Office, Adolf Eichmann, broke the news to the German Jews. On 23 October,[9] five days after the departure of the first RSHA convoy of Jews out of Berlin,[10] Eichmann's immediate superior, SS-Brigadeführer Heinrich Müller of the Gestapo, issued a related set of instructions to the offices of the Sipo (*Sicherheitspolizei*, or Security Police) and the SD (*Sicherheitsdienst*, or Security Service). This same Gestapo chief, on 1 August 1941, had wired coded instructions to the commanders of the four Einsatzgruppen (operational task forces) to the effect that "the Führer is to be kept informed continually from here about the work of the Einsatzgruppen in the East."[11] It was doubtless "the Führer's wish" to be continually updated on the mass shootings conducted by Einsatzgruppen A, B, C, and D. Since we find that this expression of Hitler's will, equivalent in force to a command, was closely connected with the mass shootings that occurred outside Riga in November and December of 1941, the following comments are worth quoting. Dr. Werner Best has said: "I can attest that, seen 'from below,' that is, from the perspective of those who received the orders, the formulas 'der Führer wünscht' [the Führer wishes] and 'der Führer hat befohlen' [the Führer has ordered] were perfectly syn-

---

8. 10 a Js 39/60, p. 173.
9. Ibid., p. 179.
10. Robert M. W. Kempner, *Der Mord an 35,000 Berliner Juden*, offprint (Heidelberg, 1970), 185.
11. Müller, SS-Brigadeführer RSHA IV A 1 b, B. Nr. 576 B/41 g FT (coded), Berlin, 1 August 1941. Fa 213/3, Institut für Zeitgeschichte.

onymous. . . . At the receiving end as well . . . the word 'wish' was used as an equivalent to 'order.'" And according to Richard Schulze-Kossens: "The verbal expressions 'der Führer wünscht,' 'es ist des Führers Wunsch' [it is the Führer's wish], and 'was des Führers Wunsch ist' [which is the Führer's wish] . . . are identical in meaning. Although these are not direct orders, they are, nonetheless, to be interpreted as such. If, therefore, he were to tell me to signal to the Leibstandarte [Hitler's bodyguard] . . . 'it is my wish that they do this and that immediately,' then the commander of the Leibstandarte naturally would view this as an order. The 'wish' is always communicated by a third party and is not explicitly passed on as a Führer-order. But it does indeed have the force of an order."[12]

The planned killing of all Jews that could be seized was a comprehensive task. To synchronize the simultaneous liquidations of great masses at the appropriate sites required a procedure thought out with absolute precision down to the smallest detail. Also needed was an organization that would ensure the swift and regular flow of Jews to be delivered to the extermination camps. In the summer of 1941, in line with directives issued by the Führer,[13] three commissions were handed out: one from the Reichsführer-SS Heinrich Himmler to the Commandant of Auschwitz, Rudolf Höss,[14] another, likewise from Himmler, to Christian Wirth,[15] and a third, dated 31 July 1941, passed on by Göring to Heydrich. Himmler's assignment to Höss was issued verbally, as were

---

12. Dr. Werner Best to author, 20 August 1980; Richard Schulze-Kossens to author, 25 October 1980.
13. Heydrich's statement at the Wannsee Conference on 20 January 1942, "that he had been commissioned by Reich Marshal Göring on the Führer's instructions" (notes by Martin Luther, 21 August 1942, NG 2586 J).
14. Notes by Höss, "Die Endlösung der Judenfrage im KL Auschwitz," (Cracow, November 1946).
15. Dr. Konrad Morgen, affidavit SS-67, 19 July 1946, Nuremberg.

those to the killing specialist of the euthanasia program, Christian Wirth. Göring's written commission resulted in the postponed Wannsee Conference of 20 January 1942.

Since 1936 it had become common practice to pass on the powers that Göring had received by the ordinance of 18 October 1936 to special deputies whose spheres of jurisdiction overlapped the normal departmental competence. Fritz Sauckel, authorized personally by Hitler to supervise the deployment of labor forces,[16] likewise derived his powers via Göring from the ordinance of 18 October 1936. But apart from direct assignments from Hitler, Sauckel operated independently. When conflicts arose with Albert Speer, the Reich Minister for Armament and Production, Sauckel looked not to Göring for assistance, but to Hitler. Göring was only the formal middleman; he transferred "his competencies for directing the highest Reich officials" onto others, as Hitler authorized him to do.[17] By the same token, it was Himmler, rather than Göring, who was Heydrich's actual superior in the latter's function as "the deputy for the preparation of the Final Solution of the European Jewish question." It was from Reichsführer-SS Himmler that Heydrich received the order to proceed with the execution of the Final Solution of the Jewish question.

In the summer of 1941,[18] Himmler disclosed to Rudolf Höss, "without the presence of an adjutant,"[19] that the Führer had ordered "the Final Solution of the Jewish question" and that now "whatever Jews we can reach" were to be eliminated "without exception" during the war. Höss would

---

16. B. A. Sijes, "Adolf Eichmann und die Deportation der in den Niederlanden wohnenden Juden," Führer-decree of 21 March 1942, p. 57, Rijksinstituut voor Oorlogsdocumentatie.

17. Ibid., p. 13.

18. "I am unable to pinpoint the date exactly at this time" (Höss, Cracow, November 1946).

19. Ibid., p. 1.

receive further details from Adolf Eichmann, who would see him. Eichmann did contact Höss shortly afterward, in Auschwitz, where the large-scale operations were to be "forced through."[20] Eichmann further initiated Höss into the plans for the liquidation actions that had been envisaged for the individual countries.

First destined for Auschwitz were the Jews in Upper East Silesia and the adjacent parts of occupied Poland; simultaneously at first, and thereafter depending upon their location, the Jews from Germany and Czechoslovakia; finally, those from the West—France, Belgium, and Holland. The logistics of the liquidations were discussed: "Only gas could be considered."[21] To eliminate the anticipated masses by shootings alone would have been physically impossible, and also too great a strain on the SS men who would have to perform this assignment—especially "in view of the women and children."

At the time of their discussion in Auschwitz, neither of the two men knew yet which gas would be considered for the mass liquidations. In any case, Eichmann ruled out "the use of carbon-monoxide gas through nozzles in shower facilities, a method that had been applied in the elimination of mental patients at a few locations in the Reich," because it would require "too many new buildings," and because "the procurement of sufficient quantities of gas for such great numbers [would be] very problematic." But after Zyklon B had been tested on Russian prisoners of war in Auschwitz in autumn 1941 and had proven its effective-

20. Cf. Himmler to Greiser, telegram of 10 June 1944: "Please see this affair, now as before, through to the finish"; and Hitler's answer to Himmler, Obersalzberg, 19 June 1943: "that the evacuation of the Jews . . . must be ruthlessly implemented and endured" (NS 19 [neu] 1947, Bundesarchiv, Koblenz).

21. Höss, Cracow, p. 2.

ness in "bringing about instantaneous death,"[22] Höss passed the news on to Eichmann during the latter's next visit to Auschwitz, "and we decided," Höss writes, "to employ this gas in future mass exterminations."[23]

22. Ibid., p. 3.
23. Ibid., p. 4.

Before Rudolf Höss and Adolf Eichmann determined which gas would be used in the mass liquidations of European Jews at Auschwitz, the RFSS Himmler had witnessed the shooting, which he personally initiated, of between 120 and 180 Jewish men and women—Russian civilians from Minsk who had not been active as partisans.[1] On the basis of this gruesome personal experience, he ordered that a better means of killing be found; this did not, however, prevent the Einsatzgruppen from following through the orders they had received at the beginning of the Russian military campaign. By the end of 1941 they had shot approximately one million people to death.[2]

Did individual leaders of the Einsatzkommandos ask Himmler *who* it was that bore the responsibility for the mass exterminations of the Jews? One of these Einsatz leaders, at any rate, did venture to ask. In the middle of August 1941, in Minsk, on the very day when the 120 to 180 Jewish civilians were shot, the head of Einsatzkommando unit 8, Obersturmbannführer (Lieutenant Colonel) Dr. Otto Brad-

---

1.   Dr. Otto Bradfisch, 9 June 1958, on the events in Minsk: "The shooting of the Jews was not a matter of destroying elements that represented a threat either to the fighting troops or to the pacification of the field of operations behind the lines; it was simply a matter of destroying Jews for the sake of destroying Jews" (10 a Js 39/60, p. 134).
2.   Gerald Reitlinger, *The Final Solution*, 3d ed. (London, 1971), 545.

fisch, put the key question to Himmler. As Bradfisch recalls: "As soon as Himmler arrived in Minsk, I turned to him and asked him who was taking responsibility for the mass extermination of the Jews. Himmler made this conversation the occasion for a speech, in which he told the members of Einsatzkommando 8, as well as those members of the Security Police who were present, not to worry—the orders had been personally given by Hitler. It was a question, then, of a Führer-order, which had the force of law, and he and Hitler alone bore the responsibility for these orders."[3] Himmler's private reply to Bradfisch before the execution had been no different: "Himmler answered me in a fairly sharp tone that these orders had come from Hitler as the supreme Führer of the German government, and that they had the force of law."[4]

The question of responsibility was raised again during this same period of time, by the director of department III in Himmler's command staff, the SS and Police Judge Horst Bender. "Himmler categorically stated that this measure had been personally ordered by Hitler, out of political and military considerations, and it therefore stood above all jurisdiction, including the SS and police jurisdiction."[5]

It should also be noted here that of the 6,500 German Jews who were deported to Minsk, only 11 survived the action.[6]

Bruno Streckenbach, a department head of the Reich Main Security Office, who was entrusted with select-

3.　Dr. Otto Bradfisch, 10 a Js 39/60, p. 135.
4.　Ibid.
5.　10 a Js 39/60, July 1962, p. 584; the statement of 19 July 1962 was confirmed for the author by Mr. Horst Bender on 5 May 1980.
6.　H. G. Adler, *Theresienstadt 1941–1945: Das Antlitz einer Zwangsgemeinschaft*, 2d ed. (Tübingen, 1960), 21; cf. Karl Löwenstein, "Minsk, im Lager der deutschen Juden," supplement to the weekly newspaper *Das Parlament*, 7 November 1956. Löwenstein, the only internee to be sent from Minsk to Theresienstadt, speaks of nine survivors. All the rest were liquidated on 28 and 29 July 1942 and 8 May 1943.

ing the personnel of the Einsatzgruppen, also brought up the subject of the mass exterminations before Heydrich and Himmler. Heydrich's response, in September 1941, was "that it was pointless to criticize this operation or to oppose it. This was strictly a matter of a Führer-order; for in connection with this war, which represented the final, violent clash of two irreconcilably opposed *Weltanschauungen*, the Führer had expressed his resolve to find simultaneously a solution to the Jewish problem."[7] Himmler's comments struck a similar, "though much sharper note" when, following Heydrich's death, Streckenbach again raised the issue: "Himmler vehemently forbade any criticism. Further, he stressed that this was a matter of a 'Führer-order,' and that he considered it his historical obligation to carry out the order, which affected the police and the Wehrmacht equally, with whatever means he had at his disposal."[8]

Gottlob Berger, Chief of the SS Main Administrative Office, also broached the subject of the mass liquidations with Himmler, once prior to, and a second time following, Heydrich's death. On the first occasion, Himmler "was visibly pained, and he cited as authority orders from Hitler."[9] On the next occasion, Himmler indicated that he shared Berger's view "that it would have been better not to have created the so-called Einsatzgruppen."[10]

Now what did the Reichsführer SS have to say about the responsibility and authorizations for the mass exterminations of the Jews in his secret speeches? Four crucial excerpts will clarify this point:

1. Himmler's secret address of 26 January 1944 before an audience of generals who had gathered in the munici-

----

7. Bruno Streckenbach, 13 November 1962, 10 a Js 39/60, Staatsanwaltschaft Munich.
8. Ibid., fol. 6.
9. Gottlob Berger, 15 October 1962, 10 a Js 39/60.
10. Ibid.

pal theater in Posen is described at length in a statutory declaration made by Freiherr von Gersdoff:[11]

At the end of January 1944 I had to attend a meeting that was held in connection with a training course for commanding generals and commanding officers of army corps. The meeting was convened by the highest-ranking National Socialist political officer, General Reineke, and was held in the municipal theater of Posen, the former capital of the so-called Warthegau. Three hundred generals, admirals, and general staff officers from the German Wehrmacht were present.

On 26 January 1944, the Reichsführer SS and Chief of Police Heinrich Himmler gave a briefing on the domestic and foreign security situation. In this context, he also dealt with the Jewish question. Naturally I can no longer recall the exact wording of his remarks. But I can assure you that the following represents, if not the very words he spoke, then at least the gist of these: "When the Führer gave me the order to carry out the total solution of the Jewish question, I at first hesitated, uncertain whether I could demand of my worthy SS men the execution of such a horrid assignment. . . . But this was ultimately a matter of a Führer-order, and therefore I could have no misgivings. In the meantime, the assignment has been carried out, and there is no longer a Jewish question."

2. On 5 May 1944 in Sonthofen, the Reichsführer-SS Himmler had the following to say on this same complex of issues: "Please understand how difficult it was for me to perform this soldierly command,

---

11. Confirmation for author by Rudolf-Christoph Freiherr von Gersdoff in a statutory declaration of 12 December 1979. Cf. Himmler's notes for his speech of 26 January 1944:

     Jewish Question: tremendous calm in G.G. [Generalgouvernement] since solution of Jewish question.
     Race war
     total solution
     obviate possibility of creating avengers for our children.
     (NS 19/HR 14, Bundesarchiv, Koblenz.)

which I followed and performed out of obedience and the fullest conviction."[12]

3. On 24 May 1944, Himmler's words on the ordered Final Solution were as follows: "Another question that was of decisive importance for the internal security of the Reich and of Europe as a whole was the Jewish question. It was resolved uncompromisingly as ordered and with complete understanding."[13]

4. And on 21 June 1944: "It was the most dreadful assignment and the most awful commission that an organization could ever receive: the commission to solve the Jewish question."[14]

These remarks by Himmler, the authenticity of which is beyond all doubt, need only the following commentary: This dreadful assignment, this most awful commission, this soldierly order can only have been given to the Reichsführer SS by Adolf Hitler: no one else stood between them in the chain of command. Since Himmler had received this liquidation order from his Führer, the Reichsführer SS wished to make it clear to his listeners that, for all his obedience, had the commission not come from "the highest level" he could *never* have given the command on his *own* initiative.[15] David Irving's contention, in his book *Hitler's War*, that "never before [5 May 1944] and never after, did Himmler

12. T 175/92/3475, U.S. National Archives.
13. T 175/94/4609, U.S. National Archives.
14. NS 19/HR 19, Bundesarchiv, Koblenz.
15. Cf. on this Werner Best to author, 16 September 1979: "The measures, however, . . . can only have been ordered by Hitler, in my opinion, not by Müller or Heydrich or even Himmler. Measures of this import—also considering their impact on German relations with the enemy states and on foreign affairs—can in my opinion only have been ordered by Hitler." Cf. also Werner Grothmann to author, 30 January 1978: "It is my conviction that Heinrich Himmler neither took decisive steps nor initiated them without having received directives to do so"; and Horst Bender to author, 21 June 1980: "I, too, am . . . of the personal opinion that Himmler never would

hint at a Führer order" is completely unfounded.[16] No less erroneous is Irving's comment on page 576 of the same book, "He [Himmler] could not have been more explicit as to his own responsibility" for the Final Solution of the Jewish question, whereby Irving posits a scenario in which Himmler gave orders without Hitler's knowledge and against his will. Likewise unfounded is the assertion made on page 576 of *Hitler's War* and reiterated on page 630, that on 6 May (sic; the intended date is 5 May) 1944, Himmler alluded for the first time to an order from above.[17] Rather, on 26 January, 5 May, 24 May, and 21 June, 1944, Heinrich Himmler left no doubt in the minds of his listeners as to the Führer-order he had received that called for the extermination of the European Jews. And on 4 and 6 October 1943, in his two addresses before the summoned SS and NS functionaries, Himmler disclosed a successful liquidation of Jewish women and children; but not even in his speech of 6 October 1943 did he assume the sole and ultimate responsibility for the mass murders, as we shall see shortly. It is at any rate correct that, in his address to the Einsatzkommandos in Nikolaev, the Reichsführer SS assumed the responsibility "alone with Hitler," while in his address to Einsatzkommando 8 in Minsk he made not just one, but two references to the order from Hitler, before proceeding to apprise the assembled ranks of the responsibility that he shared with Hitler for the mass killings.

Hitler's statesmanlike concern not to be associated with the bloody business carried out by the executive agen-

have dared—especially in fundamental matters of state policy—to make moves in opposition to Hitler or act independently in this. In my estimation Himmler was a subaltern relative to Hitler."

16.   David Irving, *Hitler's War* (London and New York, 1977), pp. 630–31.

17.   "He first hinted at having had superior orders on 6 May 1944" (ibid., 576).

cies, as well as the semantically perverse ruse he used to achieve this aim, find their counterpart in Himmler's own semantic and tactical prudence, which stemmed from the extermination order given him for the Final Solution of the Jewish question. This prudence will be revealed in further analysis of his secret addresses of 4 and 6 October 1943 in Posen, as well as of those made during the first half of 1944.

It seems natural and promising to begin by asking, why did RFSS Himmler indicate "in all candor" before the SS Gruppenführers on 4 October 1943 and before the Gauleiters and Reichsleiters on 6 October the full scope of the liquidations ("I mean now the evacuation of the Jews, the extermination of the Jewish race")[18] without also confirming in *both* of these secret sessions with SS and NS dignitaries that this was an order originating from above? And why, then, in 1944, in his secret speeches before the generals, did he so obviously find it necessary to shift the question of the order he had received into the foreground and to qualify it as "the most dreadful assignment" and "most awful commission"? The answers are apparent in the context of these speeches.

On 4 October 1943, Himmler once again wanted to bring home unmistakably to his Gruppenführers their joint responsibility: "The majority of you will know what it means when one hundred corpses lie in a pile together, when five hundred lie there, or a thousand."[19] With this reminder Himmler sought to bind the "highest-ranking bearers of the will" of the Führer as a whole to their collective responsibility. None of the assembled SS Gruppenführers

18. Heinrich Himmler, secret speech in Posen before SS Gruppenführers on 4 October 1943, PS 1919-1MG, vol. 29, pp. 65–66, Bundesarchiv, Koblenz.
19. Ibid.

would even for a moment have seen in "faithful Heinrich" the *initiator* of the assignment. In this same speech, Himmler further reminded his audience of their comrades who had been lined up against walls and shot on 30 June 1934 because "they had committed misdeeds";[20] and he drew an analogy between the firing squad's compliance with the execution orders on that day and the duty to be done in connection with the present mass liquidations, which, as Himmler added two days later before the Gauleiters and Reichsleiters, would be "carried out by the end of the year."[21] Commitment to joint responsibility, moral support, allayment of possible niggling doubts—this was the pièce justicative of the RFSS. As he stood before the assembled leaders of the Black Order, Himmler did not need to indicate that he was at the receiving end of the commands. Everyone knew.

Two days later, it was the Gauleiters' and Reichsleiters' turn to hear the same story in slightly modified form: "Then the question arose: What about the women and children? I decided to find a perfectly clear-cut solution to this too. For I did not feel justified in exterminating the men— that is, to kill them or to have them killed—while allowing the avengers, in the form of their children, to grow up in the midst of our sons and grandsons." Here Himmler appears to be acknowledging responsibility for the Final Solution—if so, then for the first time in his six secret talks. However, he is *not* taking the ultimate responsibility on this occasion either, for he goes on to say: "For the organization that had to carry out this mission, it was the most difficult that we have received to date."[22] In this address, too, Himmler is demon-

20. 10a Js 39/60, p. 177, Staatsanwaltschaft Munich.
21. Himmler, secret speech in Posen on 6 October 1943, p. 18, Bundesarchiv, Koblenz.
22. Ibid., p. 17.

strating that the SS and he, the Reichsführer SS, had an assignment to complete. He does *not* say that his organization had to carry out a mission that he himself had originally ordered. On 6 October 1943, Himmler's object was to implicate the top-level dignitaries of the National Socialist party, "this political instrument of the Führer,"[23] in a commitment to joint responsibility; moreover, to responsibility "for an act, and not just an idea."[24]

Although to have spoken in front of the SS Gruppenführers of "the highest possible order" would have been almost ridiculous, in front of the Gauleiters and Reichsleiters Himmler deemed it appropriate to speak of the most difficult assignment "that we have received to date." And although it is highly unlikely that the Gauleiters and Reichsleiters regarded the RFSS as the architect of the planned annihilation of the Jews, Himmler did not want to leave any room for doubt about his precise place in the chain of command, just as he did not want the assembled NS dignitaries to be left in any doubt about the joint responsibility they had incurred as the highest-ranking executives of the will in the National Socialist party.[25]

In his secret speeches of 1944 before the generals, Himmler hoped to win his audience's complete understanding for his obedient compliance with the "given soldierly order."[26] While he was drafting his speeches, he may well have recalled the "repeatedly stressed" assurance that Hitler had given Field Marshal Keitel, that he, the Führer, would "delib-

23. Ibid., p. 18.
24. Ibid., p. 20.
25. Cf. Baldur von Schirach, *Ich glaubte an Hitler* (Hamburg, 1967), 296.
26. Cf. p. 54 and n. 15 above. Cf. also Kunrat von Hammerstein, *Spähtrupp* (Stuttgart, 1963), 192. Von Hammerstein reports here that when Himmler, in his speech in Posen on 26 January 1944, announced the extermination of Jewish men, women, and children, all but five of the generals and admirals present applauded.

erately dissociate the Wehrmacht from everything that, in the eyes of the public and of the world, . . . could taint it. Such dirty work was the province of the police."[27] Equally present in Himmler's mind, both during his preparations for the addresses of 1944 and during their delivery, may well have been the agreements struck by the OKH and Himmler's apparatus,[28] and the resultant authorizations for Himmler and his Sonderkommandos and Einsatzgruppen—the consequences of which had been calculated in advance by Hitler. Finally, Heinrich Himmler was well aware, as he stood before the generals in 1944, that both his executive organs and the Wehrmacht had to answer to the orders of the same highest-ranking superior, Hitler.[29] He accordingly saw the virtue of presenting himself before the generals as a military subordinate. In addition, now that the orders had been performed, he had even more pressing reasons to instill in these officers a sense of their joint responsibility.

It is worth mentioning in this context that a month before his death, Reinhard Heydrich also commented on the orders issued by Hitler for the mass liquidations. As Otto Wagner reports:

> In May 1942 a conference was held in Prague on the subject of the new allocation of competencies among Intelligence and the SD. The participants included Admiral Wilhelm Canaris and his division chiefs as well as SS-Obergruppenführer Heydrich and the heads of depart-

27. Cf. p. 37 n.1.
28. OKH Q.M. Gen. Eduard Wagner to Sipo- and SD-Chief Heydrich, 4 April 1941, First Draft of Order for the Deployment of Sonderkommandos (special duty units) and Einsatzgruppen in the Field of Operations, Bundes-archiv-Militärarchiv, Freiburg, R.W. 4/575. Cf. Gen. Franz Halder, geheime Kommandosache of 11 June 1941, paragraph 4: "Einsatz der Sicherheitspolizei," 2 Hz/V 1928, pp. 3–4, Bundesarchiv-Militärarchiv, Freiburg.
29. Field Marshal Keitel, notes of 16 February 1946, p. 14, in author's possession.

ments of the Reich Main Security Office. On the fringes of the conference a heated discussion arose when members of Intelligence pointed out the negative effects that liquidations in the occupied territories would have on the civilian population and on the morale of the German troops. Heydrich reacted quite vehemently and explained that neither he nor the RSHA had prompted these liquidations, but that it was on Adolf Hitler's personal command, and his alone, that these shootings would occur.[30]

30.   Otto Wagner, Colonel (retd.) in former OKW Foreign Intelligence Department, statutory declaration of 21 December 1979 to author. These comments by Heydrich were the subject of a conversation during a visit in 1942 to 1943 by Canaris and his division chiefs in the headquarters of Oberst Wagner in Sofia.

6

Having reproduced Himmler's unambiguous references to instructions received from above, we turn once more to Hitler's endeavor to camouflage his wishes for liquidation, his intense and studied efforts to avoid, at all costs, being brought into connection with the measures he himself had initiated.[1] His remark of 19 November 1941 illustrates this endeavor. The Jews had been denied legal emigration from Germany since October 1941,[2] a prohibition resulting from an earlier change in policy: "The Führer has now authorized as a solution the evacuation of Jews to the East, instead of emigration."[3] Thus, Himmler's emigration prohibition of October 1941 had been sanctioned beforehand, and in fact ordered, by Hitler. Yet on 19 November, Hitler made the following statement at his headquarters, as recorded by Martin Bormann: "If today a few citizens wept because Jews had to emigrate from Germany, that would be just typical of these bourgeois creatures."[4] Note that Hitler continues to talk in terms of Jewish

1. Cf. pp. 20–21.
2. 10a Js 39/60, p. 179.
3. Noted by Martin Luther, 21 August 1942, re: Göring's commissioning of Heydrich, which Heydrich disclosed to the assembled officials at the so-called Wannsee Conference on 20 January 1942.
4. *Adolf Hitler, Monologe im Führerhauptquartier: 1941–1944,* ed. W. Jochmann (Hamburg, 1980), 143.

emigration, despite the fact that he had already authorized the *evacuation* of Jews to the East. What is more, on 17 September 1942, Hitler's closest confidant in matters relating to the Final Solution jotted down the following in his briefing notes under the heading "IV: Nationality and Settlement": "Jewish emigration, how should it proceed further?"—this question *one year after* the Führer and the RFSS had issued a general proscription on emigration for Jews in the Reich and the occupied territories.[5]

With this much established, we are now in a position to make better sense of Hitler's remark in the Führer's Headquarters on the evening of 5 November 1941: "Words are for the Jew not a means to expressing his thoughts, but rather a way of disguising what he is thinking. The lie is his source of strength, his weapon."[6] These two sentences represent nothing less than an exact projection of Hitler's own thoughts and actions at the time. In the same spirit of concealment and conscious deception, Hitler continued on 24 July 1942 to speak in terms of the Madagascar Plan—a plan which the preparations for Operation Barbarossa had rendered obsolete sixteen months before!

On 27 March 1942, Hitler's Propaganda Minister, Josef Goebbels, confided to his diary:

> The Jews will now be relocated from the Generalgouvernement to the East, starting with Lublin. A fairly barbaric procedure will be used here, one that cannot be precisely described. Not many of the Jews will be left over. Roughly speaking, one can be sure that 60 percent of them will have to be liquidated, while we will be able to put only 40 percent into labor detachments. The former Gauleiter of Vienna, who is in charge of this operation, is taking the appropriate precautions and employing a

5. Himmler's briefing notes, p. 85, Bundesarchiv, Koblenz.
6. *Adolf Hitler, Monologe im Führerhauptquartier*, ed. Jochmann, 130.

method that is not too terribly conspicuous. . . . The emptying ghettos in the cities of the Generalgouvernement will now be filled with Jews who have been deported from the Reich, and from these ghettos, after a certain period has elapsed, the process will be renewed.[7]

Eleven days before Goebbels's diary entry of 27 March 1942, the above-named former Gauleiter of Vienna, Odilo Globocnik, then SS and Police Leader in Lublin, had started up the machinery of death in the Belzec camp permanent gas chambers.[8] Adolf Hitler never inspected those extermination camps, unlike the RFSS, who did so several times. However, we now know of Odilo Globocnik's visit to the New Reich Chancellery in Berlin, in 1942.[9] Globocnik— "Globus" to his superiors and friends—was responsible, as head of Action Reinhard, for the extermination operations at the Belzec, Sobibor, Treblinka, and Majdanek (Lublin) camps, functioning together with camp inspector Christian Wirth.[10] On that visit Globocnik attended meetings without the officer who had accompanied him to the chancellery.[11] At this point it ought to be mentioned that in the first phase of Action Reinhard, between 16 March and 28 October 1942, approximately 40 percent of the Jewish men, women, and children in occupied Poland were gassed with carbon monoxide in the four camps named above.[12]

7. Quoted by Eberhard Jäckel, *Frankfurter Allgemeine Zeitung,* 25 August 1977, p. 17, from Institut für Zeitgeschichte, F 12/8, fols. 803–4.

8. Gerald Reitlinger, *The Final Solution,* 3d ed. (London, 1971), 573.

9. E. L. in confidential communication to author, 17 December 1979.

10. Cf. pp. 24–25, 25 n. 21.

11. E. L. to author, 9 May 1979: "I was once in the company of Globocnik in the New Reich Chancellery and had the opportunity to take a look around while he was in conference; similarly in the Reich Main Security Headquarters and in the Main Administrative Office of the Waffen SS."

12. According to careful assessments of the official Polish investigative commission, the statistics of Jewish men, women, and children from the Generalgouvernement and other occupied European countries who died in concentration camps are as follows: Belzec, about 600,000; Sobibor,

Globocnik's companion on that day can no longer recollect whether the visit to the New Reich Chancellery took place in the "spring" or "autumn of 1942."[13] We know that Hitler was present in Berlin from 28 September to 3 October 1942 and that Himmler made the entry "Conditions Gen. Gouv. Globus" in his notes from a briefing with the Führer of 7 October 1942; we know, in other words, that the Führer and his Reichsführer SS discussed the operations that came under Globocnik's supervision. On 9 November 1942, Odilo Globocnik was promoted to the rank of SS Gruppenführer.[14] As Globocnik can only have spoken with Hitler, Himmler, or Reichsleiter Bouhler in the New Reich Chancellery, competent sources can tell us whether Himmler was in a position, or whether it was his practice, to have his subordinates report to him while he was in Berlin. On this, Richard Schulze-Kossens informs us: "That Himmler could call in to the Reich Chancellery any SS leader for a briefing is, I believe, totally out of the question. And I also feel that he scarcely would have dared to request such authority from Hitler."[15] To the same question Werner Grothmann responded: "I can inform you that to the best of my recollection Himmler did not hold personal conferences in the Reich Chancellery—that is, with conferees summoned by him expressly for the purpose. That would have been absolutely contrary to normal practice. When he was

---

250,000; and Treblinka, 700,000. On 3 October 1942, 310,000 Jews were "resettled" from the Warsaw ghetto (Czeslaw Pilichowski, *No Time-Limit for These Crimes* [Warsaw, 1980], 156).

13. E. L. to author, 17 December 1979. Hitler was in Berlin on 15 to 16 March, 25 to 26 April, 22 and 30 May, and 23 June 1942. On 27 September he flew from Vinnitsa to Berlin; the return flight was on 4 October 1942, late morning.

14. Helmut Krausnick et al., *Anatomy of the SS State* (London, 1968), 583.

15. Richard Schulze-Kossens to author, 5 February 1980.

in Berlin, he held his conferences in the Reichsführung SS in the Prinz-Albrechtstrasse; otherwise, in his own headquarters, wherever they happened to be located at the time."[16] Therefore, a conference held privately between Globocnik and Reichsleiter Bouhler is likely. Bouhler's department was located at Voßstrasse 4, Berlin W. 8.

16. Werner Grothmann to author, 26 January 1980.

7

The Execution of the Final Solution in the Occupied East

The shootings in the occupied eastern territories were conducted in the first instance against the resident Jews. However, the fate of the Jews in the Reich and in the western European areas under German influence or occupation was no different from that of the *Ostjuden*. After the start of the Russian campaign, the "Final Solution of the European Jewish question" meant nothing other than physical extermination. "Elimination" was one of the more frequently used *termini technici*, like "evacuation," a code word that has been discussed above.[1] Instant, on-the-spot solutions as practiced by the Einsatzkommandos in Russia were admittedly impracticable in the occupied West. Consequently, "elimination" was systematically preceded by relocations through convoys and by longer or shorter enforced stays in camps or ghettos.[2] At first Jews were employed also

---

1. Cf. p. 21.
2. Cf. Himmler's handwritten notes from his briefing with the Führer on 6 December 1942, NS 19/275, Institut für Zeitgeschichte: "3. Jews in France 600−700,000." Adjacent to this, the handwritten word "abschaffen" (to get rid of) is checked off. This word also had a place in the realm of the semantic cover-up. Seventy thousand Jews from France were "gotten rid of"; 2,800 returned to France. Compare the briefing of 17 December 1942: "3. Declarations of consent from parents for voluntary army service of sons—are being done away with [*abgeschafft*]. Lammers" (NS 19 neu/1447, fol. 55, Bundesarchiv, Koblenz). The word "abschaffen" was here used in its original sense.

as a temporary work force in munitions factories, especially in the Generalgouvernement, but, in time, annihilation plans almost without exception enforced the replacement of Jews by Poles. Seen in their developing framework and taken in their entirety, the measures that were aimed against the Jews after the beginning of the Russian campaign in essence represent merely the components and stages of a liquidation process which was pursued and adapted according to the local exigencies conditioned by political, geographical, economic, and personal factors.

Beginning 18 October 1941, the first death convoys organized by the Reich Main Security Office left Germany for the East. This measure was adopted in response to the commission Heydrich received on 31 July 1941 from Göring "on the Führer's instructions":[3] namely, to carry out the "aimed at Final Solution of the Jewish question"—an instruction, then, whose execution was agreed upon and formalized at the so-called Wannsee Conference of 20 January 1942.[4] In the course of these "evacuations," in the period between 15 November 1941 and 14 December 1942, an additional twenty-nine convoys with 28,564 German Jews arrived in Kovno and Riga. Of these, less than 800 survived the war.[5] A more scrupulous examination of individual statements and documents that should be viewed in connection

---

3. Notes by Martin Luther, 21 August 1942, NG 2586 J.
4. Cf., on the topic of the Wannsee Conference, the Eichmann Interrogation: "That was truly . . . a landmark in the . . . totality of the developments. . . . In any case, it was late summer. I will tell you now how I know that it was late summer when Heydrich ordered me to see him. I reported to him, and he said to me: 'The Führer has ordered the physical extermination of the Jews.' These are the words he said to me" (unpublished transcripts of tape 5, 31 May 1960, p. 169, Israel National Archives; photocopy in author's possession). Cf. *Eichmann Interrogated*, ed. Jochen V. Lang (New York, 1983).
5. Gertrude Schneider, *Journey into Terror* (New York, 1979), 155–75. Cf. "g. Rs, Gesamtaufstellung der im Bereich des EK3 der EGA bis zum 1. Dezember 1941 durchgeführten Exekutionen," 3253/63 Fb 76 (a), Institut für Zeitgeschichte.

with this phase of the Final Solution will give us a clearer insight into the process leading to the extermination orders, and the language in which they were couched.

On 30 January 1939, Hitler issued a threat from the Reichstag that he reiterated on 30 January 1941. The text of this threat ran as follows: "Today I want to be a prophet once again: If the international Jewish financial establishment in and outside Europe should succeed once again in plunging the peoples of the world into war, then the result will not be a Bolshevization of the globe and thus a victory for Judaism, but the annihilation of the Jewish race in Europe."[6] It is significant that the threat was taken up for a third time during the week of 7 September 1941, now in special broadsheet form, in a publication of the propaganda department of the National Socialist party. This edition of the *Wochensprüche* (Weekly Words of Wisdom) was circulated on a massive scale—immediately prior to the introduction of the Star of David[7] and about a month before the start of the convoys to the East.

Again significant is the fact that one month after the first departure of the Berlin convoys to the East, Minister of Propaganda Goebbels felt it necessary to remind his readers precisely of this threat of annihilation, which the Reich Chancellor had made on 30 January 1939. Goebbels then added, in the 16 November 1941 issue of *Das Reich*: "We are witnessing the fulfillment of this prophecy at this very moment."

Consider the words of Julius Streicher on 25 December 1941 in his journal *Der Stürmer*: "The deadly risk that this

6. *Frankfurter Zeitung*, 1 February 1939; *Neue Zürcher Zeitung*, 31 January 1939.
7. See Robert M. W. Kempner, *Der Mord an 35,000 Berliner Juden*, offprint (Heidelberg, 1970), 182. Victor Klemperer remarks: "I ask myself today again: which was the most difficult day for the Jews during those twelve years of hell? . . . 19 September 1941. From that day on, Jews had to wear the Star of David" (*Lingua Tertii Imperii*, 3d ed. [1957; reprint Leipzig, 1970], 204).

curse of God in Jewish blood should propagate itself interminably admits of only one solution: the extermination of this race, whose father is the devil." Three days later, on the evening of 28 December in the Führer's Headquarters, Hitler commented on Streicher and his *Stürmer:* "Streicher's picture of the Jew in *Der Stürmer* is too idealized. The Jew is much more common, much more bloodthirsty and satanic than Streicher painted him."[8] This utterance typifies perhaps better than any other his unlimited and pathological hatred for the Jews, the very core of the dictator's *Weltanschauung.*

At this critical point in his political and private life, Adolf Hitler saw himself perhaps more than ever before as a fighting prophet, and as such he thought in terms of black and white, good and evil, this way or that—with tragic consequences for the German nation. The fighting prophet who seeks to vindicate the "truth" characteristically sets out to destroy whatever he perceives to be in competition with his own cause on the battleground of ideology. For Hitler, this adversary was represented first and foremost by an entity that "rivaled his own brown church—the red anti-church of Bolshevism."[9] Hitler's hatred for Jews and its by-product, the compulsive craving for destruction, were tied closely to his delusion that the whole world was caught in the clutches of a "magical nation" and its spellbinding ideology. From his fanatical black-and-white perspective, Hitler perceived this counterforce as a second anti-church which was stamped by its own prophets, and he was convinced that it posed a continual and vital threat to his closest beliefs. This rival church had no right to existence within the sphere of influence of the greater Germany and must accordingly be liquidated. And so the death convoys began rolling east-

8.   *Adolf Hitler, Monologe im Führerhauptquartier: 1941–1944,* ed. Werner Jochmann (Hamburg, 1980), 158.
9.   Werner Best, "Betr. Adolf Hitler" (written in Copenhagen), 17 March 1949, p. 9.

ward on 19 October 1941 from Berlin to Lodz, Minsk, Kovno, Riga, and finally, starting at the end of November 1942, to Auschwitz, until January 1945.

On 25 October 1941, Amtsgerichtsrat (lower court judge) Dr. Wetzel, since July 1941 the Adviser on Jewish Affairs with the Reich Ministry for the Occupied Eastern Territories and prior to that Head of the Race Politics Office of the Nazi party, drafted for his minister Alfred Rosenberg an important letter to Hinrich Lohse, the Reichskommissar Ostland stationed in Riga. This top secret draft dealt with the "solution of the Jewish question" and was directly related to Lohse's report delivered to Wetzel on 4 October 1941 in the Reich Ministry for the Occupied Eastern Territories, likewise "re: the solution of the Jewish question." Wetzel wrote Lohse as follows:

> With regard to my letter of 18 October 1941, please be informed that Oberdienstleiter [Chief Executive Officer] Brack from the Führer's Chancellery has stated his readiness to assist in the construction of the necessary accommodation(s) and gassing apparatuses. At the present time we do not have on hand a sufficient quantity of the apparatuses, so they first must be constructed.[10] Brack's

10.   Minutes of transcripts from the interrogation of Friedrich Jeckeln, 21 December 1945:
Q: Were gassing vans used in the Ostland?
A: Yes, they were used for the extermination of Jews.
Q: Where and when were these gassing vans used in the Ostland?
A: Through the above-named commanders of the SD and Gestapo in the Ostland I learned that between three to five gassing vans were used in the liquidation of Jews in Salaspils and Riga in the second half of 1942. In the course of a conversation at the end of 1942 and beginning of 1943, the commander of the SD and Gestapo in Latvia, Dr. Lange, told me about the use of such trucks and described the setup to me. He requested that I come over to have a look, but I declined. He also told me how the people inside the vehicles began to scream loudly and bang on the walls with their fists after they had been inside for five minutes, then lost consciousness, and finally also their lives.
(Historical State Archives, Latvian S.S.R., Riga.)

view is that, since construction of the apparatuses within the Reich would present far greater difficulties than on-site production, the most expedient course of action is to send his people directly to Riga, in particular his chemist Dr. Kallmeyer, who will take the necessary steps from there. Oberdienstleiter Brack further points out that the procedure in question is not without its hazards, and that therefore special safety precautions are needed. Under these circumstances, I ask you to contact Oberdienstleiter Brack in the Führer's Chancellery through your Higher SS and Police Leader. Please request from him the dispatching of the chemist Dr. Kallmeyer and any further assistants that are needed. I might further point out that Sturmbannführer Eichmann, the Adviser on Jewish Affairs in the Reich Main Security Office, is in complete accord with this procedure. According to information received here from Sturmbannführer Eichmann, camps for Jews will be set up in Riga and in Minsk, where Jews from the Altreich [Germany proper] might also be sent. Jews are currently being evacuated from the Altreich to Litzmannstadt [Lodz] and other camps, from which points those fit for work will be transferred to work forces in the East. Given the present situation, Jews who are not fit for work can be eliminated without qualms through use of the Brack device. Incidents such as those that took place during the shootings of Jews in Vilna, according to a report I have on my desk,[11] can hardly be sanctioned, keeping in mind that the executions were undertaken openly, and the new procedures assure that such incidents will no longer be possible. Jews fit for work, on the other hand, will be transported to work forces in the East. That the men and women in this latter group must be kept apart from each other goes without saying. Please keep me informed as to any further measures you take.[12]

---

11.   Per Gerald Reitlinger, "On July 17, 1941, seven hundred Jewish hostages from Vilna were shot at the train station in Ponary (Punar)" (*The Final Solution* 3d ed. [London, 1971], 228). Cf. Marc Dvorjetski, *Ghetto à l'est* (Paris, 1949), 25, 38. "The city of Vilna was almost entirely 'Jew-free' by 7 September 1941, after further mass shootings had taken place at the beginning of the month."

12.   NO-365, U.S. National Archives.

As we can see in this document, Jews unfit for work, who in the course of the "resettlements" had been or were to be transported to Lodz, Kovno, Minsk, and Riga, were destined to be gassed—already at this time, that is, three months prior to the so-called Wannsee Conference, during which the "Final Solution procedures" were formalized and finalized among high-ranking functionaries. In other words, the planning of the Final Solution and its procedures, visible—for all the camouflaging and code language—in the minutes of the Wannsee proceedings of 20 January 1942, were already well under way three months earlier.

It is further apparent in Wetzel's letter to Lohse that Sturmbannführer Eichmann, Heydrich's Adviser on Jewish Affairs in the RSHA, had informed Wetzel, the Adviser on Jewish Affairs in the Ministry for the Occupied Eastern Territories, about the first experiences with Zyklon B in Auschwitz in autumn 1941. After Zyklon B had been tested on Russian prisoners of war and had demonstrated its effectiveness in "bringing about instantaneous death," Höss passed this piece of information on to Eichmann, "and we decided," Höss writes, "to employ this gas in future mass exterminations."[13]

From Wetzel's letter we also learn of the plans of the central office of T4, directed by the Führer's Chancellery.[14] In this extermination agency SS-Oberführer Viktor Brack, of the Führer's Chancellery—an immediate subordinate to the head of the Führer's Chancellery, Reichsleiter Bouhler—played an essential role. On Bouhler's instructions, T4 sought to send the gassing specialists of the recently phased-out euthanasia program in the Reich to the extermination camps under construction in the East—which was in

13. M. Broszat, ed., *Kommandant in Auschwitz: Autobiographische Aufzeichnungen von Rudolf Höss*, Quellen und Darstellungen zur Zeitgeschichte, vol. 5 (Munich, 1958), 155.
14. Cf. pp. 20–23.

fact done—in order that their valuable experience in killing with carbon monoxide, an expertise acquired at the permanent gas chambers in the euthanasia liquidation institutes,[15] might now be "put to good use" in the planned mass annihilation of European Jews.

Thus Heydrich ordered Eichmann late in the summer of 1941 to visit Lublin and survey in that area the practical side of the preliminaries to the Final Solution that would be implemented there under the supervision of Lublin SS and Police Leader Odilo Globocnik. Upon his arrival Eichmann found, to his great surprise, Police Captain Wirth "at work on a special assignment for the Führer,"[16] his uniform jacket off and "shirt sleeves rolled up," helping with preliminary work to seal the first gas chamber.[17] Seeing this, SS-Sturmbannführer Hoefle, Eichmann's escort from Lublin, instructed Wirth "that he should now explain this installation to me." Wirth explained that "everything had to be sealed up tight, because a Russian submarine engine was to be operated here. The fumes would be conducted inside, and then the Jews would be asphyxiated."[18]

Eichmann filed a report on what he had seen in the East, submitting one copy to Heydrich and one to his immediate superior in the Reich Main Security Office, SS-Brigadeführer Müller—the same Müller who on 1 August 1941 had wired the enciphered instructions to the commanders of the four Einsatzgruppen: "The Führer is to be kept informed continually from here about the work of the Einsatz-

15. Cf. pp. 23–24, nn. 14–17.
16. Cf. p. 25, nn. 19–21.
17. Eichmann Interrogation, 31 May 1960, transcript of tape 5, p. 172; photocopy in author's possession. According to the statement by Dr. Hans-Bodo Gorgass, Hadamar (euthanasia institute), Wirth was sent to Poland by the "Foundation" in late summer of 1941 to create an institute in the Lublin area (affidavit by Dr. Gorgass, Trials of War Criminals, vol. 1, p. 803).
18. Eichmann Interrogation, 31 May 1960, transcript of tape 5, pp. 172–73.

gruppen in the East."[19] Not much later, before the end of 1941, Müller again sent Eichmann out for an extermination camp report, this time to Kulmhof (Chelmno), located in the Warthegau of Gauleiter Greiser.[20] There Eichmann witnessed the gassing of a group of Jews in one of the Saurer gassing vans stationed at the Kulmhof castle. For Eichmann it was "the most horrifying thing I had ever seen in my life. The gassing van drove up to a somewhat long pit, the doors were opened, and the corpses were tossed out. It was as if they were still alive, their limbs were so supple. Simply tossed out; and I can still picture the way a civilian pulled teeth out with a pair of pliers. Then I cleared out."[21]

In Wetzel's top secret draft document to the Reichskommissar for the Ostland Hinrich Lohse, the liquidation foreseen for the deported European Jews who were physically incapable of work is glossed by the technical term "beseitigt" (eliminated). "Beseitigen" (to eliminate) is a code word used by Hitler himself and transmitted to us in several documents. In his second address before the commanders of the Wehrmacht on 22 August 1939, one week before the invasion of Poland, Hitler says: "Our top priority: the destruction of Poland. Our objective: the elimination of vital forces, not the attainment of a defined position. Any vital force forming anew must immediately be destroyed again."[22] And in the minutes recorded in the top secret military document (*geheime kommandosache*) of 12 September 1941 of a briefing held in the Führer's Headquarters, we read under point 1: "High-ranking political figures and leaders (commissars) are to be eliminated."[23] In both Franz Halder's and Helmuth Greiner's OKW wartime logbooks under the

19. Fa 213/3, Institut für Zeitgeschichte.
20. Cf. p. 22 n. 10.
21. Eichmann Interrogation, 31 May 1960, transcript of tape 5, p. 176.
22. Nürnberg-Dokument 1014-PS.
23. Nürnberg-Dokument 884-PS.

respective dates of 31 August and 2 September 1942, we find entries directly concerned with this same policy: "The Führer has ordered that, upon penetration into the city, the entire male population be eliminated, since Stalingrad with its one million uniformly communist inhabitants is extremely dangerous."[24]

Three weeks following Wetzel's top secret draft to Lohse, the RFSS Himmler held a fifteen-minute telephone conversation with Sipo Chief Heydrich. Once again we find, in Himmler's handwritten entry under "telephone conversations made by the RFSS" for 17 November, the remark "elimination of the Jews." It referred to the liquidation of both the total population of Jewish inhabitants in Riga and the Jews who had been transported from Germany since 18 October. Further, we know that the Higher SS and Police Leader Friedrich Jeckeln received liquidation orders on 10 to 11 November 1941 in the "Gestapo-Haus, Prinz-Albrecht-strasse Berlin"; then again at Himmler's headquarters in Lötzen, sometime between 9 December and the end of the month, and a third time on 25 January 1942, between 11:30 A.M. and 1:00 P.M., again in Lötzen.[25] This information we owe to Jeckeln's interrogation transcript of 14 December 1945, a document we will consider in depth below. The liquidation order of 10 to 11 November from Himmler and Hitler to the newly named Higher SS and Police Leader Ostland contains the words: "Tell Lohse it is my order, which is also the Füh-

24. As reported by Gen. Franz Halder in OKW-KTB III, p. 514. ("Conference with Field Marshal List at Hitler's Headquarters and individual notes from conference of 31 August 1942. Halder added that the female population must be shipped off.") Also reported by Captain Helmuth Greiner in OKW-KTB, Memoranda, 2 September 1942, p. 669, Bundesarchiv-Militärarchiv, Freiburg.

25. Per Himmler's appointment calendar of 25 January 1942, NS 19 DC/vorl. 12, Bundesarchiv, Koblenz. Between 7 and 15 November 1941 and from 5 December 1941 to the end of the year, Himmler's appointment calendar shows no entries.

rer's wish."[26] The execution of the order was later confirmed by the head of Einsatzgruppe A, Dr. Franz Walter Stahlecker, on 5 January 1942 in his Einsatzgruppen report: "In the meantime, the Higher SS and Police Leader in Riga, SS-Obergruppenführer Jeckeln, has begun a shooting action, and on Sunday, 30 November 1941, he eliminated ca. 4,000 Jews from the Riga ghetto and from an evacuation convoy that originated in Germany."[27] On that Sunday, however, not 4,000 but 14,000 Jewish inhabitants of the city of Riga were massacred in the pits in the Rumbuli Forest outside Riga, together with 1,000 German Jews from Berlin.[28] An additional 13,000 were murdered on 8 December by the bullets of the SD marksmen.

Here we must add that Himmler, in a telephone conversation from the Führer's Headquarters with Heydrich in Prague on 30 November 1941, discussed—too late—a reversal of a previously given general order. (Of this discussion Himmler noted, in a handwritten entry in his telephone log book, "Jewish convoy from Berlin. No liquidation.") There were several reasons for this singular attempt. It may well have been a response to the Wehrmacht's repeated remonstrances relating to the urgent need for all available transport at this time, and it may also have reflected a last, momentary hesitation before America's entry into the war a few days later. But Himmler's action is explained most clearly by Eichmann's statement on 6 March 1942 during a conference in the RSHA, Office IV B 4 (Jewish Affairs):

> SS-Obersturmbannführer Eichmann made some introductory remarks concerning the further evacuation of fifty-

26. Shorthand minutes from Jeckeln's interrogation on 14 December 1945 (Major Zwetajew, interrogator; Sergeant Suur, interpreter), p. 2, Historical State Archive, Riga. Cf. also p. 46 n. 12.
27. Nürnberg-Dokument NO-3257.
28. Verdict of the assize court of Hamburg (50) 9/72 of 23 February 1973, pp. 53–120; and Gertrude Schneider, *Journey into Terror*, 12–14.

five thousand Jews from the Altreich [Germany proper], the Ostmark [Austria], and from the Protectorate. . . . In this connection, SS-Obersturmbannführer Eichmann pointed out that the guidelines that had been issued especially with regard to age, frailty, etc. had to be observed as closely as possible. In the convoys to Riga, forty to forty-five cases of unjustified evacuation were reported in a complaint lodged with Gauleiter Lohse by the Jewish elders in Riga and then passed on to SS-Obergruppenführer Heydrich. . . . In order that individual police offices would no longer be faced with the temptation of deporting those elderly Jews whose presence was disagreeable to them, Eichmann reassuringly explained that these Jews remaining in the Altreich would very probably during that summer or autumn be deported to Theresienstadt, which had been allocated as a "ghetto for the aged."[29]

Himmler knew full well that in the first convoys of German Jews to Riga and Minsk there were men who had earned military decorations in the First World War, and others who were over sixty-five. Holders of the Iron Cross First Class and the Silver Medal of Valor as well as the Verwundetenabzeichen were subsequently deported, beginning in June 1942, to the "ghetto for the aged" in Theresienstadt.

29.   Eichmann Trial, document 119, Düsseldorf, 5 March 1942.

8

The Mass Shootings Outside Riga, 30 November and 8 December 1941

The actual site of execution lay about five miles outside Riga in the direction of Dünaburg [Daugavpils], between the highway and the railroad, both of which connect Riga and Dünaburg. The railroad tracks and the road there run a near-parallel course, with the railroad tracks running to the north of the road. The site lies in the vicinity of the railroad station at Rumbuli; its terrain is sandy and slightly hilly, sparsely wooded, and forms part of the Rumbuli Forest. In the center of this site was a densely forested area; this was the location of the actual execution site, with prepared pits designed to accommodate about thirty thousand bodies. The approaching columns of Jews coming from Riga along the highway between Riga and Dünaburg had to turn left from the highway onto a dirt track which led up to the small patch of woods. In the process they were funneled into a narrow cordon, which was formed by SS units, a contingent of the Special Task Unit Riga, and Latvian units.

The columns of Jews advancing from Riga, comprising about one thousand persons each, were herded into the cordon, which was formed in such a way that it narrowed greatly as it continued into the woods, where the pits lay. The Jews first of all had to deposit their luggage before they entered the copse; permission to carry these articles had only been granted to give the Jews the impression that they were taking part in a resettlement. As they progressed, they had to deposit their valuables in wooden boxes, and, little by little, their clothing—first overcoats, then suits, dresses, and shoes, down to their under-clothes, all placed in distinct piles according to the type of clothing.

On this particular day (30 November 1941), the air temperature in Riga, measured at two meters above ground, was −7.5°C at 7:00 A.M., −1.1°C at 1:00 P.M., and 1.9°C at 9:00 P.M. On the previous evening, 29 November 1941, there had been an average snowfall of seven centimeters. On 30 November between 7:00 A.M. and 9:00 P.M., it did not snow.

Stripped down to their underclothes, the Jews had to move forward along the narrow path in a steady flow toward the pits, which they entered by a ramp, in single file and in groups of ten. Occasionally the flow would come to a standstill when someone tarried at one of the undressing points; or else, if the undressing went faster than expected, or if the columns advanced too quickly from the city, too many Jews would arrive at the pits at once. In such cases, the supervisors stepped in to ensure a steady and moderate flow, since it was feared that the Jews would grow edgy if they had to linger in the immediate vicinity of the pits. . . . In the pits the Jews had to lie flat, side by side, face down. They were killed with a single bullet in the neck, the marksmen standing at close range—at the smaller pits, on the perimeter; at the large pit, inside the pit itself—their semi-automatic pistols set for single fire. To make the best of available space, and particularly of the gaps between bodies, the victims next in line had to lie down on top of those who had been shot immediately before them. The handicapped, the aged, and the young were helped into the pits by the sturdier Jews, laid by them on top of the bodies, and then shot by marksmen who in the large pit actually stood on the dead. In this way the pits gradually filled.[1]

The executions of the Jews who had been "evacuated" from the Riga ghetto began at 9:00 in the morning and continued—in the large pit—well into the evening. Prior to this action, a convoy had arrived in Riga in a German train

1.   Riga Trial (50) 9/72, verdict of 23 February 1973, pp. 69–73.

with over one thousand German Jews from Berlin, and between 8:15 and 9:00 A.M. the group was liquidated. The Jews had been pulled off the train, herded immediately up to the pits, and shot. When darkness fell the shootings in the large pit were still going on.

"Staff members not allocated any specific tasks by Jeckeln were present as observers. Moreover, others were at the execution pits during the shootings: Wehrmacht and police officers, members of the civil administration, and Latvian officers, as well as Stahlecker, with the officers of his command post. They stood for the most part on top of the earthen walls that ringed the pits."[2]

There were some, however, who did not stand around the pits and were not to be connected in any way with the mass liquidations: the staff of the Intelligence Headquarters in Riga, whose head had received a top secret signal from Admiral Wilhelm Canaris shortly before the executions began. The contents of this signal ran something like this: "It is unworthy of an Intelligence officer to be party to, or even merely present at interrogations or maltreatments."[3] "Interrogations or maltreatments," of course, "meant the murder of the Jews."[4]

In retrospect the historian could say that this secret order was the logical expression of the Admiral's personal attitude. But how did Chief of Intelligence Canaris come to know about the impending mass liquidations that were to occur outside Riga—through the Führer's Headquarters, through the OKH, or through the Intelligence Headquarters Ostland in Riga?

2.   Ibid., p. 75.
3.   Frau Gertrud Meyer in letter to naval Capt. Herbert Wichmann (retd.), 11 December 1979.
4.   Herbert Wichmann to Lt. Col. Franz Seubert (retd.), 11 December 1979; and Herbert Wichmann to author, 22 December 1979 and 25 January 1980.

As I already stated in a written deposition during the OKH trial in Nuremberg, one day early in the winter of 1941, the commander of the Brückenstab [Bridge Inspection Staff] of Riga[5] appeared unbidden and of his own volition at my headquarters in Angerburg, East Prussia, where part of the OKH headquarters was located. It must have been *at the very latest* the beginning of December. The officer was in an extremely agitated state, but as he talked I gradually began to piece together his story: en route to Riga he had heard curious, inexplicable gunfire and screaming, which he followed to the source. Because of a breakdown in the usual security, he reached a point so close to the scene of murder that he was able to see everything. He also mentioned the brutal laughter of the SD people. This experience had left him in such a bewildered state that I had to calm him down before I could ask him what he wanted of me. His answer was that I should immediately notify Admiral Canaris, so that Canaris could step in. I told him that Canaris had nothing to do with matters of internal policy, since he was in charge of counterintelligence. The responsibility lay with the Commander in Chief of the Army, General von Brauchitsch, and the competent department was the Special Duties Department (General Staff Colonel Albert Radke). I called his attention to a Führer-order that stated that the Wehrmacht was to keep out of such matters of political necessity and should, moreover, be grateful to have nothing to do with these "very difficult" tasks.[6] Then I pointed out to Bruns that, in view of this Führer-order, to pass on his report would put him in personal danger. Bruns, however, insisted on pursuing the matter. I conferred with Radke over the phone and was told to prepare a written account of the whole affair.[7] I gave Bruns a room that happened to be free, and he wrote up his report. I never knew

5. Then Colonel, later Major General, Walter Bruns.
6. Cf. p. 37, n. 1.
7. From 1 September 1940 to 20 February 1943, Albert Radke was OKH-General Staff of Army—Army Section—Dept. of General Special Duties, Colonel General Staff (RAD: 1 February 1942); Deutsche Dienststelle, Berlin, to author, 21 February 1980.

that Bruns had been informed by Captain Dr. Schulz-Du Bois. I then passed the papers with my signature on to the Special Duties Department . . . My office (General of Engineers and Fortifications with the Commander in Chief of the Army) never heard another word about this matter. . . . I did not phone Canaris. . . . There was no point in trying, from my position, to put an end to these murders in Riga or anywhere else. Not even a commander in chief could have done so, since the matter was purely political.[8]

This account proves that at the end of November or beginning of December, the former Chief of Staff of the General of Engineers in the OKH forwarded Bruns's official report on the events in Riga to Major in the General Staff Albert Radke in the Special Duties Department, OKH.[9] The question now is whether Radke was in a position to pass this report on to the Chief of Counterintelligence, Admiral Canaris, and furthermore, whether Radke could possibly have been on intimate terms with Canaris.

As to the first question, it should be pointed out that communications from the Special Duties Department, OKH, operated on a "two-track" system, since reports could be sent up either to General Halder in OKH or to Admiral Canaris.[10] As to the second question, whether Radke could have passed Bruns's report on to Canaris by virtue of personal connections, we know the following: "After a brief term at the war academy he [Radke] headed the Intelligence Office in Münster for several years, until the fall of 1937 or the spring of 1938. I also know for a fact that Oberst Radke served on the staff of the Commander in Chief of the Army. Of course,

8. Erich Abberger to author, 16 October 1978.
9. Head of this Special Duties Dept. at this point was Lieutenant General for Special Duties with the OKH Eugen Müller; Deutsche Dienststelle to author, 1 October 1980.
10. Dr. G. Meyer of the Militärgeschichtliche Forschungsamt, Freiburg, to author, 9 July 1980.

Radke knew Canaris well."[11] We can safely presume that the Special Duties Department in the OKH informed Canaris of the shootings that occurred outside Riga on 30 November and 8 December 1941.

Next, we should examine the testimony offered by Major General of Engineers, Walter Bruns, at the so-called OKW trial (case XII) in Nuremberg. Bruns stated that he had "filed his report in duplicate" when he learned of the occurrences outside Riga: one copy he sent to the Northern Army Group, and the other he immediately handed in himself at the OKH in Angerburg at the office of the General of Engineers. Prior to filing his report, Bruns had been told by a certain Administrative Officer Werner Altemeyer in Riga that the operation resulted from a "Führer-order."[12]

According to his testimony, when Bruns learned "on the Friday before the first Sunday of Advent" in 1941, that is, on 28 November, that liquidations were scheduled for Riga in the immediate future, he urged Administrative Officer Altemeyer to postpone the action at least until he, Bruns, had received some sort of response to his personal inquiries. Then Bruns immediately contacted the OKH in Angerburg in person. On Sunday, 30 November, the day of the first mass shooting in the Rumbuli Forest outside Riga, Bruns dispatched two officers to the execution site. When these two officers, whom Bruns failed to identify in Nuremberg, returned from their mission, they gave him an oral report of what they had witnessed. Bruns ordered them to submit an official written report. Later he drove to the OKH in Angerburg. "I arrived there Monday morning and saw Colonel Abberger. I gave Abberger this report." Abberger made several inquiries over the phone to determine where Bruns

11. Hans Crome to author, 3 March 1980.
12. Nuremberg, Case XII, 18 February 1948, p. 841.

might intercede most effectively to prevent a recurrence of the shootings. From these telephone conversations made in Bruns's presence, he, Bruns, gathered that "the only proper channel for the report was through Admiral Canaris," as Abberger afterward confirmed; Abberger would see to it at once.[13] The Admiral should then notify the Führer of the matter at the appropriate time. Abberger asked Bruns if he agreed to having his written report passed on, which could be dangerous for Bruns. On this note the representations which Colonel Bruns of the Brückenstab Riga had made in the OKH came to a close.

It should be mentioned that Colonel Abberger referred Bruns's official report not to Admiral Canaris—for he was not permitted to do so—but instead to General Staff Major Albert Radke, Special Duties Department in the OKH.[14] The question remains, on whose information did Bruns base his statements in Nuremberg? At the trial he mentioned, without naming them, "two officers" who had furnished him directly with eyewitness reports of the shootings.

At the end of April 1980 I received a statutory declaration from Erika Ilse Schulz-Du Bois, widow of the former Captain of the Engineer Reserves, Otto Schulz-Du Bois, together with the photocopy of a letter, dated January 1942, from Captain Schulz-Du Bois to his wife.[15] This statement reads as follows: "I came across the attached pages a short time ago in a bundle of old war letters. The handwriting is unmistakably that of my husband Otto Schulz-Du Bois, who died in 1945. At the top right of the document is written in another hand: January, 1942. This I recognize to be my

13. Ibid., p. 844.
14. Erich Abberger to author, 28 October 1978.
15. Statutory declaration by Erika Schulz-Du Bois to author, Frankfurt am Main, 13 March 1980. The original letter by Capt. Dr. Schulz-Du Bois, together with a statutory declaration by Frau Erika Schulz-Du Bois, was donated to the archive of the Institut für Zeitgeschichte.

own writing. I am certain that these pages were part of a letter that my husband wrote to me and then gave to a friend who was going home on leave. The information and opinions contained in the letter were much too sensitive to be entrusted to the army postal service." In this letter from Dr. Otto Schulz-Du Bois we read:

On the way back to Riga after my leave [in Frankfurt am Main], I stopped off again at the Commander in Chief's, where I had been with the Colonel [Bruns] upon setting out from Riga. Among other things, I checked to see what had become of the report I had submitted at my previous visit, on the Jewish situation in Riga. I learned from the office that dealt with such matters that the excesses described in my report—the scale and the bestiality of the liquidations—had proved to be beyond anything known even to this office, which had seen plenty of atrocities before. The report was passed on to the highest-level agency responsible for things of this kind, and eventually came into the hands of the highest-ranking officer in Intelligence, a general. The justification given for this attention was that such things posed a threat to the morale of the troops who had to witness them. This officer in Intelligence, who had open access to Hitler, is reported to have given the Führer once again an urgent account of the atrocities and consequences of such methods, whereupon the Führer is said to have replied, "You're getting soft, sir! I *have* to do it, because after me no one else will!" . . . As for the Jewish situation, there were two or three more days of what took place on 30 November 1941. Half of the women employed by us were "resettled," as they now call it. . . . I also saw concentration camps filled with German Jews. Four thousand from Württemberg were kept on a single farm [i.e., Camp Jungfernhof, Riga], poorly fed and penned up in barns; naturally they dropped like flies. It was strange suddenly to be surrounded by Swabian accents. Many of the children were wearing warm ski outfits, and everyone bore up quite admirably under the circumstances. In what used to be the local ghetto, on the other hand, one could hear Berlin accents. I recently saw children standing at the barbed wire, all of them well clothed, begging the Jews who worked in the city: "Ah Uncle, a piece of bread, ah Uncle!" But in the meanwhile even this, I am told, has been stopped! How long will it be until these Jews, too, are "re-settled" to the pine forest, where I recently saw mounds of earth heaped up over five large pits, sharply sagging in the middle, and despite the cold a sickly, sweet odor lingered in the air.

From this letter it is now apparent that beyond the report on the liquidations of 30 November 1941, submitted by Bruns to Abberger and from there on to Radke of the Special Duties Department in the OKH, a second official report on the shootings also was made to this department in the OKH by Dr. Schulz-Du Bois, an officer serving in Bruns's Bridge Inspection Staff. The identity of the person who received Bruns's report can no longer be determined. Colonel Abberger did not receive the report, nor did he see Schulz-Du Bois with Bruns in the OKH on that day.[16] In his statement on these events,[17] Brigadier Otto Richter, then Lieutenant Colonel and Chief of Staff with the General of Engineers, of Northern Army Group, testified that in December 1941 he had visited Colonel Bruns at the officers' clubhouse in Riga. On that evening, Bruns told Richter that "one of his officers in the Bridge Inspection Staff had allegedly witnessed shootings while on a reconnaissance mission in the vicinity of Dünaburg. The officer who reported this incident had evidently been in a greatly agitated state of mind."

This testimony, along with Dr. Otto Schulz-Du Bois's letter, confirms that Captain Schulz-Du Bois was an eyewitness to the mass shootings of Jews outside Riga on 30 November 1941 and that the statements made by Colonel

16. Erich Abberger to author, 18 February 1980.
17. Nuremberg, Case XII, 23 April 1948, p. 2589.

Bruns, Schulz-Du Bois's commanding officer, were based on this captain's eyewitness account. A second eyewitness could not be found.

Early in June 1980 I received a notarized record written by Dr. Hans Holzamer and a notarized statement on Holzamer's account by Frau Erika Schulz-Du Bois. Holzamer's account reads as follows:

> A written record of my recollection of a report made by my friend, Dr. Otto Schulz-Du Bois, then Captain of the Engineering Corps Reserves, about his experiences during 1941 in Riga, in the surrounding region of Riga, and in the OKH.
>
> One day, most probably in 1942—a more exact date is beyond my recollection—my wife and I received an invitation from an old friend on home leave, who wished to tell us about his horrifying experiences in Riga and its vicinity and what happened in the High Command of the Army.
>
> We were both deeply moved by the Schulz-Du Bois story—devastated by the appalling acts to which he had become a most reluctant witness and filled with admiration for our friend's persistent courage. Afterwards, this story became a frequent theme in discussions with our friends and acquaintances, and as a result, the facts have rooted themselves firmly in my memory.
>
> At the time, Dr. Schulz-Du Bois was stationed in Riga. One day, a young man wearing the Star of David asked Schulz-Du Bois to find out what had become of his (the young man's) mother, in whose apartment the Captain was living at the time.
>
> Captain Schulz-Du Bois went first to the warden of the Latvian prison and inquired after the woman. The warden was astonished that a German officer should make inquiries about a Jewish woman, and he referred him to the SS Commandant in Riga. Captain Schulz-Du Bois then contacted the commander, who expressed a similar amazement at the interest of a German officer in a Jewess. Then the SS Commandant quite calmly explained: "Fifty thousand Jews once inhabited Riga. We have liquidated

half of them already. The other half must still perform work for us, but then they too will be liquidated." In the course of the conversation, the officer asked my friend, "Have you ever shot down children?" My friend replied, "Have you no children?"

Sometime afterward, Schulz-Du Bois was in his vehicle on a routine inspection of roads and bridges, when he heard intermittent but persistent reports of gunfire. He decided to investigate. The first thing he came upon was a huge heap of clothes, then men, women, children, and elderly people standing in a line and dressed in their underclothing. The head of the line ended in a small wood by a mass gravesite. Those first in line had to leap into the pit and then were killed with a pistol bullet in the head.

Six SS men were busy with this grisly chore. The victims maintained a perfect calm and composure. There were no outcries, only light sobbing and crying, and soothing words to the children. My friend wrote up an objective account of what he had seen and handed it in as a routine report to his superior. [This superior was Colonel Bruns, commander of the Brückenstab Riga.] In the report he maintained that such atrocities would weaken, if not sap entirely, the morale of the army. This report made its way to the High Command of the Army, to which my friend thereupon was summoned.

As I remember, Admiral Canaris then read the report to Hitler. Hitler's words to Canaris were: "You're getting soft. I have to do it; after me no one else will." All of this was duly recorded by my friend in documentary form, and he gave a few close friends, including my wife and myself, a full account of the affair. Schulz-Du Bois regrettably died in February 1945 of a sudden heart failure. His written record no longer exists. With the occupation of Frankfurt by the American army, the house of the Schulz-Du Bois family passed into the occupied zone, and the family was forced to evacuate at short notice. In their disarray, they left the document behind. It was later discovered that all their papers had been burned.

Frau Erika Schulz-Du Bois appended the following notarized statement, dated 27 May 1980, to Holzamer's record:

> I have read the above record of the recollections of Herr Dr. Med. Hans Holzamer and agree with it in all its essentials, to the best of my judgment twenty-seven years after the event.
>
> Beyond everything else, I distinctly remember that when Hitler had been presented with my husband's report, he answered: "You're getting soft. I have to do it, because after me no one else will."
>
> The written report which my husband made concerning his experiences in and around Riga and in his headquarters has unfortunately been lost.[18]

On 25 and 29 November 1941, five convoys of German Jews[19] from Munich, Berlin, Frankfurt, Vienna, and Breslau were massacred in Kovno in Fort IX,[20] without any prior screening to determine which were fit for labor and which were not. On Sunday, 30 November, at 1:30 P.M., the RFSS Himmler telephoned Heydrich in Prague from the bunker of the Führer's Headquarters, the Wolf's Lair (Wolfsschanze). Himmler knew full well that he had already issued the first liquidation orders for Riga to the newly appointed Higher SS and Police Leader for the Ostland, Friedrich Jeckeln, on 10 and 11 November from his headquarters in the

18. Dr. Hans Holzamer to author, 28 May 1980; Frau Erika Schulz-Du Bois to author, 28 May 1980. These documents have likewise been placed in the archive of the Institut für Zeitgeschichte.
19. From 16 November 1941, all German Jews were no longer under the protection of the law upon leaving the German border, and on 25 November the decree concerning the abrogation of German citizenship became law (RGB1 1/S. 40).
20. Jäger Report, geheime Reichssache 1 December 1941, 3253/63, Fb 76 (a), Institut für Zeitgeschichte.

Prinz-Albrechtstrasse: "Tell Lohse it is my order, which is also the Führer's wish."[21] Now Himmler recalled that on 27 November a Jewish convoy with over one thousand people from Berlin had departed for Riga, arriving there on the evening of 29 November, and had been left standing on a railway siding, in order for these Jews to be liquidated the following morning. Himmler instructed Heydrich to cancel the scheduled liquidation of this Berlin convoy. Heydrich's response to the RFSS was, however, a confirmation that all of the Berlin Jews on this convoy had been shot at 8:15 that morning in the Rumbuli Forest, ahead of their fourteen thousand companions in misfortune from Riga, and that the action was continuing as ordered.

21. Cf. p. 76 n. 26.

ALL GERMANY KNEW ABOUT THE EXTERMINATION CAMPS, AND THE WHOLE NATION DIDN'T CARE.

TENDERS FOR "GAS OVENS" & "CREAMATION OVENS" WERE PUBLISHED OPENLY IN GERMAN NEWSPAPERS OF 1938 AN STIPULATIONS AS TO HANDLE 10,000 [TEN THOUSAND] PERSONS PER DAY WERE GIVEN. GERMAN CIVILIAN WORKERS MADE THEM AND BUILT THEM ON SITE IN THE CAMPS BEFORE GOING HOME AGAIN IN FULL KNOWLEDGE OF HAVING TESTED THEM FOR A WHOLE WEEK. WHO "RECYCLED" THE MILLIONS OF SHOES, COATS, SUITS ETC. SENT TO GERMANY DIRECT FROM THE CAMPS? NOT TO MENTION THE CONTENTS OF THE NOW EMPTY JEWISH HOMES, PICTURES, POTS, PANS, CARPETS ETC.? very true 90 THE WHOLE GERMAN NATION KNEW. THEY SHOULD BE OCCUPIED FOR EVER.

9   The Wannsee Conference

In the senior-administrative-level policy agreement for the "Final Solution of the European Jewish question," formulated on 20 January 1942 during the Wannsee Conference, the procedural guidelines for the future exterminations of physically healthy Jews were laid down once and for all: liquidation through labor.[1] Heydrich, who presided over this fateful conference and ultimately "gave the finishing touches" to the minutes of the proceedings, which had been prepared by Eichmann,[2] prudently refrained from documenting any mention regarding the "special treatment" of Jews who were *not* fit for labor. From Adolf Eichmann, however, we know what the topics of this conference in fact were:

> What I know is that the gentlemen convened their session, and then in very plain terms—not in the language that I had to use in the minutes, but in absolutely blunt terms—they addressed the issue, with no mincing of words. And my memory of all of this would be doubtful, were it not for the fact that I distinctly recall saying to

1.   Wannsee Conference, minutes of the proceedings, geheime Reichssache, p. 71.
2.   Eichmann Trial, session 107, 24 July 1961, F 1/RH. On 25 January 1942, Brigadeführer Franz Stahlecker, head of Einsatzgruppe A in Riga, received a secret dispatch signed by Heydrich and containing the contents of the Wannsee minutes (Historical State Archives, Riga).

myself at the time: look, just look at Stuckart,[3] the perpetual law-abiding bureaucrat, always punctilious and fussy, and now what a different tone! The language was anything but in conformity with the legal protocol of clause and paragraph. I should add that this is the only thing from the conference that has still stuck clearly in my mind.

Presiding Judge :	What did he say on this topic?
Answer :	In particular, Mr. President, I would like to . . .
Question :	Not in particular—in general!
Answer :	The discussion covered killing, elimination, and annihilation.[4]

What Heydrich did not wish to see entered into the minutes of the Wannsee Conference had already been set forth in the secret draft sent on 25 October 1941 from Minister for the Occupied East Rosenberg's Adviser on Jewish Affairs Wetzel to the Reichskommissar of the Ostland, Hinrich Lohse, in Riga: that the Jews who were unfit for labor must be exterminated.[5] Following the Wannsee Conference, the agreed-upon selection process began in the German-Jewish concentration camp in Riga. Selections took place on 5 and 9 February and 14 and 26 March 1942, as well as on 2 November 1943—after twenty-seven thousand Jewish citizens of Riga had already been shot on 30 November and 8 December 1941.[6]

The minutes of the Wannsee Conference of 20 January 1942 registered the commander of the Security Police in Riga, Dr. Rudolf Lange, as fourteenth on the list of conference

3. Dr. Wilhelm Stuckart was the State Secretary in the Ministry of the Interior.
4. Eichmann Trial, Session 107, 24 July 1961, E 1/RV.
5. Cf. p. 71.
6. Between 27 November 1941 and 14 December 1942, twenty-four convoys with 23,625 persons left the Reich for Riga.

Plates

„ *Nordafrika* "

FRR

☒ -(Fernschreiben

9. 6. 1942

Geheime Kommandosache
Cheffache!
Nur durch Offizier!

An

1.) Pz.Armee Afrika
über Dtsch.Gen.b.Obkdo.d.Ital.Wehrmacht, <u>Rom</u>

nachr.: 1.) OKH / Gen Qu
2.) Gen.z.b.V. bei OKH
4.) Ob.d.L. / Gen Qu
5.) OKW / W R

 Nach vorliegenden Meldungen sollen sich bei den freien
franz. Verbänden in Afrika zahlreiche deutsche politische
Flüchtlinge befinden.

 Der Führer hat angeordnet, dass gegen diese mit äusserster
Schärfe vorzugehen ist. Sie sind daher im Kampf schonungslos
zu erledigen. Wo das nicht geschehen ist, sind sie nachträglich
auf Befehl des nächsten deutschen Offiziers sofort und ohne
weiteres zu erschiessen, soweit sie nicht vorübergehend zur
Gewinnung von Nachrichten zeitweilig zurückbehalten werden
sollen.

 Schriftliche Weitergabe dieses Befehls ist verboten. Die
Kommandeure sind mündlich zu unterrichten.

<u>OKW/WFSt/Qu</u> (Verw.)
Nr.55 994/42 g.Kdos.Chefs.

Plate 2 SS-Sturmbannführer Christian Wirth, inspector of the Sobibor, Belzec, and Treblinka extermination camps (Zentrale Stelle der Landesjustizverwaltungen, Ludwigsburg).

Plate 3 Higher SS and Police Leader Ostland Friedrich Jeckeln, prisoner in Riga, 1945 (USSR State Archives, Moscow).

Plate 1 Führer-order to Field Marshal Rommel (translation on p. 37). Instead of orally conveying the order to the commanders as stipulated, Rommel had it burned (Bundesarchiv-Militärarchiv, Freiburg im Breisgau).

Plate 4 The arrival of Reichsführer-SS Heinrich Himmler at the concentration camp in Auschwitz, where on 17 July 1942 he witnessed the gassing of a convoy of Dutch Jews (Archives of the Polish Ministry of Justice).

Plates 5a&b 15 and 16 December 1941, Skede Beach outside Libau. Shooting of Jewish citizens (mostly women and children) from Libau (Liepaja). The pictures were taken by a member of the Libau Gestapo (Latvian Historical Archives, Liepaja).

- NO 3342 -
(- NO 511 -)

Der Reichsführer-H
Feld-Kommandostelle
den 29. Dezember 1942

Betr.: Meldungen an den Führer über
Bandenbekämpfung.

M e l d u n g Nr. 51

Russland-Süd, Ukraine, Bialystok.

Bandenbekämpfungserfolge vom 1.9. bis 1.12.1942

1.) Banditen:

a) festgestellte Tote nach Gefechten (x)

August:	September:	Oktober:	November:	insgesamt:
227	381	427	302	1337

b) Gefangene sofort exekutiert

125	282	87	243	737

c) Gefangene nach längerer eingehender Vernehmung exekutiert

2100	1400	1596	2731	7828

2.) Bandenhelfer und Bandenverdächtige:

a) festgenommen

1343	3078	8337	3795	16553

b) exekutiert

1198	3020	6333	3706	14257

c) Juden exekutiert

31246	165282	95735	70948	363211

3.) Überläufer a.G. deutscher Propaganda:

21	14	42	63	140

(x) Da der Russe seine Gefallenen verschleppt
bzw. sofort verscharrt, sind die Verlustzahlen
auch nach Gefangenenaussagen erheblich höher
zu bewerten.

-2-

318

V.69

Plate 6   Report of the Reichsführer SS to Hitler (see pp. 3, 110n 9, and 129). Item 2c records the murder of 363,211 Jews in the period from 1 September through 1 December 1942 (Bundesarchiv, Koblenz).

Plate 7   Gassing van used to liquidate Jews at the Kulmhof
(Chelmno) extermination camp
and near Konitz (Archives of the
Polish Ministry of Justice).

Plate 8a   Imprisoned SS guards
from the Majdanek camp with
Zyklon-B cans (Archives of the
Polish Ministry of Justice).

Plate 8b   Gas mask used by SS
"Disinfector," who poured Zyklon-
B crystals into vents on the roof of
the gas chamber (Państwowe
Muzeum, Oswiecim).

BIRKENAU EXTERMINATION CAMP
OSWIECIM, POLAND
25 AUGUST 1944
WOMEN'S CAMP
GAS CHAMBER AND CREMATORIUM II
GATE
GUARD TOWER
CONVOY
PRISONERS
GROUP ON WAY TO GAS CHAMBER
CREMATORIUM
UNDRESSING ROOM
GAS CHAMBER AND CREMATORIUM III
ZYKLON-B VENT
GAS CHAMBER
PRISONERS

Plates 9a&b The Auschwitz-Birkenau extermination camp, photographed on 25 August and 21 December 1944. The later photo shows the partial destruction of the extermination installation (U.S. National Archives, Modern Military Branch, Reference Collection).

BIRKENAU EXTERMINATION CAMP
OSWIECIM, POLAND
21 DECEMBER 1944

GAS CHAMBERS IV (DESTROYED) AND V

SECTION BII DISMANTLED

FILTRATION PLANT

UNDRESSING ROOM DISMANTLED

FENCE DOWN

CREMATORIUM PARTIALLY DISMANTLED

GAS CHAMBERS II & III

ADOLF HITLER

Mein politisches Testament.

Seit ich 1914 als Freiwilliger meine
bescheidene Kraft im ersten, dem Reich aufge-
zwungenen Weltkrieg einsetzte, sind nunmehr
über dreissig Jahre vergangen.

In diesen drei Jahrzehnten haben mich
bei all meinem Denken, Handeln und Leben nur
die Liebe und Treue zu meinem Volk bewegt. Sie
gaben mir die Kraft, schwerste Entschlüsse zu
fassen, wie sie bisher noch keinem Sterblichen
gestellt worden sind. Ich habe meine Zeit, meine Arbeitskraft und meine Gesundheit in diesen
drei Jahrzehnten verbraucht.

Es ist unwahr, dass ich oder irgend-
jemand anderer in Deutschland den Krieg im Jahre

Plate 10 In his "Political Testament" Hitler again gave free
rein to his hatred of Jews (see pages one and three of the
Johannmeier original. Imperial War Museum, London).

1939 gewollt haben. Er wurde gewollt und ange-
stiftet ausschliesslich von jenen internationalen
Staatsmännern, die entweder jüdischer Herkunft
waren oder für jüdische Interessen arbeiteten.
Ich habe zuviele Angebote zur Rüstungsbeschrän-
kung und Rüstungsbegrenzung gemacht, die die
Nachwelt nicht auf alle Ewigkeiten wegzuleugnen
vermag, als dass die Verantwortung für den Ausbruch dieses Krieges auf mir lasten könnte. Ich
habe weiter nie gewollt, dass nach dem ersten
unseligen Weltkrieg ein zweiter gegen England
oder gar gegen Amerika entsteht. Es werden Jahr-
hunderte vergehen, aber aus den Ruinen unserer
Städte und Kunstdenkmäler wird sich der Hass gegen das, letzten Endes verantwortliche Volk immer wieder erneuern, dem wir das alles zu verdan-
ken haben: Dem internationalen Judentum und seinen
Helfern!

Ich habe noch drei Tage vor Ausbruch des
deutsch-polnischen Krieges dem britischen Bot-
schafter in Berlin eine Lösung der deutsch-polnischen Probleme vorgeschlagen - ähnlich der im
Falle des Saargebietes unter internationaler
Kontrolle. Auch dieses Angebot kann nicht weg-
geleugnet werden. Es wurde nur

verworfen, weil die massgebenden Kreise der eng-
lischen Politik den Krieg wünschten, teils der
erhofften Geschäfte wegen, teils getrieben durch
eine, vom internationalen Judentum veranstaltete
Propaganda.

Ich habe aber auch keinen Zweifel darüber
gelassen, dass, wenn die Völker Europas wieder
nur als Aktienpakete dieser internationalen Geld-
und Finanzverschwörer angesehen werden, dann auch
jenes Volk mit zur Verantwortung gezogen werden
wird, das der eigentlich Schuldige an diesem mör-
derischen Ringen ist: Das Judentum! Ich habe weiter keinen darüber im Unklaren gelassen, dass dieses Mal nicht nur Millionen Kinder von Europäern
der arischen Völker verhungern werden, nicht nur
Millionen erwachsener Männer den Tod erleiden und
nicht nur Hunderttausende an Frauen und Kindern
in den Städten verbrannt und zu Tode bombardiert
werden dürften, ohne dass der eigentlich Schuldige, wenn auch durch humanere Mittel, seine Schuld
zu büssen hat.

Nach einem secnsjährigen Kampf, der einst
in die Geschichte trotz aller Rückschläge als ruhm-

vollste und tapferste Bekundung des Lebenswillens
eines Volkes eingehen wird, kann ich mich nicht von
der Stadt trennen, die die Hauptstadt dieses Reiches
ist. Da die Kräfte zu gering sind, um dem feindli-
chen Ansturm gerade an dieser Stelle noch länger
standzuhalten, der eigene Widerstand aber durch
ebenso verblendete wie charakterlose Subjekte
allmählich entwertet wird, möchte ich mein Schick-
sal mit jenem teilen, das Millionen anderer auch
auf sich genommen haben, indem ich in dieser Stadt
bleibe. Ausserdem will ich nicht Feinden in die
Hände fallen, die zur Erlustigung ihrer verhetz-
ten Massen ein neues, von Juden arrangiertes Schau-
spiel benötigen.

Ich hatte mich daher entschlossen, in
Berlin zu bleiben und dort aus freien Stücken in
dem Augenblick den Tod zu wählen, in dem ich glaube,
dass der Sitz des Führers und Kanzlers selbst
nicht mehr gehalten werden kann. Ich sterbe mit
freudigem Herzen angesichts der mir bewussten un-
ermesslichen Taten und Leistungen unserer Soldaten
an der Front, unserer Frauen zuhause, den Leistungen unserer Bauern und Arbeiter und dem in der Geschichte einmaligen Einsatz unserer Jugend, die
meinen Namen trägt.

Dass ich ihnen allen meinen aus tiefstem
Herzen kommenden Dank ausspreche, ist ebenso
selbstverständlich wie mein Wunsch, dass sie
deshalb den Kampf unter keinen Umständen aufgeben
mögen, sondern, ganz gleich wo immer, ihn gegen
die Feinde des Vaterlandes weiterführen, getreu
den Bekenntnissen eines grossen Clausewitz. Aus
dem Opfer unserer Soldaten und aus meiner eigenen
Verbundenheit mit ihnen bis in den Tod, wird in
der deutschen Geschichte so oder so einmal wieder
der Samen aufgehen zur strahlenden Wiedergeburt
der nationalsozialistischen Bewegung und damit
zur Verwirklichung einer wahren Volksgemeinschaft.

Viele tapferste Männer und Frauen haben
sich entschlossen, ihr Leben bis zuletzt an das
meine zu binden. Ich habe sie gebeten und ihnen
endlich befohlen, dies nicht zu tun, sondern am
weiteren Kampf der Nation teilzunehmen. Die Führer
der Armeen, der Marine und der Luftwaffe bitte ich,
mit äussersten Mitteln den Widerstandsgeist unserer Soldaten im nationalsozialistischen Sinne zu
verstärken unter dem besonderen Hinweis darauf,
dass auch ich selbst, als der Gründer und Schöpfer
dieser Bewegung, den Tod dem feigen Absetzen oder
gar einer Kapitulation vorgezogen habe.

Möge es dereinst zum Ehrbegriff des
deutschen Offiziers gehören - so wie dies in
unserer Marine schon der Fall ist - dass die
Übergabe einer Landschaft oder einer Stadt
unmöglich ist und dass vor allem die Führer
hier mit leuchtendem Beispiel voranzugehen
haben in treuester Pflichterfüllung bis in den
Tod.

participants. Together with the Latvian Sondereinheiten (special units), under SS-Sturmbannführer Viktor Arajs, Lange oversaw the Final Solution in Latvia, as head of the Einsatzkommando 2 C Special Duties, a formation of Einsatzgruppe A in Riga.[7] Both Lange and Arajs were responsible to the head of Einsatzgruppe A, Dr. Stahlecker, who in turn answered to the Higher SS and Police Leader Ostland, Friedrich Jeckeln. The thirteen names that preceded Lange's on the list of participants at Wannsee were: SS-Oberführer Dr. Schöngarth, Commander of the Security Police in the Generalgouvernement; SS-Gruppenführer Müller; SS-Obersturmbannführer Eichmann; SS-Gruppenführer Hofmann, head of the Race and Settlement Main Office; Ministerial Director Kritzinger, from the Reich Chancellery; SS-Oberführer Klopfer, from the Party Chancellery; Undersecretary of State Luther, from the Foreign Office; State Secretary Dr. Bühler, from the Office of the Governor-General; State Secretary Dr. Freisler, from the Department of Justice; State Secretary Neumann, the Deputy Representative for the Four Year Plan; State Secretary Dr. Stuckart, of the Reich Ministry of the Interior; Chief Reich Administrative Officer, Dr. Leibbrandt; and Gauleiter Dr. Meyer, from the Ministry for the Occupied Eastern Territories. SS-Sturmbannführer Lange was well equipped—and doubtless invited by Heydrich to the conference for that reason—to describe his practical experiences with the Final Solution to the other participants gathered on 20 January 1942 at Grosser Wannsee, no. 56/58.

7. After 199 days of court proceedings, on 21 December 1979, the Hamburg assize court condemned the former SS-Sturmbannführer of the Latvian Legion and former Police Major Viktor Arajs to a life term in prison. Arajs had been living an underground existence in Frankfurt for twenty-five years after the war under a false name and was arrested in 1975.

When Heydrich postponed the conference from 9 December 1941 to 20 January 1942, it was not simply the Japanese attack on Pearl Harbor on 7 December and Germany's subsequent declaration of war on the United States on 11 December that weighed in the balance. On 8 December 1941, Lange's services as supervisor at the execution pits in the Rumbuli Forest outside Riga, and later in the Bikerniek Forest, could not be spared.

10

The Interrogation of Friedrich Jeckeln

In his interrogation on 14 December 1945,[1] the Higher SS and Police Leader Jeckeln detailed the operations that fell within the framework of the Final Solution in the East:

> The shootings were carried out under the direction of Colonel Dr. Lange, Commander of the SD and Gestapo in Latvia. Knecht was in charge of security at the liquidation sites.[2] I, Jeckeln, took part in the shootings on three occasions; the same holds for Lange, Knecht, Lohse, and Lieutenant Colonel Osis, commander of the traffic police in Riga.

Q : Who did the shooting?

A : Ten or twelve German SD soldiers.

Q : What was the procedure?

A : All of the Jews went by foot from the ghetto in Riga to the liquidation site. Near the pits, they had to deposit their overclothes, which were washed, sorted, and shipped back to Germany. Jews—men, women, and children—passed through police cordons on their way to the pits, where they were shot by German soldiers.

1. Minutes from Jeckeln's interrogation on 14 December 1945 (Major Zwetajew, interrogator; Sergeant Suur, interpreter), pp. 8–13, Historical State Archives, Riga.
2. Max Knecht was the commander of the municipal police in Latvia.

Q : Did you report the execution of the order to Himmler?

A : Yes, indeed. I notified Himmler by phone that the ghetto in Riga had been liquidated. And when I was in Lötzen, East Prussia, in December 1941, I reported in person, too.[3] Himmler was satisfied with the results. He said that more Jewish convoys were due to arrive in Latvia, and these were to be liquidated by me also.

Q : Go into more detail.

A : At the end of January 1942,[4] I was at Himmler's headquarters in Lötzen, East Prussia, to discuss organizational matters regarding the Latvian SS legions. There Himmler informed me that additional Jewish convoys were due to arrive from the Reich and from other countries. The destination point would be the Salaspils concentration camp, which lay one and a quarter miles from Riga in the direction of Dünaburg. Himmler said that he had not yet determined how he would have them exterminated: whether to have them shot on board their convoys or in Salaspils, or whether to chase them into the swamp somewhere.

Q : How was the matter resolved?

A : It was my opinion that shooting would be the simpler and quicker death. Himmler said he would think it over and then give orders later through Heydrich.

Q : What countries were the Jews in Salaspils brought from?

A : Jews were brought from Germany, France, Belgium, Holland, Czechoslovakia, and from other occupied countries to the Salaspils camp. To give a precise count of the Jews in the Salaspils camp would be difficult. In any case, all the Jews from this camp were exterminated. But I would like to make an additional statement while we are on this topic.

---

3. I.e., to Himmler's "Hochwald" headquarters in Lötzen.
4. I.e., 25 January 1942, 11:30 A.M. – 1:00 P.M.; per RFSS appointments book, NS 19 DC/vorl. 12, Bundesarchiv, Koblenz.

On the same day Himmler made the following handwritten entry, re: his telephone conversation "from the Wolfsschanze 17 [i.e., 5:00 P.M.] SS Gr.F. Heydrich Prague: Jews into the concentration camps" NS 19/neu 1439 Bundesarchiv, Koblenz.

Q : What statement would you like to make?

A : I would like to state for the record that Göring shares in the guilt for the liquidations of Jewish convoys that arrived from other countries. In the first half of February 1942 I received a letter from Heydrich. In this letter he wrote that Reich Marshal Göring had gotten himself involved in the Jewish question, and that Jews were now being shipped to the East for annihilation only with Göring's approval.

Q : This does not diminish your guilt. Describe your role in the Jewish liquidations in Salaspils.

A : I have already said that I discussed the extermination of Jews in Salaspils with Himmler in Lötzen. That alone makes me an accessory to this crime. Beyond that, Jews were shot in the Salaspils camp by forces recruited from my SD and Security Police units. The commander of the SD and Gestapo in Latvia, Lieutenant Colonel Dr. Lange, was directly in charge of the shootings. Other officers who reported to me on the shootings of Jews in the camp were the commander of the SD and Gestapo in the Baltic States, Major General Jost; Colonel of Police Pifrader; and Colonel of Police Fuchs.

Q : Specifically, what did they report to you?

A : They reported that two to three convoys of Jews were to arrive per week, all subject to liquidation.

Q : Then the number of Jews shot in Salaspils ought to be known too, isn't that correct?

A : Yes, of course. I can give you the approximate figures. The first Jewish convoys arrived in Salaspils in November 1941. Then, in the first half of 1942, convoys arrived at regular intervals. I believe that in November 1941, no more than three convoys arrived in all, but during the next seven months, from December 1941 to June 1942, eight to twelve convoys arrived each month. Overall, in eight months, no less than fifty-five and no more than eighty-seven Jewish convoys arrived at the camp. Given that each convoy carried a thousand men, that makes a total of 55,000 to 87,000 Jews exterminated in the Salaspils camp.

Q : This figure sounds low. Are you telling the truth?

A : I have no other, more exact figures. It should be added, however, that before my arrival in Riga, a significant number of Jews in the Ostland and in White Ruthenia were exterminated. I was informed of this fact.[5]

Q : By whom, specifically?

A : Stahlecker; Prützmann; Lange; Major General Schröder, the SS and Police Leader in Latvia; Major General Möller, the SS and Police Leader in Estonia; and Major General Wysocki, the SS and Police Leader in Lithuania.

Q : Be specific. What did they report?

A : Schröder reported to me that over and above those Jews who had been exterminated in the ghetto in Riga an additional 70,000 to 100,000 Jews were exterminated in Latvia. Dr. Lange directly oversaw these shootings. Möller reported that in Estonia everything was in order as far as the Jewish question was concerned. The Estonian Jewish population was insignificant, all in all about 3,000 to 5,000 and this was reduced to nil. The greater part were exterminated in Reval. Wysocki reported that 100,000 to 200,000 Jews were exterminated—shot—in Lithuania, on Stahlecker's orders. In Lithuania, the Jewish exterminations were overseen by the commander of the SD and Gestapo, Lieutenant Colonel of Police Jäger. Later Jäger told me that he had become neurotic as a result of these shootings. Jäger was pensioned off and left his post for treatment. All told, the number of Jews exterminated in the actions in the Baltic East reached somewhere in the vicinity of 190,500 to 253,500.[6]

Such were the words of the Higher SS and Police

5. Jeckeln was promoted on 31 October 1941 to Higher SS and Police Leader for northern Russia (H.Q. Riga); Jeckeln, personnel file, Berlin Document Center. A second promotion to the rank of Leader of the SS Upper Section, "Ostland," occurred on 11 December 1941 (Bundesarchiv, Koblenz [NS 19 neu/2846]).

6. In reply to telegram number 1331 from the Security Police of Riga (dated 6 February 1942), SS-Standartenführer Karl Jäger reported the following from Kovno on 9 February 1942: "Re: executions through 1 February 1942, by the Einsatzkommando 3A: Jews: 136,421. Total: 138,272, of these, women: 55,556; children: 34,464" (Institut für Zeitgeschichte 3253/63 Fb 76 [a]).

Leader Friedrich Jeckeln in his interrogation of 14 December 1945. A telegram from the High Command of the Northern Army Group, Section IIb, delivered "by courier" to the OKH and dated 17 August 1944,[7] indicates that on 27 January 1942, Jeckeln received the KVK (*Kriegsverdienstkreuz*, or war service cross) First Class with swords, as "a token of appreciation for services rendered in this war that we have waged under compulsion, recognition for which cannot be expressed by conferment of the Iron Cross."[8] Evidently, the Kriegsverdienstkreuz was also bestowed upon participants in "executions" and special actions. This fact emerges from the following correspondence, dated 14 and 20 November 1941, between the camp commandant of Gross-Rosen and the inspector of concentration camps:[9]

> re: Conferment of the Kriegsverdienstkreuz.
> re: My telegram to you, no. 2719, of 14 Nov. 1941.
>
> The Commandant's Office has submitted to date two lists recommending the conferment of the Kriegsverdienstkreuz. In both of these appear SS personnel who participated in executions. We herewith request confirmation as to whether these names should be listed once again in the roll currently under preparation. Further requested is information as to whether in the recommendation lists under "Reasons and Comments of Immediate Superior" there should be specified, "Execution, i.e., special action" or whether a general, routine reason should be given.
>
> The Camp Commandant
> Signed, Rödl
> SS Obersturmbannführer

7.   Personal Data for the Nomination of SS-Obergruppenführer Jeckeln for the Knight's Cross, 18 August 1944, per telegram: Reichsführer-SS Himmler, 2. Gruppenführer Fegelein, Führer's Headquarters. Bundesarchiv-Militärarchiv, Freiburg.

8.   E. Döhle, 1943, p. 25, as reported to author by Dr. Adalbert Rückerl, Zentrale Stelle für Landesjustizverwaltungen, Ludwigsburg, 22 August 1979.

9.   Zentrale Stelle für Landesjustizverwaltungen 436/31, 437/31.

This inquiry was answered on 20 November 1941 by the acting inspector of concentration camps, SS-Obersturmbannführer Liebehenschel:

> In the lists of recommendation for the conferment of the KVK to SS members who participated in the executions, under "reasons" enter: "completion of vital war assignments." The word "execution" should under no circumstances be mentioned. In the lists to be handed in, the names already submitted should be cited once again.
>
> I.V. [by order of the Chief Inspector]
> Signed, Liebehenschel
> SS Obersturmbannführer

During the prosecution of liquidation camp personnel, it was repeatedly acknowledged that the persons referred to in the correspondence above were given the KVK.[10] There can be no doubt that the Higher SS and Police Leader Friedrich Jeckeln received the KVK First Class with swords in recognition of his faithful performance: his organization of the mass shootings in Riga, "on orders from the highest level" (*auf höchsten Befehl*).

10. Dr. Adalbert Rückerl to author, 22 August 1979.

11

On 28 November 1941, the Construction Department in the staff of the Higher SS and Police Leader Ostland once again, on the order of Jeckeln, inspected the five pits that had been dug a few days earlier by three hundred Russian prisoners of war.[1] These pits measured approximately twelve square yards and were roughly eight to ten feet deep; and each was fitted with a ramp, "so that the victims could descend into the pit."

On the very day of these inspections, Adolf Hitler received the Grand Mufti Haj Amin Husseini from Jerusalem for talks at the Reich Chancellery in Berlin. Present at this meeting were Reich Foreign Minister Joachim von Ribbentrop and Ambassador Fritz Grobba. Excerpts from the minutes of the Hitler-Husseini talks follow.[2] This detailed record is invaluable, for it pinpoints certain facets of Hitler's state of mind at the time of the talks.

> The Grand Mufti first thanked the Führer for the great honor of a personal reception. He further wished to take the opportunity to express his gratitude on behalf of the

1. Riga Trial (50) 9/72, pp. 57–58.
2. Record by Dr. Paul Otto Schmidt on the conference between the Führer and the Grand Mufti of Jerusalem in Berlin on 28 November 1941, geheime Reichssache 57 a/41, Records Dept. Foreign and Commonwealth Office Pa/2.

entire Arab world, particularly for the continual interest in Arab, and especially Palestinian, affairs which the great Führer of the *Grossdeutsche Reich* [Greater German Reich] had demonstrated, and for the unequivocal support he had shown in his public speeches. The Arab nations were deeply convinced that Germany would win the war, and that the interests of the Arab world would consequently be safeguarded. The Arabs were, moreover, natural allies of Germany, as could be seen by their mutual enemies: the British, the Jews, and the communists. As a result, the Arabs were prepared to collaborate wholeheartedly with Germany and to lend support to the war effort, not only through perpetrating acts of sabotage and encouraging political destabilizations, but materially, by forming an Arab Legion.[3] The Arabs would make better allies than

3. When, in 1941, news of the successful escape of the Grand Mufti of Jerusalem and of the Prime Minister of Iraq Rashid Ali El-Gailani to Germany became known, Chief of Foreign Intelligence Admiral Canaris contacted the Arab leaders.

In agreement with the Foreign Office, which was entrusted with the care of foreign nationals living in German asylum, permission to collaborate with the Arab leaders was granted. A few hundred, mainly youthful, adherents of the Grand Mufti and of the Iraqi Prime Minister had adventurously traveled to Europe to carry on the fight against the British and French colonial powers. Among them were Palestinians, Syrians, Iraqis, and Egyptians. As many as were capable of bearing arms were consolidated into the "Arab Legion" in the vicinity of Athens, and the most capable were detached to the Brandenburg Division by the Foreign Intelligence Office for training as radio operators. Directly after the conclusion of the French campaign in 1940, another detachment was added to Section IH West in the Foreign Intelligence Office and assigned to reconnoiter the Anglo-American army in the Near and Middle East, as well as French military forces in North Africa. The head of this detachment was the former Captain F. S., cover name "Angelo." When the British succeeded, in 1941, in quelling the rebellion in Iraq (it was strategically important for Britain to secure Iraq as a line of communications and supplies between India and Egypt), the Grand Mufti (who had personally supported the Iraqi struggle), the Prime Minister of Iraq Rashid Ali El-Gailani, and all their collaborators were forced to leave the country. They reached Italy and Germany by way of Iran. On 22 November 1940, the Axis powers issued a manifesto in which they declared their commitment to the struggle for the freedom of the Arab peoples.
(Franz Seubert, *Die Nachhut*, no. 4 [1968]: 7)

perhaps it would seem at first, both in light of geographical considerations and because of the sufferings that the British and Jews had inflicted on the Arabs. In addition, the Arabs had close ties with all Muslim nations, which could also benefit the common cause. The Arab Legion could be mustered with ease. An appeal by the Mufti to the Arab nations and the prisoners of Arabic, Algerian, Tunisian, and Moroccan nationality who were currently held in Germany would yield a multitude of combat-ready volunteers. The Arab world was firmly convinced of a German victory, by virtue not only of the large army, brave soldiers, and brilliant military strategists at Germany's disposal, but also because Allah could never grant victory to an unjust cause. The Arabs were seeking to win independence and unity for Palestine, Syria, and Iraq from this war. They had full confidence in the Führer, who could heal the wounds inflicted on the Arab nations by Germany's enemies.

The Mufti then recalled a document he had received from the German government, which stated that Germany had occupied no Arabic lands, that it recognized and sympathized with the Arab struggles for independence and liberation, and that it would support the elimination of the national Jewish homeland. A public declaration today to this same effect would be of immense propagandistic value in the campaign to mobilize the Arab nations. . . . The Führer responded that the fundamental attitude of Germany toward these issues . . . was self-evident. Germany had declared an uncompromising war on the Jews. Such a commitment naturally entailed a stiff opposition to the Jewish homeland in Palestine, a cause that had become the political rallying point for Jewish interests and their destructive influence. Germany also knew the allegation that the Jews were playing the part of economic pioneers in Palestine to be false. There only the Arabs worked, not the Jews. Germany was determined to challenge the European nations one by one into a settlement of the Jewish question, and, when the time came, Germany would turn to the non-European peoples with the same call.

At the present time, Germany was engaged in a life-or-death struggle against the two power bases of Jewry, Britain and Russia. In theory, the economic systems of Britain and Russia were polar opposites, but in practice, Jewry in both countries was pursuing a common objective. The present war was of decisive importance: politically, it represented a conflict of interests between Germany and England; ideologically, it represented a showdown between National Socialism and Judaism. Of course, Germany was prepared to offer positive and practical aid to its Arabian partners, who were faced with the same contest. For, in a struggle for existence, especially where the Jews could enlist the assistance of the British war machine for their own purposes, platonic assurances were pointless. . . . The Führer then made the following declaration, requesting the Mufti to lock it deep in his heart:

1. He (the Führer) would carry on the fight until the last traces of the Jewish-communist European hegemony had been obliterated.

2. In the course of this fight, the German army would—at a time that could not yet be specified, but in any case in the clearly foreseeable future—gain the southern exit of the Caucasus.

3. As soon as this breakthrough was made, the Führer would offer the Arab world his personal assurance that the hour of liberation had struck. Thereafter, Germany's only remaining objective in the region would be limited to the annihilation of the Jews living under British protection in Arab lands.[4]

---

4. The collaboration between the Grand Mufti and Intelligence eventually subsided. "The Arab leaders had found an equal partner for discussing their political views—especially in respect to the Jewish question—in the SD, to whom they finally became totally subservient" (Franz Seubert, *Die Nachhut*, 1968, 4:7). "The Grand Mufti of Jerusalem was a close collaborator with Office VI, RSHA. Husseini's trip to Germany was organized by the Office VI agent in Ankara, Moyzish, while the head of the Press and News Division of the Foreign Office, Dr. Paul Karl Schmidt, brought the Grand Mufti, effectively disguised by head bandages, from Ankara to Berlin by plane" (Schellenberg Interrogations, final report, RG 238, U.S. National Archives Collection of World War II War Crimes Interrogations, App. 5). Cf. on this the statement by Dieter Wisliceny: "After the Grand

Such were Adolf Hitler's thoughts and designs on 28 November 1941. Three days later, now in the close-drawn circle of his personal intimates and possessed by the monstrous hatred that dictated his every move, Hitler was driven by the inner need to justify his decisions. He once again brought up the key issue, here in a thinly veiled form: "Many Jews have not been conscious of the destructive character of their existence either. But whoever destroys life exposes himself to the risk of death, and the Jews will be no exception. Who is to blame, the cat or the mouse, if the cat eats up the mouse? The mouse, which never in its life did anything to harm a cat?" Hitler had made up his mind well before Heydrich formally extended the invitations to the conference on the Wannsee.[5]

Mufti El Husseini had come to Germany, he paid a visit to Himmler. Shortly afterward, the Grand Mufti visited the Head of the Office for Jewish Affairs in Dept. IV, Obersturmbannführer Adolf Eichmann, in the latter's offices in Berlin, Kurfürstenstrasse 116. The exact date escapes me now; it could have been the end of 1941 or the beginning of 1942. I was with Eichmann in Berlin a few days later, and he gave me a thorough rundown on this visit" (IMT, 26 July 1946).

5. *Adolf Hitler, Monologe im Führerhauptquartier: 1941–1944*, ed. W. Jochmann (Hamburg, 1980), 148.

12

It should come as no surprise that certain officials within the Reich Ministry of the Interior in Berlin were notified immediately of the mass shootings in the Baltic East, and in particular of the shootings that occurred outside Riga on 30 November and 8 December 1941. A few days after the Rumbuli Forest liquidations, the Assistant Adviser on Racial Affairs in the Reich Ministry of the Interior, Dr. Werner Feldscher,[1] received a firsthand account of the massacre "from a fully reliable source, a friend."[2] Feldscher passed this on to his immediate superior, the Adviser on Jewish Affairs, a lower-rank senior civil servant, Dr. Bernhard Lösener, who on 21 December made an urgent appointment with his and Feldscher's superior, Secretary of State Dr. Wilhelm Stuckart:

> I told him that my colleague, Dr. Feldscher, had received an eyewitness account of the way in which deported German Jews had recently been massacred in Riga. . . . I told Stuckart that this outrage had affected me as it would any feeling human being; and that in the present case I was also affected as an adviser in the Ministry of the

---

1. Werner Feldscher, Oberregierungsrat and Assistant Adviser on Racial Affairs, 15 February 1943, personnel file, Berlin Document Center.

2. Document NG-19449-A, Lösener affadavit, 24 February 1948, RG 238, Case XI (Weizsäcker et al.), vol. 64a, U.S. National Archives.

Interior, since Jews of German citizenship were involved.[3] My conscience and my position at the Ministry were now irreconcilable. They would remain so even if the present policy on mixed marriages and on the offspring from these unions were to prove untenable. Stuckart's reply to this was, word for word: "Herr Lösener, don't you realize that all of this is being done on orders from the highest level?"[4] I said, "There is a judge inside me who tells me what I have to do." Stuckart answered that if my conscience did not allow me to continue, he would relieve me at once from my position; but first he would need to consider how I might otherwise be employed.

Fifteen months elapsed before Stuckart's promise materialized and Lösener was released from his post as Adviser on Jewish Affairs, to be transferred to another desk. On account of his complaints Lösener remained a lower-rank senior civil servant until the end of the war.[5]

State Secretary Stuckart knew perfectly well, on 21 December 1941, what the Final Solution of the Jewish question involved. One month later (20 January 1942), Sipo Chief Heydrich would explicitly disclose what had long been a matter of tacit knowledge—which he would have formalized and announced on 9 December, at Grosser Wannsee 56/58, had the SS-Sturmbannführer Dr. Lange not been busy on 8 and 9 December acquiring "the practical experience that is of crucial significance to the impending Final Solution of the Jewish question."[6]

3. Cf. p. 89 n. 19.
4. "'On orders from the highest level' can only mean that an order or a command came from Hitler himself" (Richard Schulze-Kossens to author, 1 December 1979).
5. "I left the Reich Ministry of the Interior in March 1943, at which time I was transferred to the Reich Administrative Court and employed as a judge" (Lösener affadavit, 24 February 1948, vol. 64a, p. 6, U.S. National Archives).
6. Per minutes of the proceedings of 20 January 1942, re: the Final Solution of the Jewish Question, NG 2586, p. 5, Berlin Document Center. Cf. Heydrich's letter of 8 January 1942, to Gruppenführer Otto Hofmann, in

In the "Besprechungsprotokoll" (minutes of the proceedings) from Wannsee, which Heydrich personally sent over to the Undersecretary of State in the Foreign Office, Martin Luther, we read not only that the Führer had "sanctioned" the evacuations to the East, but also that these evacuations "constitute only temporary solutions." Spelled out, this means that only for a limited period would the Jews evacuated to the East still be subjected to maximal hard-labor assignments in ghettos or in so-called transit camps.

> Pursuant to the Final Solution, the Jews are to be put into labor detachments in the East, under the appropriate supervision. The Jews who are *fit for labor* [italics added] will be marshalled into large work columns, divided by sex, and conducted into regions in the East to build roads, whereby a great many will unquestionably die off through attrition. The eventual remainder will have to be dealt with accordingly, since this will doubtless be the more resistant lot, representing a natural selection, which, if released, would constitute the germ of a new Jewish revival. (Witness the lessons of history.) In the course of the practical realization of the Final Solution, Europe will be thoroughly combed, from west to east.

From this excerpt emerges the fact that the Jews were to be split into two distinct groups, those capable of work and those not, and that even this selection ultimately made no difference: survivors and casualties alike were to undergo "special treatment." From among those fit for labor, it was already determined in advance ("unquestionably") that "a

---

which Heydrich informs Hofmann, who had also been invited, that because of occurrences in which "a few of the invited men" were involved, the conference had to be postponed until 20 January (Gerald Reitlinger, *The Final Solution*, 3d ed. [London, 1971], 101). Cf. also Heydrich to Undersecretary of State Martin Luther in the Foreign Office, on 29 November 1941: "I am therefore inviting you to a discussion followed by breakfast on 9 December 1941, 12:00, in the office of the International Criminal Police Commission in Berlin, at Grosser Wannsee 56/58" (FOSD 372043/4).

great many"—that too was already determined—would "die off." Extermination through "labor" or through other avenues—such was the fate allotted the Jews.

As the following verbal exchange will illustrate, Heydrich and Eichmann were not the only participants of the Wannsee Conference to know about the planned mass liquidation using Zyklon B in permanent "liquidation sites":

Dr. Servatius :	Witness, you yourself had a preview of the preparations for the liquidations in the East before the conference took place. Is that not so?
Defendant [Eichmann] :	Yes, indeed.
Dr. Servatius :	Did the participants in the conference have any prior knowledge of this type of final solution?
Defendant :	I have to presume so, since by the time of the conference the war against Russia had already gone on for six months, and as we have ourselves seen from the documentary evidence, the Einsatzgruppen were in complete control of these territories. And the centrally placed, key figures of the Reich administration were naturally aware of the situation.[7]

Adolf Hitler, certainly, had precise knowledge of the way in which the Einsatzgruppen were operating in the East. Already on 1 August 1941, Gestapo Chief Müller of the Reich Main Security Office transmitted a coded directive to the commanders of the four Einsatzgruppen, advising them that "the Führer [was] to be kept informed continually from

7. Eichmann Trial, Session 79, 26 June 1961, BI/FL, Israel State Archives. In this session Eichmann also remarked: "And the greatest surprise of all was surely, as far as I can remember, Bühler, but above all, Stuckart, the perpetually cautious and perpetually dilatory Stuckart, who here suddenly revealed himself with an unprecedented élan."

here about the work of the Einsatzgruppen in the East" and that "to this end, visual materials of special interest, such as photographs," were needed. Müller requested "the speediest possible delivery."[8]

Adolf Hitler's involvement in the Final Solution did not end with his request for continual updating on the progress of the Einsatzgruppen.[9] He also issued orders covering all aspects of the gassings. This, at least, is the picture that emerges when we fill in the background to the so-called Gas Chamber Letter of 25 October 1941, which was sent to the Reichskommissar for the Ostland, Hinrich Lohse.[10] Its author, the Adviser on Jewish Affairs in the Ministry for the Occupied Eastern Territories, Lower Court Judge Dr. Wetzel, sketched in the details surrounding this top secret draft document in his interrogation on 20 and 21 September 1961:

> On 24 October 1941, I went to Brack's office in the Führer's Chancellery on Voßstrasse. Brack said . . . that he had an assignment for me. I was to convey the following message to Minister Rosenberg: Minister Rosenberg should inform Reichskommissar Lohse that he, Brack, had a gassing apparatus ready for shipment to Riga. Brack told me that the gassing apparatus was to be used on the Jews, and that Eichmann had agreed that this gassing van should be sent to Riga. Jewish convoys would also be sent to Riga and Minsk. . . . In the course of this briefing, Brack told me that this was a matter of a Führer-order or Führer-commission.[11]

8. RSHA IV A I b, B. Nr. 576 B/41 g, FT (enciphered), signed "Müller, SS Brif" (Fa 213/3, Institut für Zeitgeschichte).
9. Cf. "Reports to the Führer, re: campaign against gangs," report number 51, for 1 September to 1 December 1942: prisoners executed, 8,565; gang accomplices and suspects executed, 14,257; Jews executed, 363,211. (See plates.) Submitted to Hitler, 31 December 1942 (NS 19/291, Bundesarchiv, Koblenz).
10. Cf. p. 71 n. 12.
11. Hearing of Dr. Erhard Wetzel, 20–21 September 1961, 2JS 499/61, Staatsanwaltschaft Hannover.

Asked how he, Wetzel, as a judge, could account for his having been a party to unlawful murder, the defendant replied:

> I have already explained: Brack explicitly told me that this matter resulted by order of the Führer, and that in conformity with this assignment I had to report to the Reich Minister Rosenberg, who in turn would notify the Reichskommissar Ostland. I was only acting as deputy, and I do not feel in any way answerable for these things. To refuse the assignment and simply walk out of the Reich Ministry was out of the question. I was informed that the position in the Ministry for the Occupied Eastern Territories would constitute military service. Had I refused the assignment, especially being a member of the party, I would have faced internment in a concentration camp.[12]

That the top levels of the National Socialist regime were closely informed about the ordered actions by now scarcely needs mentioning. Thus, for instance, Minister of Propaganda Josef Goebbels wrote the following in his journal on 27 March 1942:[13]

> The Jews will now be relocated from the General-gouvernement to the East, starting with Lublin. A fairly barbaric procedure will be used here, one that cannot be precisely described. Not many of the Jews will be left over. Roughly speaking, one can be sure that 60 percent of them will have to be liquidated, while we will be able to put only 40 percent into labor detachments. The former Gauleiter of Vienna, who is in charge of this operation,[14] is taking the appropriate precautions and employing a method that is not too terribly conspicuous. . . . The emptying ghettos in the cities of the Generalgouvernement will now be filled with Jews who have been deported from

12. Ibid., p. 31.
13. F 12/8, fols. 803–4, Institut für Zeitgeschichte.
14. I.e., the SS and Police Leader in Lublin, Odilo Globocnik.

the Reich, and from these ghettos, after a certain period has elapsed, the process will be renewed.[15]

In the summer of 1942, at the start of the long prepared-for major extermination actions in the eastern parts of the Generalgouvernement—a concert of operations that was slowly building up to a crescendo-like Final Solution of the Jewish question in Europe—SS-Obergruppenführer Gottlob Berger, acting as the chief liaison officer to the Ministry for the Occupied Eastern Territories, presented Himmler with a proposal for an ordinance defining the term "Jew" for the occupied East. Himmler's response was: "I strongly advise against publishing any ordinance on the term 'Jew.'[16] All these silly rules and regulations will only serve to tie our own hands. The occupied East will be freed of Jews (*judenfrei*). The Führer has laid upon my shoulders the execution of this very difficult order. Moreover, no one can relieve me of this responsibility. I have therefore forbidden any further meddling in the matter."[17]

The "*Entjudung*" (literally: "de-Jewification") of the occupied East was now, "in conformity with the Führer's wish,"[18] well on its way toward realization. After the bomb attack made on Heydrich in Prague on 27 May 1942 and his subsequent death on 4 June, the project was pushed for-

15. From the convoys that left the Lublin district, approximately 40 percent went to Sobibor, 39 percent to Belzec, 14 percent to Treblinka, and 7 percent to Majdanek (Adalbert Rückerl, *NS-Vernichtungslager* [Munich, 1977], 128), quoted from W. Scheffler declaration, Sobibor trial proceedings, Schwurgericht, Hagen.

16. RFSS to SS-Gruppenführer Gottlob Berger, 28 July 1942, RG 238, U.S. National Archives.

17. Cf. pp. 56–58; RFSS to Gottlob Berger, geheime Reichssache, one copy, 28 July 1942, RG 238, No. 626, U.S. National Archives.

18. RFSS on 2 October 1942, to SS-Obergruppenführer Pohl, head of the Economy Administration Main Office; SS-Obergruppenführer Friedrich-Wilhelm Krüger, HSSPF Ost (Cracow); SSPF Odilo Globocnik, Lublin; and SS-Obergruppenführer Karl Wolff, head of the Personnel Staff of the RFSS (G. T-175, R. 22, pp. 7359–60, Bundesarchiv, Koblenz).

ward with redoubled zeal by Eichmann's section IV B 4 (Jewish Affairs) in the RSHA. "The plan," as Eichmann wrote on 22 June, "is to evacuate . . . in the first instance" 40,000 Jews from the occupied territory in France, 10,000 Jews from Belgium, and another 40,000 from Holland, beginning in mid-July. The destination point was to be Auschwitz, and the loads would average 1,000 persons per day. Eichmann assumed "that no objections to these measures had been raised on the part of the Foreign Office either."[19]

The direct preparation for the deportations of West European Jews was made in June and July of 1942,[20] during which time the late Heydrich's position as Chief of Sipo and the SD remained unfilled. Up to the time of his assassination, Heydrich had functioned jointly as acting Reich Protector of Bohemia and Moravia and as Chief of Sipo and the SD (the head of the RSHA combined the offices of Chief of Sipo and Chief of the SD). Since Heydrich's successor, Kaltenbrunner, was not named until January 1943, it follows that Eichmann benefited from the temporary vacuum: from June 1942 to January 1943, in matters regarding the Final Solution of the European Jewish question Eichmann probably was directly answerable to Himmler, and the scope and range of his independent activities, not to mention responsibilities, were consequently enlarged.

It seemed obvious to the National Socialist leadership that the assassination attempt on Reinhard Heydrich, the "man with the heart of iron," had been intended in the first instance for the head of the RSHA, and not the Reich

19. NG-183 (Case 11. Pros. Doc. book 60-B) (B 76), Bundesarchiv, Koblenz.
20. On 11 June a conference was held in the RSHA in Berlin, attended by the advisers on Jewish affairs from France, Belgium, and Holland. The consensus reached here was that 15,000 Jews should be deported from Holland (B. A. Sijes, "Adolf Eichmann und die Deportation der in den Niederlanden wohnenden Juden," p. 84, Rijksinstituut voor Oorlogsdocumentatie).

Protector of Bohemia and Moravia. It was presumed that the attack had been organized, if not carried out, by Jewish terrorists.[21]

Immediately after the attempt, Goebbels made the following journal entry:

> A bomb attack has been made on Heydrich in a suburb of Prague. . . . We must recognize that an attempted assassination like this might form a precedent unless we proceed against it with extremely brutal countermeasures. But such a danger is really nonexistent; we shall have no problem crushing this attempt at creating chaos in the Protectorate and the occupied territories.
>
> My campaign against the Jews in Berlin will be waged along similar lines. I am currently having a Jewish hostage list put together. Sweeping arrests will follow. I have no intention of possibly letting a twenty-two-year-old East European Jew—characters of this type were found among the assassins at the anti-Soviet exhibition—fire a bullet into my belly. Ten Jews either in a concentration camp or six feet under are preferable to one roaming at large. There is no room for sentimentalism here.[22]

A few days later, Goebbels made the following entry:

> Unfortunately, Heydrich is in critical condition. . . . The details of the assassination remain a mystery. . . . In any case, we are taking adequate reprisals against the Jews. I have given the go-ahead for the arrest of five hundred Jews in Berlin, as planned, and have made clear to the leaders of the Jewish community there that for every Jew-

---

21.   The British-educated Czech noncommissioned officers, Jan Kubis and Josef Gabcik, were flown into the Protectorate and carried out the order as radioed in mid-May 1942 by Czech President Eduard Beneš, who was in exile in London, to the Czech resistance leaders at their secret radio station "Libuse" in the vicinity of Pardubice: "In the interests of the Western Allies, the attack must be carried out as planned" (Charles Wighton, *Heydrich* [London, 1962], 271).

22.   "Fragmente aus Goebbels' Tagebuch," 28 May 1942, III21g 16/5c, pp. 27–30, Rijksinstituut voor Oorlogsdocumentatie.

ish act of terrorism or sedition, one hundred or one hundred fifty of the Jews in our hands will be shot. On the heels of the Heydrich assassination a whole crowd of Jews were charged with conspiracy and shot in Sachsenhausen. The more of this filthy race we eliminate, the better things will be for the security of the Reich.[23]

23. Ibid., pp. 19ff., 31 May 1942. Goebbels's entry of 30 May 1942 records the following statement by Hitler, with whom Goebbels had conferred on that day in the Reich Chancellery: "The Führer's assessment of the political situation is practically identical to mine. He foresees the possibility of a rise in assassination attempts if we do not proceed with energetic and ruthless measures in the Protectorate against those circles which are receptive to assassinations. He accordingly required that all restraint be dispensed with, and that the interests of the security of the Reich be placed above the interests of single individuals from whom we can expect little good" (Goebbels's diary entry of 30 May 1942, pp. 38–39, Institut für Zeitgeschichte).

13

The Camp of the
German Jews in Minsk

Two months before his death, Heydrich had flown to Minsk to deliver in person a stern reprimand to Wilhelm Kube, the Generalkommissar for White Russia based at Minsk. For, in his preliminary inspection of the 7,300 Jews who had been deported in November 1941 from Hamburg, Düsseldorf, Frankfurt, Bremen, Berlin, and Vienna to the Minsk camp for German Jews,[1] Kube had noticed, to his great consternation, that two of the young women prisoners from Germany had fully Aryan features. He had also become absolutely incensed when he learned from the Jewish elder, Dr. Frank, that among the deportees were men with military decorations from the First World War.[2] Gauleiter Kube, one of the earliest members of the Nazi party and a confirmed anti-Semite, sud-

---

1. Karl Löwenstein, "Minsk," supplement to the weekly paper *Das Parlament,* 7 November 1956.
2. Cf. Adolf Eichmann to the leader of seventeen State Police offices and to the inspectors of the Security Police and SD in Vienna, Prague, Danzig, Berlin, 17 April 1942, (secret):

> re: evacuation of Jews
> re: FS-decree of 20 November 1941, B. Nr. Roem. 4B4 2963/41 G
> Concerning evacuation of Jews to Minsk and Riga.
> Referring to the above-mentioned FS-decree, please be informed that Jews in possession of the decoration for combat injuries are likewise not to be evacuated to the East. (Bundesarchiv, Koblenz)

This directive resulted from the fact that convoys to Riga and Minsk in November 1941 included Jews with war decorations.

denly felt obliged to protect his Jews, who, he realized, belonged "to our cultural milieu." Kube therefore promptly filed a complaint with Reinhard Heydrich, in which he stated that "during the evacuation of Jews from the Reich, the guidelines on who was to be evacuated had not been properly observed," and he attached a list of names. Thus it came about that on 2 March 1942, Generalkommissar Kube withheld his German Jews from a mass shooting which was conducted in Minsk under the supervision of Sturmbannführer Dr. Eduard Strauch, at which 3,412 Jews were killed. This unheard-of behavior by Kube in turn provoked a formal complaint from the SS:[3]

> On 1 March 1942, an action against the Russian ghetto in Minsk was to take place. . . . To conceal the action, the elder of the Jews was to be told that five thousand Jews were being resettled.[4] The council of elders was to select and organize the required numbers. Each Jew was allowed two kilograms of luggage. The actual intentions of the Security Police were evidently disclosed by the Generalkommissariat. . . . As a result of this betrayal, none of the Jews presented themselves at the appointed time. There was no choice but to round them up by force. Resistance ensued, and the deployed units had to use firearms.

Having removed his office Jews from the camp for German Jews twenty-four hours before the action on 2 March, and in the process managing to frustrate the liquidation of the occupants of the Minsk ghetto on that same day, Kube had to endure the wrath of Heydrich upon the latter's visit to Minsk, shortly after the successful completion of the sty-

3. Helmut Heiber, "Aus den Akten des Gauleiters Kube," *Vierteljahrshefte für Zeitgeschichte* 4 (1956): 87.
4. Karl Löwenstein, who was relocated to Theresienstadt on 13 May 1942 from the camp for German Jews in Minsk, was told by the SS that twenty-five thousand Russian Jews had been executed. It seems likely, however, that exaggerated figures like this were given verbally by the SS for the purpose of terrorizing the surviving Jews. The official figure is bad enough.

mied liquidation. "I regret," Kube read in a letter from Heydrich,. written on 21 March, "having to furnish this kind of justification, six and a half years after the decree of the Nuremberg Laws";[5] and in the written complaint submitted by the SS against Kube, we find the telling remark of the complainant, Dr. Strauch, Commander of the SD in White Russia: "Generalkommissar Kube appears to have promised to the German Jews, who before my time were delivered to the ghetto five thousand strong, that life and health would remain theirs."[6] Nothing of the kind had been foreseen in the guidelines drawn up at Wannsee, and Heydrich demanded of Strauch the complete liquidation of all the Jews still alive in the Minsk region. Thus, on 28 and 29 July 1942, the Russian and German ghetto in Minsk was reduced from 19,000 to 8,794 inhabitants.[7]

The complaint registered by the SS, the harsh reprimand by Heydrich, and Heydrich's death on 4 June in Prague together achieved Kube's required unconditional obedience in the execution of orders given for the Final Solution. On 31 July a submissive Kube, evidently concerned about his position, wrote to his friend, the Reichskommissar Ostland, Hinrich Lohse, in Riga:

> Following lengthy talks with the SS-Brigadeführer Zenner and the extraordinarily diligent head of the SD, SS-Obersturmbannführer Dr. Strauch, in the last ten weeks in White Russia we have liquidated roughly 55,000 Jews. . . . In the city of Minsk about 10,000 Jews were liquidated on 28 and 29 July. Of these, 6,500 were Russian Jews, predominantly women, children, and the aged; the rest were Jews unfit for labor, mainly from Vienna, Brünn, Bremen, and Berlin. The latter had been sent to Minsk last year in ac-

5. Heiber, "Aus den Akten des Gauleiters Kube," 67.
6. Ibid., 90.
7. PS 3428, IMT XII, 67 and Case XI, transcript 142.

cordance with the Führer's orders. .... In Minsk proper, there are 2,600 Jews from Germany left.[8]

Reichskommissar Lohse commented on Kube's report on 7 August, during a conference chaired by Göring in the headquarters for the Four Year Plan: "Only a few Jews are still alive. Tens of thousands were eliminated."[9] Kube himself survived the last "resettlement" in Minsk by only a week. On 22 September he was killed by a bomb which had been planted under his bed by an agent of the partisans, his maid. For Himmler, who had expressed his dissatisfaction with the SS critic Kube to the latter's highest superior, the Minister for the Occupied Eastern Territories Rosenberg, Kube's assassination meant one less problem to solve.[10]

8. Israel State Archives 1098.
9. Minutes of the discussion, IMT, Document 170, USSR.
10. Heinz Höhne, *Der Orden unter dem Totenkopf* (Munich, 1976), 342.

14

Reichskommissar
of the Ukraine,
Erich Koch

Minister for the Occupied East Alfred Rosenberg did not only have Wilhelm Kube's disobedience to contend with. The self-willed Reichskommissar for the Ukraine and the district Bialystok, Erich Koch, gave Rosenberg even greater trouble. Koch's political career was launched in 1928, when he was made Gauleiter of the Nazi party for East Prussia at the recommendation of the notorious Julius Streicher. In 1933 Koch became a member of the Prussian State Council, and later that same year, on 1 June, he became president of the province of East Prussia. On 15 August 1941, Hitler appointed Koch as head of the civil administration in the Bialystok district, stipulating: "The head of the civil administration is immediately subordinate to me and takes his instructions from me."[1] Hitler further had the good sense to make contingent policy provisions in this same decree of 15 August: "In differences of opinion that cannot be settled through direct negotiation, my decision is to be obtained through the Reich Minister and the head of the Reich Chancellery." Five days later, Hitler nominated Koch once again, now to the position of Reichskommissar for the Ukraine, with headquarters in Rovno.[2]

1. R 43 II/132 a, Bundesarchiv, Koblenz.
2. R 43/II/690 b, Bundesarchiv, Koblenz.

To the degree that Koch was not subordinate to the administration of the Generalgouvernement, he regarded his policies for the Ukrainian area of the occupied East as the expression of views that were coordinated at the highest level. This is clear from a memorandum recorded by Minister Rosenberg after a meeting with Hitler on 14 December 1941: "Then I came to the topic of my relationship with the Reichskommissar for the Ukraine, Koch. I told the Führer that through various remarks Koch had given officers of the Wehrmacht High Command the impression that he alone had direct access to the Führer, and that, beyond this, he intended to govern without Berlin. His assertions were of the following order: that he determined policy and that he regarded his policies as the expression of a coordination at the highest level. . . . I requested that the Führer not receive Koch alone, but in my presence. The Führer immediately agreed to this."[3]

Koch's position is emphatically stated in a communication addressed to his superior, Minister Rosenberg, and dated 16 March 1943. For Koch, everything hinged on the significance of the assignments he had received from his Führer, Hitler: "As a Gauleiter of long standing, I am accustomed to taking my concerns and wishes directly to the Führer. Nor was this prerogative of mine ever queried by my Minister while I was president. It should be stressed that the Führer frequently handed me his policy directives, and that on certain occasions he also expressed his views on Ukrainian policies in the company of my subordinates. . . . In my talks with the Führer, I frequently set policy guidelines for the East. . . . I have always been concerned to carry out my duties as defined by the directives from the Führer."[4] In par-

3. Trial of Erich Koch, Archives of the Ministry of Justice, Warsaw, 1958.
4. Professor K. M. Pospieszalski, "Die Kompetenz des Angeklagten

ticular, Koch was closely briefed on Hitler's policies regarding the Final Solution, and he understood Hitler's logic of using the partisan war as a pretext for annihilating the Polish intelligentsia and leadership and, notably, the Jews. Koch also knew that on 16 July 1941, Hitler had told Rosenberg, Lammers, and Keitel: "The Russians have ordered the commencement of the partisan war behind our front. This partisan war has its virtues, too, since it will give us an opportunity to destroy those who resist us."[5] Koch, who in any case had long found the Slavic *Untermenschen* (subhumans) repugnant, took Hitler's words as a cue for unleashing a ruthless policy of exploitation and oppression in Volhynia and Podolia. "Koch knew," a former Wehrmacht officer who had been stationed in Lutsk later testified, "how to turn forty million Ukrainians against Germany in a single year, in spite of the fact that German soldiers were once greeted with flowers, bacon, and vodka."[6]

One notable instance of Koch's behavior is given in the complaint filed by Rosenberg on 2 April 1943, according to which Koch drove the villagers from all 175,000 acres of the Zuman district and then had the land converted into a private hunting estate.[7] A firsthand report made to Rosenberg affords an insight into the tyrannical methods and tactics the Reichskommissar of the Ukraine used:

> The entire Zuman district was cleared on orders from the highest level. Germans and Ukrainians alike alleged

Erich Koch als des Oberpräsidenten und Gauleiters der Provinz Ostpreussen und Chefs der Zivilverwaltung des Bezirks Bialystok in Bezug auf die Lage der polnischen und jüdischen Bevölkerung," ibid., pp. 26ff.

5. Nuremberg document 1221-PS, U.S. National Archives; Gerald Reitlinger, *Ein Haus auf Sand gebaut* (Hamburg, 1962), 273.

6. R. Grabow, "Zur Sache Gauleiter und Reichskommissar Koch, Königsberg-Rowno," trial of Erich Koch, Archives of the Ministry of Justice, Warsaw, 1958.

7. Trial of Erich Koch, IV. K. 109.

that the entire Zuman was to become a game preserve for the Reichskommissar. The removal of the villagers was begun in the bitter cold of December 1942. Hundreds of families had to pack up their entire belongings overnight and then were resettled thirty-six miles away. Hundreds of other families from Zuman and the vicinity, though, were shot down by a police battalion, "because of their communist leanings."

No Ukrainian, however, is willing to believe this last argument, and even the Germans are skeptical of the reasoning: for if it were true, if the shootings had in fact been for the sake of national security, then at the same time it would have been necessary to execute communist-contaminated elements in other departments as well. The consensus, however, is that these people were killed off indiscriminately and without due process for the simple reason that, given the short time available and the great numbers involved, the resettlement would have been unworkable otherwise; and what is more, the new relocation site lacked the space that would have been needed to accommodate the original population.[8]

On 19 May, Rosenberg and Koch confronted each other in the presence of Hitler and Reich Minister Lammers. Bormann's minutes of the meeting[9] give us an idea of Hitler's views on the dispute between Rosenberg and Koch, and "on acute questions of eastern policy": If partisans operate in the Ukraine, Rosenberg felt, this could be ascribed to "Koch's incompetent political leadership." The Minister for the Occupied East further indicated that "the authority of the Reich could not tolerate Koch's conduct." Hitler, however, emphasized: "In view of a necessarily harsh administration, one cannot gain the political consent of the Ukrainians. All historical experiences attest that conquered subjects cannot be treated as confederates; the super-smart

8. Ibid., IV. K. 110.
9. RSHA, R. 58/1005, 10 June 1943, Bundesarchiv, Koblenz.

people should reflect on the Romans, who had attempted to do so with the Gauls. . . . Only weakling generals can possibly believe that we will win the Ukrainians over to our side by arming them. They fail to see the inevitable second step of such a concession."[10]

Hitler's Russian policy was diametrically opposed to the policy Erich Koch despised and successfully sabotaged, the "soft approach" developed by the Balt Alfred Rosenberg and his closest collaborators in the Ministry for the Occupied Eastern Territories. Hitler's more vigorous approach entailed nothing less than carving up the "gigantic Russian pie," syphoning off labor forces and relocating them in Germany, levying tributes of vital food supplies, decimating the eastern populations, and then filling the vacuum with German farmers.

Himmler was to hear on 5 October 1943 from the journalist Melitta Wiedemann that Hitler's *Untermensch* slogans about the eastern peoples had "helped Stalin wage a national war."[11] Wiedemann had already reproached the Reichsführer SS on 26 May: "The *Untermensch* theory with regard to the eastern populations, especially the Russians, has been refuted by experience. They are good fighters; they sacrifice everything for their fatherland; they often build weapons that are at least as good as our own."[12] However,

10. Ibid., pp. 6–7.
11. Personal Staff of the RFSS, excerpt from a letter of 5 October 1943 by Melitta Wiedemann, Archiv Wulf.
12. Letter of Melitta Wiedemann to Himmler, 26 May 1943, U.S. National Archives, RFSS, film roll 38. At the beginning of 1944, Himmler's Intelligence Chief Schellenberg held a lengthy discussion with Walther Hewel, von Ribbentrop's liaison officer in the Führer's Headquarters. Schellenberg pointed out that the German handling of the occupied territories was virtually crippling German foreign policy. Schellenberg asked Hewel to solicit from Hitler a modification of the occupation policies. Hewel answered that Hitler was not an ordinary man, but a genius who saw things in an entirely different light. Hitler was of the opinion that the occupied territories were only to be considered as a possible source of raw materials and war materials. To Schellenberg's objection that Hitler's opinion on this could change, Hewel

the Reichskommissar of the Ukraine, Erich Koch, who enjoyed Hitler's complete confidence to the very last, had no intention whatever of deviating from Hitler's theory on the inferiority of Slavs and Jews.

In the polemical pamphlet *Der Untermensch*, which was produced by Gottlob Berger's SS Main Administrative Office, we read: "The *Untermensch*, that product of nature which, on the surface, is a member of the same species, with hands, feet, and a sort of brain, with eyes and mouth, is nonetheless a creature of a totally other and horrifying kind, a mere approximation of a human, with human facial features—but mentally and spiritually, he is lower than a beast. Within this creature reigns a vicious chaos of wild, uninhibited passions: unspeakable destructiveness, the most primitive desires, unconcealed baseness."[13] One will recognize at once the close relationship between formulations of this caliber and pictures used for twelve years as anti-Semitic propaganda in Streicher's *Der Stürmer*. Of these propaganda pictures Hitler, on 28 December, 1941, said in the Führer's Headquarters: "Streicher's picture of the Jew in *Der Stürmer* is too idealized. The Jew is much more common, much more bloodthirsty and satanic than Streicher painted him."[14]

---

replied that in this regard he was in full agreement with the Führer and that, moreover, Hitler saw himself as a historical figure of such dimensions that his political statements were fully binding and never to be questioned (Schellenberg Interrogations, Report on the Case of Walter Schellenberg, Annex XXIII, RG 238, pp. 5–6, U.S. National Archives).

13. Quoted in Heinz Höhne, *Der Orden unter dem Totenkopf* (Munich, 1976), 465.

14. *Adolf Hitler, Monologe im Führerhauptquartier: 1941–1944*, ed. Werner Jochmann (Hamburg, 1980), 158.

On 16 July 1942 Hitler landed in Vinnitsa with his retinue to occupy the new advanced *Wehrwolf* Führer's Headquarters, where he would remain until 27 September, despite the swarming flies and mosquitoes. On the day of Hitler's arrival, Himmler drove up from his field headquarters in Zhitomir to discuss briefly, among other things, the Führer's plans for the Caucasus. "The Führer's view is that we should not visibly incorporate this territory into the German sphere of power, but only militarily secure oil sources and borders."[1] Whether Himmler and Hitler also went over the two-day tour of inspection that the RFSS was about to make at Auschwitz cannot be established with any degree of certainty. Conferences between Himmler and Hitler were, with few exceptions, always held in private.

On the following day, the Reichsführer Himmler went to Auschwitz for the second time. Also present were Gauleiter Fritz Bracht; SS-Obergruppenführer Ernst-Heinrich Schmauser, the Higher SS and Police Leader for Upper Silesia; and SS-Gruppenführer Dr. Hans Kammler, head of Bureau C of the SS Construction Office. On the first day of his visit, Himmler and company toured the entire

---

1.   Letter from Himmler to Walter Schellenberg, 17 July 1942 (Helmut Heiber, ed., *Reichsführer . . . Briefe an und von Himmler* [Stuttgart, 1968], 161).

campsite of Auschwitz-Birkenau. After that inspection, Himmler observed the entire liquidation procedure, as demonstrated on a newly arrived Jewish convoy. It was the convoy that had left the Dutch camp Westerbork on 15 July, coupling with a second Dutch convoy in transit through Germany on 16 July. The combined number of deported Dutch Jews aboard this train came to 2,030, from which 449 men, women, and children were selected at the loading platform in Auschwitz for immediate gassing.[2] Himmler was present to witness the unloading of this convoy, the selection of able-bodied Jews, and the gassing of the remainder with Zyklon B in bunker number two, as well as the cleanup of the bunker afterward. At this stage, the corpses of gassed victims were not yet being incinerated but interred in pits.

On the evening of 17 July, Himmler attended a reception for the guests and the heads of the SS garrison. Afterward, accompanied by Camp Commandant Höss and his wife, and by the director of the agricultural department of Auschwitz, Dr. Caesar, Himmler went to a reception hosted by the Gauleiter of Upper Silesia, Fritz Bracht, at his home in Katowice. On the following day, Himmler toured the original camp, the kitchen, and finally, the women's quarters, where he asked to observe punitive beatings "to determine their effects." Permission for beating women was granted only upon personal decision by the Reichsführer SS. At the end of the inspection, Himmler went into Höss's office for the final discussion and there ordered the commandant to hasten the expansion of Birkenau and of the armament industry at the camp, and to continue with the extermination of physically unfit Jews. Himmler then pro-

---

2. Dr. L. de Jong to author, 30 December 1977; Rudolf Höss trial, statement by Höss, p. 6; Notebooks from Auschwitz, Muzeum w Oświęcimiu, 1960, pp. 71–72.

moted Höss to Obersturmbannführer, in recognition of his commendable performance.

On 19 July the RFSS ordered that the resettlement of the entire Jewish population in the Generalgouvernement be carried out and concluded by 31 December 1942, declaring this "total cleansing" a necessary measure requiring earliest implementation.[3] In another secret letter, dated 2 October, Himmler gave more explicit instructions: Jews who had been detailed to munitions factories in the Generalgouvernement were to be "concentrated to capacity in a few Jewish camp-run industrial centers in the eastern parts of the Generalgouvernement." This communication closes with the classic formulation of the elegant Führer-order: "However, one day the Jews there, in conformity with the Führer's wish, are also to disappear."[4]

The formula, "it is the Führer's wish," was only one way liquidation orders "from the highest level" or "on highest orders" were concealed.[5] Late in July 1942, a coded radio signal from Vinnitsa was taken down and deciphered in the Lutsk radio station in the Ukraine. Signed "Adolf Hitler, Führer's Headquarters," the message was an order for the Reichskommissar Erich Koch, Rovno, Ukraine, instructing him to liquidate, within a specified period of time, all the Jews that were still alive within the general region of Rovno.[6] On the basis of this order, no less than seventy

3. RFSS to HSSPF Ost (Cracow) Friedrich-Wilhelm Krüger, 19 July 1942, Bundesarchiv R 122, p. 7914.
4. RFSS to SS-Obergruppenführer Oswald Pohl, head of the Economy Administration Main Office; SS-Obergruppenführer Krüger, HSSPF Ost; SS-Brigadeführer Odilo Globocnik, SSPF Lublin, RSHA; and SS-Obergruppenführer Karl Wolff, head of the Main Office Personal Staff (Bundesarchiv R 122, pp. 7359–60). On "the Führer's wish," see pp. 44 n. 7, 46 n. 12, and 76 n. 26.
5. Cf. p. 107.
6. Statutory declaration by Werner Isensee to author, 17 February 1978. Cf. Will Klein to author, 10 April 1979: "I was with Herr Werner Isensee at the radio station Lutsk"; and 4 May 1979: "While I was in Lutsk, there

thousand Jews were shot in the Rovno region between August and November of 1942. It is extremely likely that this figure was included in report number 51 to the Führer, signed by Himmler, which for the months of August to November 1942 shows, under the rubric "Jews executed," a total of 363,211 persons liquidated. Report number 51 was prepared in quadruplicate on the Führer-typewriter (a special typewriter with very large type) in Himmler's field-command headquarters on 29 December; it was submitted to Hitler on 31 December, as the handwritten notation by Hitler's adjutant Pfeiffer indicates.[7]

That Reichskommissar Koch received liquidation orders directly from Hitler is corroborated by the following account:[8]

> In 1941 to 1942 I was a country doctor in Lutynsk, Volhynia. There I treated a family of Russian emigrants, Kovalenko by name. The son, Dr. A. Kovalenko, who resided in Berlin for some time, a member of the NSDAP and the SA [brown-shirted storm troopers], was immediately assigned to Rovno (headquarters of Reichskommissar Koch), where he became assistant head of the medical administration. Dr. Kovalenko made frequent visits to his

was an NCO in charge of the radio station." Cf. also p. 120 relating to the direct chain of command Hitler—Erich Koch. Also Dr. Walter Labs to author, 20 July 1980: "I cannot recall whether there existed an official channel of communications for direct instructions and reports between Hitler and Koch in the Ukraine in 1942, but I consider this a distinct possibility. I cannot say anything about the technical avenues of such direct instructions, though probably information was passed through the Wehrmacht, since few other communication channels were available." Richard Schulze-Kossens to author, 10 October 1979: "On 7 September 1942, Hitler received the Reichskommissar Koch in the new Führer's Headquarters 'Wehrwolf,' in Vinnitsa."

    7. "Reports to the Führer, re: campaign against gangs," report number 51, from southern Russia, Ukraine, Bialystok, 29 December 1942 (NS 19/291, Bundesarchiv, Koblenz) (see plates).

    8. Statement by Prof. Dr. Joseph Parnas to author, 20 July 1978.

parents in Lutynsk and also to me, to thank me for the medical care I was giving his parents. Dr. Kovalenko said to me, "Erich Koch told us that he is directly subordinate to Hitler." The Führer had ordered the total and speedy liquidation of the Jews, on the grounds that they were spreading Bolshevism and organizing partisans. Kovalenko said: "Koch instructed us, his entire staff, to participate, armed, in the liquidation of the Jews in Rovno."[9] I was also there to witness this massacre, but I was unarmed. When Dr. A. Kovalenko's father died, the doctor, assistant head of Koch's medical administration, came to Lutynsk for the burial, . . . together with a number of other functionaries from Koch's Reich Commissariat. At the dinner following the funeral (called the *siypa*), they told me: "We have shot all the Jews. It was Hitler's order, carried out by Koch."

I was in the partisan movement from 1942 to 1943. In January 1943, Colonel Anton Brynski secretly contacted me and said, "You have a pocket of resistance in Rovno. You must organize the poisoning of Koch. A young Polish woman works in his kitchen." I went to Rovno, where I was Dr. Kovalenko's guest. I contacted the Catholic priest there, with an eye to the planned poisoning of Koch. The prospects of killing Koch looked good, until the Polish girl in his kitchen was dismissed and sent to work in Germany. The remaining Ukrainian women were utterly devoted to Koch.

In 1969 to 1970 I was a prisoner in Bartchevo prison, where Erich Koch was also imprisoned.[10] Since I was con-

---

9. The first action took place on 6–7 November 1941. Fifteen thousand Jews were shot. The next large-scale action took place on 13 July 1942; over six thousand persons were killed.

10. After the fall of East Prussia, Erich Koch managed to escape aboard the icebreaker "Ostpreussen" and to avoid arrest for four years with the help of forged papers. He had let himself be discharged as a major under the name of Rolf Berger and was living at the time of his arrest (the end of May 1949) in Haasenmoor, near Hamburg, while working as a farm laborer. On 14 January 1950, Koch was transferred to the Mokotow prison in Warsaw.

Koch was condemned to death at the beginning of March 1959 in Warsaw, after an extremely fair trial lasting five months. He denied to the end all personal culpability. The court found him guilty for his responsibility in

sidered politically dangerous, I was locked up in the isolation cell number 14, next to Koch's cell. I saw him both in his cell and in the prison courtyard. He was seventy-four years old and ran like a man of fifty. His physician was Dr. Olszynska, but other physicians in the prison were my former students at the medical academy in Lublin. Koch said, "I received the orders to liquidate directly from Hitler. I was not guilty. Orders are orders. I had to obey."

Hitler and the RFSS could depend on Reichskommissar and Gauleiter Koch. In the summer of 1942, large-scale roundup actions were carried out in a number of Ukrainian cities. Then the liquidations that had been ordered took place, often in somewhat remote, specially constructed execution sites. After these mass killings four hundred Jews only, all of whom worked in a German workshop in Lutsk, were left in that town.

Shortly before Christmas 1942,[11] the German workshop in Lutsk, Ukraine, was shut down. The workshop itself was a large, multi-story factory building, fenced around several times with barbed wire and heavily guarded by military police sentries. Inside, about four hundred Jewish artisans, many of them women, performed various services for the Germans employed at the Generalkommissariat in Lutsk, as well as for certain circles of the Wehrmacht, from sergeant upwards—services such as shoemaking, cabinetmaking, watchmaking, tailoring, or fur-trimming. They were, in other words, the typical eastern Jewish artisans who were known and sought after for their great skill. All the other, "nonproductive," Jews had previously been liquidated, apart from a small number who lived difficult lives in the woods as

---

the deaths of four hundred thousand Poles and Polish Jews. Koch, now eighty-nine years old, is interned in Bartchevo as a war criminal.

11.   The exact date was 12 December 1942 (Dr. Henrik Stein to author, 31 March 1981).

partisans. In and around Lutsk alone, forty thousand Jews were said to have been shot. The Jewish workers were selected beforehand and then quartered in barracks. The German management that ran these shops, set up in all the larger cities, charged the German clientele the requisite sums, and part of the proceeds went into the maintenance of the Jews, which consisted of a very slim diet and a bit of *machorka* (Russian tobacco). The Germans were strictly forbidden to tip a Jewish worker if he had done a particularly good job. This policy was variously broken, depending upon the client. These workshops were kept very busy. It was well known in the East that the Jewish artisan was a very diligent and precise worker. The factory in Lutsk operated for about a year.

Shortly before Christmas 1942, the Germans in Lutsk received word that the workshops would be shut down and that the Reichskommissar had ordered the liquidation of the four hundred Jews. Since just before Christmas a large number of orders had been placed in the workshops, and every German who was planning to go home on leave wanted to take his things with him, a great clamor arose—not among the Jews, who were still ignorant of what lay in store for them—but among the Germans. They protested and appealed to Generalkommissar [Area Chief Administrator] S. in the hope that he could arrange for a postponement of the liquidation until after Christmas. The Generalkommissar was himself a customer at the workshop, and the officials and employees of the Generalkommissariat were favored clients. (Under Herr Koch's administration, social classes were sharply demarcated. His clubhouse for officials in Rovno, for instance, sported a large sign that read, "Entrance for officers and personnel of the Wehrmacht strictly forbidden." Guests were allowed inside by invitation only, even when the Russians were already in Kiev.)[12] Herr Koch, in

12. On 22 September 1942, the day that Generalkommissar Kube was killed in Minsk by a bomb that had been planted under his bed, an attempt was made on Reichskommissar Koch in Rovno on the street, from a Wehrmacht Mercedes (Reinhold Grabow to author, 25 October 1978).

Rovno, refused. He had everything he needed and was not interested in the workshops in Rovno and Lutsk. Just the same, many Germans did not take the threat of a liquidation seriously. The Jews, in the meantime, had also heard about it. They no longer finished anything; they dragged out their repairs and orders. To avoid unrest among the Jews, the Germans were forbidden to ask for their goods back all at once. Everything, it was believed, could be retrieved after the extermination. But the Germans were mistaken!

When, on 12 December, a detachment of Ukrainian auxiliary police marched in under the command of Police Major G. to take away the Jews, they opened fire. The Jews had a few weapons smuggled in through secret channels, so that they could at least make a respectable last stand. It finally came to a fight that was decided by hand grenades and anti-tank guns. The German workshop went up in flames with all its goods and materials. It was completely destroyed; and with it, the four hundred Jews.

During the course of the "battle," the General of the Wehrmacht assigned to Lutsk (Stölk) appeared on the scene, drawn by the sound of gunfire. He yelled out to the SS and Police Leader for Lutsk, who in the meantime had arrived on the "battlefield," to find out who had ordered the shooting. If there was to be any shooting in Lutsk, he and the Wehrmacht had to know about it. Civilians were not allowed to conduct private wars—a brave piece of bellowing that met with the delight of all the Germans who had gathered. The SS Leader responded: "This doesn't concern you in the least. Orders from Herr Reichskommissar Koch. We are under civilian administration here, so the Wehrmacht has absolutely no say in the matter."[13]

13. The Führer and Supreme Commander of the Wehrmacht, Führer's Headquarters, 11 October 1941: "On 20 October 1941, at 12:00 noon, the following sector will be eliminated from the field of operations of the Army, viz. the rear region of the army in the south, viz. center: the course of the Row from Bar to where it meets the Bug—the stretch of the Bug to Perwomaisk—Nowo Ukrainka . . . II. The civil administration of this region will be taken over by the Reichskommissar for the Ukraine under the Reich Minister for the Occupied Eastern Territories" (Bundesarchiv R 43 II/690 b).

Later, the Wehrmacht commander took revenge by refusing to give Herr Koch's police the support of his troops when partisans set fire to Koch's hunting lodge in the Zuman forest.[14]

14.　Trial of Erich Koch, IV K. 311/58t. VII, pp. 135–37, statement by Reinhold Grabow, 25 August 1949.

16

"The Führer Has Taken Note: Destroy"

Himmler's apparatus was more than qualified to keep running statistical records on the victims of the Final Solution, and it would have been a remarkable oversight if the conscientious Reichsführer had failed to instruct his key administrative aides to do so. Such an accounting operation was in fact practiced, as the statements by Adolf Eichmann[1] and the statistical report prepared by the RFSS's "Inspector for Statistics," Dr. Korherr, confirm.[2] In December 1942, a statistician commissioned by Himmler to prepare an exact statistical report on the current status of the Final Solution appeared at Eichmann's office, Kurfürstenstrasse 112, Berlin. All the relevant records and data available in IV B 4 (Jewish Affairs) were to be put at his disposal. At the same time Gestapo Chief Heinrich Müller informed Eichmann that Himmler had requested a statistical report, to be typed on the "Führer-typewriter."[3]

On 18 January 1943, Himmler instructed his Inspector for Statistics in writing to draw up a report on the Final

1. Eichmann Interrogation, transcripts of tape, tape 37, pp. 7–16, Yad Vashem, Jerusalem.
2. "The Final Solution of the European Jewish Question," statistical report, geheime Reichssache, NS 19 (neu)/1570, Bundesarchiv, Koblenz.
3. Per Eichmann Interrogation, tape 37, p. 10; and Pierre Joffroy, *Eichmann par Eichmann* (Paris, 1970), 209.

Solution of the European Jewish question. "The Reich Main Security Office is to put at your disposal whatever materials you request or need for this purpose."[4] A second top secret document of the same date informed the head of the Reich Main Security Office, Dr. Kaltenbrunner, of Korherr's commission and made the additional comment: "The Reich Main Security Office is hereby relieved of its statistical responsibilities in this area, since the statistical materials submitted to date have consistently fallen short of professional standards of precision."[5]

According to Eichmann, Korherr worked at Eichmann's office for "eight or fourteen days," reviewing records of Jewish emigration and deportations. The figures on Jews who had been liquidated through "special treatment" could be accessed either through the Economy Administration Main Office[6] or through the RSHA. Twelve years later, Dr. Korherr wrote to Gerald Reitlinger, author of the book *The Final Solution*: "I not only received the raw data complete and intact—cf. my references on p. 9 [of the unabridged, sixteen-page-long report], 'according to the compilations of the RSHA,' and on p. 10, 'according to the information given by the RSHA'—but I also received the companion texts to the tables."[7]

On 23 March 1943, Korherr sent his sixteen-page report to the personal adviser of the RFSS, Dr. Rudolf Brandt. The date of completion indicated on the report is 31 December 1942.[8] On 9 April, Himmler informed Kaltenbrunner

4. Himmler to the Inspector for Statistics, geheime Reichssache, 18 January 1943, NS 19 (neu)/1577, fol. 3, Bundesarchiv, Koblenz.

5. Himmler to the head of the RSHA, geheime Reichssache, 18 January 1943, NS 19 (neu)/1577, fol. 2, Bundesarchiv, Koblenz.

6. Eichmann Interrogation, tape 37, p 13.

7. Dr. R. Korherr to G. Reitlinger, 28 September 1955, Wiener Library, Box 526.

8. Per Georges Wellers, supplement to the weekly newspaper *Das Parlament*, 29 July 1978, p. 26.

that he considered the report as "potentially useful for future purposes, in particular for camouflage purposes. At the present time, it may neither be published nor passed on."[9] The main concern, now as before, was "that as many Jews are transported to the East as is humanly possible. In the brief monthly reports of the Security Police, I only want figures on how many Jews per month have been shipped off and how many are currently left."[10] The following day, Himmler's personal adviser, Dr. Rudolf Brandt, sent word to Korherr that the RFSS had received his report. "He has requested that 'special treatment of the Jews' be mentioned nowhere in the document. Page 9, point 4, should read as follows: 'Transport of Jews from the eastern provinces to the Russian East: passed through camps in the Generalgouvernement, . . . through the camps in the Warthegau. . . .' No other wording may be used. I am returning the copy of the report, with the Reichsführer SS's initials, and with the request that page 9 be altered accordingly and then resubmitted."[11] On page 10 of Korherr's original version we do in fact read: "Total evacuation incl. Theresienstadt and incl. special treatment . . . 1,873,539." Brandt's letter of 10 April bears the handwritten marginal note, on the bottom left-hand side of the page: "Original personally handed to Dr. Korherr on 9. Apr. M. [Meine] 12 Apr."

Conspicuous in both Himmler's letter of 9 April 1943 and in Brandt's letter of 10 April 1943 are the corrections in the dating, from March to April, in both cases done by hand. August Meine explains: "The letter of 9 April 1943 to the Chief of Sipo and of the SD was dictated by Himmler to his secretary. She transcribed the recorded text in March 1943,

9. Reichsführer SS to Chief of Sipo and the SD, geheime Reichssache, 9 April 1943, NS 19 (neu)/1570, Bundesarchiv, Koblenz.

10. Cf. p. 66 n. 2.

11. R. Brandt to the Inspector for Statistics, geheime Reichssache, 10 April 1943, NS 19 (neu)/1570, Bundesarchiv, Koblenz.

because she had anticipated a date in March. However, Himmler must have merely given a few key phrases for his letter of 10 April 1943 to the Inspector for Statistics. This explains why the initials 'RF' fail to accompany the typist's initials. This second letter was evidently also written in March of 1943. . . . My note and the dates indicate that at the time I was in the Berlin office, and that it was there that I gave Dr. Korherr the letter and handed back to him his report."[12]

On 1 April 1943, Korherr was commissioned by Himmler, via Kaltenbrunner, to prepare an abridged version of his statistical report, "for submission to the Führer."[13] The statistical results up to 31 March 1943 were processed for Hitler's condensed version. The report, now 6½ pages long, was sent by the RSHA to Hitler a few days before 19 April; and on 19 April Korherr sent a copy of the abridged version, together with a covering letter, as a top secret paper to Dr. Rudolf Brandt in Himmler's office in Berlin. It is extremely unlikely that Korherr had a so-called Führer-typewriter in his office on Potsdamer Strasse 61, Berlin. It is equally improbable that the original report was prepared for Hitler in Himmler's field headquarters.[14]

In all likelihood, the report was typed on the "Führer-typewriter" in the RSHA. This same report to Hitler on the "Final Solution of the European Jewish Question" was eventually returned to Eichmann, bearing, as Eichmann testified, the remark: "The Führer has taken note: destroy.—H. H."[15]

This piece of correspondence gives a further indica-

---

12. August Meine to author, 26 February 1980.
13. The Inspector for Statistics to Dr. R. Brandt, geheime Reichssache, 19 April 1943, NS 19 (neu)/1570, Bundesarchiv, Koblenz.
14. "On this account, I consider it not only possible, but probable, that the report you refer to was not written in the field headquarters" (Werner Grothmann to author, 18 September 1980).
15. Eichmann Interrogation, tape 37, p. 9.

tion of the cynical and grotesquely naive game, replete with all the semantic conventions, that was played between the Führer and the RFSS in matters regarding the Final Solution—not unlike a long-term pact playfully agreed on by schoolboys, which then is adhered to with deadly earnestness and thievish glee. Of course, it went without saying that the leading figure in Germany, Head of State Adolf Hitler, could not under any circumstances afford to be saddled with the phenomenal crime that would most assuredly have been brought to light by a report containing the words "special treatment." The limits of the semantically permissible, as set by Himmler in the Korherr report, are clear from the reference to the "collapse of the Jewish masses . . . since the evacuation measures of 1942."[16]

16. "Die Endlösung der europäischen Judenfrage," statistical report, geheime Reichssache, NS 19 (neu)/1570, Bundesarchiv, Koblenz; cf. pp. 22 n. 12 and 48 n. 20.

17

An Official Report
from Auschwitz-Birkenau

As a result of the "partial identity of objectives"[1] that existed between the army and Hitler, a number of army officers joined the Waffen SS. These officers served during the Second World War as commanders of larger contingents or held other key positions within the SS main offices. One such officer was Colonel Maximilian von Herff. Von Herff had served as commander of the Giessen Panzergrenadier regiment (mechanized infantry formation) under Rommel in Africa and won the Knight's Cross of the Iron Cross for his capture of the Halfaya Pass.[2] At the promptings of the head of the Reichsführer SS's personal staff, SS-Obergruppenführer and General of the Waffen SS Karl Wolff, von Herff, following a brief orientation, was transferred from the Wehrmacht to the SS and made head of the SS Personnel Main Office on 1 October 1942.

On 22 April 1943, von Herff wrote to the Higher SS and Police Leader East, Friedrich-Wilhelm Krüger, inform-

---

1. M. Messerschmidt, *Wehrmacht im NS-Staat* (Hamburg, 1969), cited in Jürgen Förster, "Zur Rolle der Wehrmacht im Krieg gegen die Sowjetunion," supplement to the weekly newspaper *Das Parlament* 45 (1980): 15.
2. Per indictment against Karl Wolff, 10a Js 39/60, p. 210; Maximilian von Herff to head of traffic police main office, Kurt Daluege, 8 October 1942; Personnel File of Maximilian von Herff and SS-Gruppenführer Pohl to Reich Minister of the Treasury Franz Xaver Schwarz, 4 March 1942, Berlin Document Center.

ing Krüger that he was planning an official trip to the Generalgouvernement for early May, and that he also wished to pay Krüger a visit in Cracow. "On the evening of 3 May, I intend to take the train from Berlin to Mislowitz, accompanied by SS-Sturmbannführer Franke-Gricksch; from Mislowitz I will inspect the Auschwitz camp, then arrive in Cracow on 4 May, in the evening."[3] Von Herff also wanted to visit Warsaw, which in fact he did, thereby witnessing the extermination of the Warsaw ghetto, as was later confirmed by Obergruppenführer Jürgen Stroop in an official report dated 14 May.[4] Whether von Herff actually arrived at Auschwitz on 4 May cannot, despite statements to this effect, be established with absolute certainty. He may well have found it expedient to have only his capable assistant, Sturmbannführer Franke-Gricksch, visit Auschwitz.[5]

Von Herff died in 1945, in British captivity; Franke-Gricksch, however, was released from British captivity in August 1948. In October 1951, he went to visit his mother in Potsdam, where he and his wife were arrested and subsequently charged. For his activities with the SS Police division in Russia between August and the winter of 1942, Franke-Gricksch was condemned to death by the Russians in October 1951, in Karlshorst, while his wife was sentenced to twenty-five years in a labor camp. Two years later, Alfred Franke-Gricksch was reported to have died in a Russian camp. In October 1955, his wife left Vorkuta and returned to West Germany.[6]

It is certain that sometime between 4 and 16 May

3. SS Personnel File of Franke-Gricksch and SS Personnel File of von Herff, Berlin Document Center.
4. Gerald Reitlinger, *The Final Solution*, 3d ed. (London, 1971), 318; Personnel File of Maximilian von Herff, Berlin Document Center.
5. Maximilian von Herff considered Franke-Gricksch to be the second best officer in the SS Personnel Main Office (Charles W. Sydnor, *Soldiers of Destruction* [Princeton, 1977], 337).
6. Liselotte Franke-Gricksch to author, 5 and 18 September 1978.

1943, Franke-Gricksch wrote a report entitled "Resettlement of Jews" on the liquidation machinery he had seen at Auschwitz. This report, written for his chief von Herff and the Reichsführer SS, falls directly within the framework of his career with the SS[7] and his services on behalf of the Third Reich. The report of SS-Sturmbannführer Franke-Gricksch reads as follows:

Resettlement of Jews

The Auschwitz camp plays a special role in the resolution of the Jewish question. The most advanced methods permit the execution of the Führer-order in the shortest possible time and without arousing much attention. The so-called "resettlement action" runs the following course: The Jews arrive in special trains (freight cars) toward evening and are driven on special tracks to areas of the camp specifically set aside for this purpose. There the Jews are unloaded and examined for their fitness to work by a team of doctors, in the presence of the camp commandant and several SS officers. At this point anyone who can somehow be incorporated into the work program is put in a special camp. The curably ill are sent straight to a medical camp and are restored to health through a special diet. The basic principle behind everything is: conserve all manpower for work. The previous type of "resettlement action" has been thoroughly rejected, since it is too costly to destroy precious work energy on a continual basis.

7.   SS Personnel File of Franke-Gricksch, Service Record, Berlin Document Center; R. Ströbinger informed the author on 18 November 1980 about Franke-Gricksch's career: 1934 reconnoitering of the radio station "Schwarze Front"/Otto Strasser near Prague; report on this to Heydrich, which led in January 1935 to the murder of Rudolf Formis, who serviced the illegal station in Dobris near Prague from a room in the Hotel Zahori; 1935–1939 SS Hauptsturmführer in the Death's Head formations in Dachau; October 1939 until March 1941, as Intelligence Officer in Death's Head Division (SS); March 1941–July 1942 in SD Main Office and Section SD-England; August 1942 to end of the year, active service in the SS Police Division; from January 1943 until the end of the war in SS Personnel Main Office.

The unfit go to cellars in a large house which are entered from outside. They go down five or six steps into a fairly long, well-constructed and well-ventilated cellar area, which is lined with benches to the left and right. It is brightly lit, and the benches are numbered. The prisoners are told that they are to be cleansed and disinfected for their new assignments. They must therefore completely undress to be bathed. To avoid panic and to prevent disturbances of any kind, they are instructed to arrange their clothing neatly under their respective numbers, so that they will be able to find their things again after their bath. Everything proceeds in a perfectly orderly fashion. Then they pass through a small corridor and enter a large cellar room which resembles a shower bath. In this room are three large pillars, into which certain materials can be lowered from outside the cellar room. When three- to four-hundred people have been herded into this room, the doors are shut, and containers filled with the substances are dropped down into the pillars. As soon as the containers touch the base of the pillars, they release particular substances that put the people to sleep in one minute. A few minutes later, the door opens on the other side, where the elevator is located. The hair of the corpses is cut off, and their teeth are extracted (gold-filled teeth) by specialists (Jews). It had been discovered that Jews were hiding pieces of jewelry, gold, platinum, etc., in hollow teeth. Then the corpses are loaded into elevators and brought up to the first floor, where ten large crematoria are located. (Because fresh corpses burn particularly well, only 50–100 lbs. of coke are needed for the whole process.) The job itself is performed by Jewish prisoners, who never step outside this camp again.

The results of this "resettlement action" to date: 500,000 Jews. Current capacity of the "resettlement action" ovens: 10,000 in twenty-four hours.[8]

8. Typewritten copy, deposited by Charles W. Sydnor in the U.S. National Archives; one of three carbon copies from Alfred Franke-Gricksch's report, written on a service mission through the Generalgouvernement between 14 and 16 May 1943, is in author's possession.
From the summer of 1943, there were forty-six combustion chambers in

The following needs to be said concerning this description of the liquidation process in Auschwitz-Birkenau: Franke-Gricksch's account of "the execution of the Führer-order," namely, the lowering of "certain materials" into a large cellar room resembling a "shower bath" and activation and release of the "particular substances that put the people to sleep in one minute," is a fraudulent and cynical whitewashing of death by gassing. Filip Müller, a surviving witness who had been assigned to the Auschwitz-Birkenau special prisoner commando in the crematorium recalls a liquidation action as he experienced it:

> In the meantime, the SS NCOs on duty had taken their stations on the flat roof of the crematorium, from which the SS officers had addressed the crowd. Wearing protective gas masks, they removed the lids from six camouflaged openings and shook the blue-green crystals of Zyklon B into the gas chamber.
>
> Next, the motors of the trucks that were parked close by were started up. Their noise was supposed to keep the rest of the camp from hearing the screaming of the dying and their pounding against the doors of the gas chamber. We, however, had to experience everything immediately and directly. It sounded as if the Day of Judgment had come, with all the harrowing cries and calls for help, fervent prayers, the frantic banging and pounding on the door, and the whole of it drowned out by the din of the truck engines thrown into high gear. Aumeier, Grabner, and Hössler looked at their wristwatches to keep track of the time it took for everything to quiet down inside the gas chamber, in the meantime amusing themselves with macabre jokes. I heard one say, "The water in the shower rooms must be very hot today, since they shout so loudly."[9]

operation in the crematoria of the liquidation complex at Auschwitz (Wolfgang Scheffler to author, 22 June 1982).

9.   Filip Müller, *Sonderbehandlung* (Munich, 1979), 62–63.

The accounts of the SS officer and the former concentration camp prisoner concur on one fact: that the cremation capacity of the camp ovens reached up to ten thousand corpses per twenty-four hours.[10]

After his release from British captivity in August 1948 and "a few months after his return home," the former SS-Sturmbannführer Alfred Franke-Gricksch dictated to his wife an account entitled "From the Diary of a Fallen SS Leader."[11] This record was submitted as evidence at the Treblinka trial on 16 January 1965 by Franke-Gricksch's widow,[12] that is, by the widow of the man who was reported by the German Red Cross to have died in August of 1953 in a Russian camp.[13] The text of this document is reproduced here in its entirety, in order that we may scrutinize it for its truth content, especially in the light of two facts: first, the fact that on 22 April 1943, the Head of the SS Personnel Main Office, Maximilian von Herff, wrote to the Higher SS and Police Leader in Cracow, Friedrich-Wilhelm Krüger, announcing his intention to travel to the Generalgouvernement with Franke-Gricksch and his desire to inspect the Auschwitz camp;[14] and second, the fact that in the course of this trip Franke-Gricksch inspected the Auschwitz-Birkenau extermination installation and made a report of his findings for his commanding officer in the document entitled "Resettlement of Jews."

10. Ibid., 97.
11. Institut für Zeitgeschichte, ZS-1931; notarized copy in author's possession.
12. Dr. Anton Hoch provided the author with the account "From the Diary of a Fallen SS Leader," 12 June 1978.
13. Liselotte Franke-Gricksch gave the author what information she had about her husband's captivity, 5 September 1978.
14. Personalakte [personnel file] von Herff; SS-Gruppenführer und Generalleutnant der Waffen SS von Herff an Staatssekretär, SS-Obergruppenführer und General d. Pol. Krüger, 22 April 1943, Berlin Document Center.

Franke-Gricksch's record, which he deemed necessary to dictate to his wife shortly after his release from the prisoner-of-war camp in Colchester in late autumn 1948, follows.

From the Diary of a Fallen SS Leader

Reports about certain incidents in several camps in the East were increasing: suicide by a few SS leaders, continually renewed applications by a few SS leaders in these camps for frontline duty. The urgency of these letters indicates that there must be underlying reasons of a most serious nature. These matters have already been brought to the attention of the Reichsführer through numerous sources. Today, he called the Chief of the Main Office [von Herff] and myself [Franke-Gricksch] into his headquarters. "Today I [Franke-Gricksch] attended a meeting that disturbed me greatly." Not only the objective grounds and facts that were brought up by the Reichsführer in the course of the conversation, but also the striking gravity that the Reichsführer's remarks evoked and the insight that I gained into the so often humanly difficult situation of this man gave me much to reflect on. Since this discussion ranged over broad and weighty questions that are of decisive import not only for the future of our nation, but in certain respects for the whole of the white race, and since besides the Chief of the Main Office, I was the only other officer present, I recorded this discussion as soon as I left the Reichsführer's office.

Reichsführer's Headquarters, spring 1943.

As so often before, I am once again in the headquarters of the Reichsführer. We still have a little time, so we decide to go into the dining car and seize the opportunity to drink some good coffee; in the dining car you can find all those who have appointments with the Reichsführer around this time, be they comrades from the front who are to receive their decorations from the Reichsführer personally, or advisers and chiefs of main offices who, like us, have been called in for a conference. My chief runs one last time through all the points we want to present to the Reichsführer. We still do not know what it is all about and why we were so suddenly called in. Although the material we were told to bring along points to certain matters in a few eastern camps, the overall connection escapes us.

We are summoned in to see the Reichsführer, and we proceed through the simple and sparsely equipped barracks to his room, which lies at the end of one barrack. The Reichsführer greets the Chief of the Main Office with a friendly and firm gesture, then offers me his hand. A brief question about how our families are faring, and then he launches into his discourse. I will attempt to reproduce his comments as faithfully as possible:

Reichsführer (facing my chief) :   You have brought along the papers regarding the rising number of suicides among the SS leaders in certain camps. In your last report you already informed me of certain complaints and incidents brought to your attention. I have given the matter some thought. We have to act immediately to establish the reasons for the loss of leaders in these camps, so that I can take the appropriate steps to deal with the problems that have arisen in this connection. We are here concerned with an assignment whose implementation must not be delayed and must be carried out by every available means—and above all everything must be done smoothly and quietly. Therefore, I am going to order you to visit certain camps and determine exactly what the situation there is in each case. You will receive express authorization from me, and in the individual cases we are about to discuss, you will have to take very stringent measures, if necessary.

I have seen from your report, my good . . . , that you seem to think that a proportion of the leaders in these camps are not bearing up well under the psychological strain, and that they should be transferred to the front. We went over this matter once before, in our discussion of the employment of veteran front officers in concentration camps. I know your objections to it, and even though I can understand and sympathize with your view that every officer would prefer front-line duty to service in these camps, I nevertheless have to insist now that something finally be done. I realize that the men of the Waffen SS consider themselves too good for such service, but the Waffen SS represents only a fraction of the SS, and they simply have to get used to the idea that the SS has certain tasks to perform which are not always simple. I myself have sometimes wished that I could lead a respectable contingent at the front and that I need not bother about matters which give me sleepless nights.

My chief : Reichsführer, here is a list of leaders who have made several requests to return to the front. And I have also noted which leaders could replace them, so that these experienced officers might be sent to a fighting unit.

Reichsführer : My good . . . , that is pointless. You have no conception of what is involved. The officers who are presently in these camps are to stay put until their assignments have been carried out. Tell them that I understand their position, but that I also expect them to do their duty irrespective of circumstances; tell them that I realize their tasks are far more demanding than the tasks of those who are able to lead their platoons or companies on the front. I shall never forget this sacrifice of theirs, and after I have received your report, my good . . . , I shall bring all the officers from the different camps together so that I can personally have a word with them. I have not talked about these things with you yet, either. You are of course familiar with the Führer-order. Since you now have to go to these camps, you may as well be instructed as to their function, and also as to my personal opinion in this regard. Speak to the officers about my views on these matters—I believe that their awareness of my viewpoint will make the performance and strain of their work lighter to bear. I ought to stress that the remarks I am about to make are intended exclusively for your ears; you may repeat them only to the officers who have specific tasks to perform in the camps. Otherwise, you are at no time to speak about these things.

The Reichsführer said this in his terse and emphatic style. He was silent for a while, then looked at my chief and me, and continued, now in a quieter and calmer fashion. One could see from his delivery how these things still clearly move him even as he is relating them: how he is searching for his words, and how he seeks with care to avoid giving us the impression that deep down he dissents from many of these words and decisive statements.

Reichsführer :   I was with the Führer a short while ago. He told me of his intentions and plans with an ease that is rare for him—and this during an hour heavily burdened with cares—touching freely upon matters he had never mentioned before. He told me, practically word for word, "You see, Himmler, when I look at this global conflict, in which once more the best blood of the white race is being shed on both sides, time and again I must observe, to my great sorrow, that the actual driving forces, the subversive elements of the nations on earth, the real instigators of this war, are, as so often before, getting away with it completely unscathed—indeed, this time perhaps coming out of the struggle stronger than before. You see, I am often in the grip of a deep concern about the future of the white peoples, and if at this decisive juncture we should lose—and may providence spare us this fate—then these subversive elements, international Jewry, will in every sense of the word, be the ones who will come out on top. Today the whole world is babbling about the achievements of the French Revolution. But no one considers the fact that amidst all the screaming in the streets, the heads of the French nobility were rolling. Revolutionary times are governed by their own laws. Should we win the battle, no one will ask us afterward how we did it. Should we lose, then we shall at the very least have hit decisively these subversives. Therefore, Himmler, I have after much deliberation decided to blot out once and for all the biological bases of Judaism, so that if the Aryan peoples emerge weakened from this conflict, at least a crippling blow will have been dealt to those other forces. I am determined, out of a higher responsibility, to translate this recognition of mine into action, whatever the consequences."

The Reichsführer then resumed : I was deeply disturbed by this order, for it burdens us, as the Führer's most faithful adherents, with a historical obligation of incalculable proportions. I can well imagine that we shall be denounced and blackened by powers that see only the deed, but not the compelling necessity behind this action. They fail to recognize that we are the greatest executors of an order whereby our cadres will always be associated with this deed. I have suffered greatly as a result of this order and know what it means to the SS, whatever may happen. But I also see the execution of this order as a test of fidelity to the Führer, such as no other organization can and will give him. I have spoken about these things to you so that you might comprehend the magnitude of the task which the SS has been assigned and for which I must answer. Therefore, speak forcefully with the camp officers and make these facts clear to them. I cannot allow the small circle of SS leaders who have been implicated in these things, and who therefore have to bear this burden entirely for themselves, to be widened and varied through constant transfers to the front and relief replacements. Maintenance of secrecy is in this case imperative, and I urge you to stress this point when you announce my rejection of transfers. These two hundred leaders, and they alone, must bear the burden for all. At this point we cannot furnish even the SS corps of leaders with a historical justification of this undertaking. Much of it would be beyond them, and they would only evaluate the facts as such. Only at a greater distance from these events, perhaps only after decades, perhaps only after a period of fierce defamation, will the perspective that alone can reveal the real necessity of this assignment be that of the majority.

My chief : Reichsführer, should I give individual reports on the important cases, or will a written summary of the results of the trip suffice? I would be very much in favor of making negative or positive entries in the personnel papers of particular leaders, in order to assist them with an appropriate transfer after the completion of their assignments.

Reichsführer : My good man, you know my position: in a battle as great as the one we, in this ideological conflict, are faced with, the troops have to be tough. The SS leader has to be tough too, but he should not be callous. In cases where you find that one leader or another is exceeding the limits necessary to the fulfillment of his duty, that certain distinctions are beginning to blur for him, intervene immediately and report the incident to me at once. I will respond with the utmost severity wherever one of my leaders oversteps his bounds and exceeds his assigned competencies, which are already fairly wide as they stand. Understand me well: I have a feeling that some of these men believe that because of the scope of this assignment and the psychological strain it entails, they can just let themselves go. Wherever you encounter such cases, be ruthless. This very assignment, which, objectively seen, is extremely difficult to carry out, must be borne in an irreproachable fashion by every single man. He who must anesthetize himself or who forgets himself in the face of the enemy whom he holds in his power proves that he is no SS leader, and that he has not properly understood the true severity of this struggle.

The Reichsführer stood up, shook hands with my chief and me, and explicitly ordered him to report in person after the trip, besides submitting a written account. When we had left the Reichsführer's office and were passing through the barracks and the pine forest on the way to the car, my chief, deeply struck by our conference with Himmler, said to me: "Ours is not an easy assignment. We shall have to examine things with a critical eye and then write up an objective report, irrespective of how the Reichsführer might react to it. Keep extremely accurate notes on everything that happens and on any conversations you might have; for this is not just a matter of SS leaders who are facing excruciatingly difficult personal decisions; the very coat of arms of our order must be kept untarnished."

We then lapsed into a long silence, as we had been deeply moved by the earnest and imploring words of the Reichsführer; and in particular the Führer's very careful intimation—that events could possibly turn against us—afforded an insight into the situation that put us in a reflective mood.

The question now is, what lies behind this account? First, it is manifest that the title, "From the Diary of a Fallen SS Leader," is fraudulent, for Franke-Gricksch did not fall in the war; he was reported in August 1953 to have died in a Soviet camp. The author of this account evidently was anxious to cover up the fact of his postwar existence. This is understandable, in view of his report from Auschwitz and his service record during the war. Above all in his mind was the need to demonstrate the extenuating compulsion of an order, for it is certain that Franke-Gricksch did not write the report "Resettlement of Jews" on his own initiative, but rather on order from his commanding officer, von Herff. But in autumn 1948, when the above account was written, von Herff was no longer alive to testify (having died in British captivity in 1945); Alfred Franke-Gricksch therefore saw himself left with no choice but to supply, in as convincing and plausible a form as possible, the background circumstances of the report he made on the liquidation machinery at Auschwitz-Birkenau. He did not know at the time whether the Auschwitz report had already been found and registered, but he had to reckon with the possibility that sooner or later this compromising document would indeed be found.

According to his account, Franke-Gricksch and von Herff met with the RFSS in the latter's headquarters in the "spring of 1943," at which time the liquidation order of the Führer was to have been given to the SS "a short while ago"—whereas in reality, the mass liquidation was already in full swing long before then.

The Head of the SS Personnel Main Office conferred frequently with Himmler in the spring of 1943. On 1 April 1943, Himmler recorded two appointments with von Herff in the RFSS Headquarters "Bergwald."[15] Bergwald was located in Aigen (Salzburg); from there Himmler visited Adolf Hitler at the "Berghof."[16] In the account by Franke-Gricksch, however, the picture-perfect reference to Himmler's headquarters points *exclusively* to the RFSS Headquarters in Lötzen, East Prussia, called "Hochwald."[17] We asked Werner Grothmann about the "dining car" in the RFSS Headquarters and about Franke-Gricksch's description of the barrack in which, as Franke-Gricksch recounts, the meeting with Himmler took place.

> "Special train" and "barracks" are in this case no contra-diction. Hochwald was a permanent headquarters, with built-in barracks for the RFSS, a portion of his staff, and the security forces; while the special train, positioned on a railroad siding within the facilities, belonged to the head-quarters and served as lodgings for part of the staff, for a few of Minister Lammers's colleagues, and for guests in-vited for conferences. The headquarters were located in a wooded area, so that even this detail fits the headquarters

15. NS 19 (neu)/1444, Bundesarchiv, Koblenz.
16. "On 22 March 1943, Hitler arrived at the Berghof in the evening and stayed several weeks. On 12 May he returned via Munich to East Prussia" (Nicolaus von Below to Richard Schulze-Kossens, 29 May 1979).
17. Werner Grothmann to author, 25 August 1978.

in East Prussia. The description of the barrack, with the room of the RFSS at the end of it, describes precisely the barrack in East Prussia.

I knew Obergruppenführer von Herff, and I also met Franke-Gricksch.[18]

Grothmann further stated: "It is entirely possible that Franke-Gricksch sometimes accompanied von Herff to the Headquarters, but impossible that he ever entered into talks with Himmler. Your reproduced account by Franke-Gricksch certainly suggests that *on this occasion* he did participate in a conference."[19]

This record of the circumstances that led to the Auschwitz inspection trip and the report written there was evidently intended to serve not only as a personal cover document, but also as an exculpatory account for all the SS officers who had been assigned to the liquidation camps in the East, as "a vindication of those SS officers who were driven to suicide, who inwardly resisted implementation of their orders. With this account he wished to transmit to posterity the record of these officers' conflict of conscience."[20] There is, however, not a single known case of an SS leader committing suicide in a liquidation camp in the East because he could not withstand the psychological stress.

Clearly, Himmler cannot have received his first liquidation orders from the Führer "a short while ago"—that is, shortly before the spring of 1943—as Franke-Gricksch of necessity alleges. For, as we have seen, at the end of March 1943, Gauleiter Greiser (Wartheland), acting "in the name of the Führer," had already tendered thanks to Sonderkommando Bothmann, assembled at Kulmhof (Chelmno), for their accomplishments at that death camp;[21] and at the end

18. Werner Grothmann to author, 9 August 1978.
19. Werner Grothmann to author, 16 September 1978.
20. Liselotte Franke-Gricksch to author, 5 September 1978.
21. Cf. p. 8 n. 26.

of April, Dr. Kaltenbrunner called this same SS Sonderkommando into the Reich Main Security Office, imposing absolute silence on them and expressing once again "the personal gratitude of the Führer"—gratitude, that is, for their liquidation of 145,301 Jews up to 1 January 1943 in the Kulmhof (Chelmno) camp.[22] Moreover, as early as the end of August 1942, a Führer-order was delivered to Auschwitz, stipulating that "duty in Auschwitz is frontline duty."[23] The first known selection for the gas chambers at Auschwitz took place two months prior to this order.[24]

The date furnished by Franke-Gricksch for a meeting between von Herff and Himmler is a conceivable one, given the narrow range of certain other known facts: the meeting can only have taken place between early January and mid-March of 1943, since Himmler was in his Hochwald headquarters during this period; and Franke-Gricksch was not transferred to the SS Personnel Main Office until January 1943. This would place the conference held between Hitler and Himmler "a short while ago" at the time of the Stalingrad crisis.[25] It is not at all unlikely that Hitler reaffirmed his liquidation directives to Himmler during just this period, for whenever the god of war had forsaken the Füh-

---

22. This figure, taken from the statistical report on "The Final Solution of the European Jewish Question" by the Inspector of Statistics of the RFSS, Dr. R. Korherr, is cited by A. Rückerl, *NS-Vernichtungslager* (Munich, 1977), 291. Original report in Bundesarchiv; copy in document collection Zentrale Stelle für Landesjustizverwaltungen, vol. 7, pp. 417ff.

23. Statement by prisoner Josef Erber to author, 25 August 1981.

24. Report of Dr. Vrba, War Refugees Board, Washington, November 1944. Of the 1,000 Jews on board the convoy that left Paris (Drancy) on 22 June 1942, 800 were registered in Auschwitz and 200 were gassed; on this, see the handwritten list by Dr. Heinz Röthke, Eichmann's representative in Paris, re: convoys from Paris, from 29 April, 6 June, 22 June, and 28 June 1942 (original in Centre de Documentation Juive Contemporaine, Paris, vol XXVI-C, p. 254).

25. "I, too, repeatedly caught sight of Himmler in the Führer's Headquarters during the winter of 1942 to 1943" (Nicolaus von Below to author, 20 June 1981).

rer of the Third Reich, Hitler's thoughts returned to the dynamic source of his political motivation: "to blot out once and for all the biological bases of Judaism."

Soon Hitler's hatred for the Jews would resurface at a meeting with the Hungarian Regent Miklós Horthy, in the presence of the Reich Foreign Minister von Ribbentrop, on 17 April 1943. In their zeal to impress upon Horthy the need for a speedy Final Solution in Hungary, Hitler and the Reich Foreign Minister seriously overestimated Horthy's antipathy against the Jews: "The Jews were to be treated as tuberculosis bacilli, which could infect a healthy body. This was not cruel, considering that even innocent creatures of nature, such as rabbits and deer, have to be killed to prevent harm."[26]

26. Memorandum from Paul Otto Schmidt, 18 April 1943, geheime Reichssache, on the conversation between the Führer and the Hungarian Regent.
Horthy in Schloss Klessheim on 17 April 1943, A.M. (Politisches Archiv des AA, Handakten Schmidt, vol. 7 [1943]).

In conference with Hitler and von Ribbentrop on 17 April 1943, Admiral Horthy raised the question of "what he ought to do with the Jews, now that he had practically reduced their living conditions to the absolute minimum, since he could not simply beat them to death." The Reich Foreign Minister declared that "the Jews would either have to be annihilated or put in concentration camps: there were no other alternatives."

Four weeks later, Hitler's future Reich Plenipotentiary in Hungary, Edmund Veesenmayer, wrote to Himmler that Admiral Horthy's sole tie to the Reich lay in his fear of Bolshevism, and that Prime Minister Miklós Kállay (in office from March 1942 to March 1944) regarded all measures against the Jews as a crime against Hungary.[1] Kállay confirmed Hitler's worst suspicions when three months later he delivered a speech over Radio Budapest that betrayed clear signs of Hungary's battle fatigue.[2] Only Horthy's dread of a Russian invasion timed with a German withdrawal enabled the dictator to wring further concessions from the Hungarian Head of State. A second summit conference at Schloss

1. Veesenmayer to Himmler, 19 May 1943, Case XI, NG 2192, U.S. National Archives.
2. Gerald Reitlinger, *The Final Solution*, 3d ed. (London, 1971), 453.

Klessheim near Salzburg was arranged for 17 March 1944. This time, Hitler extracted from his Hungarian guest a promise to dismiss Premier Kállay. His replacement would be Döme Sztojay, already familiar to the German government as the Hungarian Chargé d'Affaires in Berlin.[3]

Dr. Paul Otto Schmidt, who as a witness kept the minutes of the Horthy-Hitler talks of 17 April and also made notes of the ultimatum of 18 March 1944, describes in his book the tactics that were used to detain Horthy at Schloss Klessheim for twenty-four hours: a mock air raid; the cutting off of telephone communications with Budapest; Hitler's order to bring Horthy back to Budapest as a prisoner, if necessary.[4] The Hungarian Head of State was not being compelled to continue to fight as an ally of Germany; that was guaranteed by the Russian advance. Rather Horthy consented, under great pressure, to relocate 800,000 Jewish citizens from Hungary—which now was to become a battleground—to the occupied East. "The Jewish question in Hungary is . . . being brought toward a swift solution. The Hungarian government has agreed to the relocation to the eastern territories of all Hungarian citizens who are considered Jews by Hungarian law."[5] Thus, the code word "relocation" (*Verbringung*) merits a place in the register of Final Solution—related semantic conventions. Wagner's explanatory note of 26 May concludes with the significant remark: "To the best of our present knowledge, about one third of the deported Jews are fit for

3.   On 16 January 1943, Undersecretary of State Martin Luther heavily reproached Ambassador Sztojay with the fact that "a country friendly to us has become a haven in the middle of Europe for nearly one million Jews. Germany could not in the long run countenance this danger without taking action" (Israel Police Archive).

4.   Paul Otto Schmidt, *Statist auf diplomatischer Bühne, 1923–1945* (Bonn, 1949), 271.

5.   Horst Wagner, Foreign Office, Dept. Inland IIa, geheime Reichssache Berlin, 26 May 1944, Israel Police Archive.

work."[6] Of the Hungarian Jews "relocated to the eastern territories"—that is, transported to Auschwitz—between 15 May and 30 June 1944, no fewer than 240,000 were gassed or shot to death.

What role did Adolf Hitler play in this macabre drama? The day after he had forced Horthy to recall the Kállay regime and to submit from then on to the orders of a Reich plenipotentiary, Hitler signed the document for Veesenmayer's appointment as Plenipotentiary in the Wolfsschanze.[7] Paragraph 4 of this top secret paper states: "For SS and police assignments involving German personnel in Hungary, and in particular for policing assignments that fall within the domain of the Jewish question, a higher SS and police leader shall be placed on the staff of the Reich Plenipotentiary and shall look to him for instructions." This provision needs the following commentary: The "Higher SS and Police Leader" ordered to Hungary in April was General of Police Otto Winkelmann, an SS Obergruppenführer. As he himself has quite correctly stated in evidence, he was never ordered to handle the Jewish question in Hungary; and he took his instructions from the RFSS.[8] Responsible for the Jewish question in Hungary on the German side was above all Adolf Eichmann, whose instructions came neither from the Reich Plenipotentiary nor from Winkelmann, but rather from Himmler and Kaltenbrunner, via the RSHA, or else from Müller. Operating "in accordance with his policy directives," on the very day that Hitler installed the Reich Plenipotentiary

6. Case XI, IMT, NG 2190, with the remark, "with the request of the Secretary of State that this memorandum be submitted to the Reich Foreign Minister."

7. The Führer, geheime Reichssache. Führer's Headquarters, 19 March 1944, signed Adolf Hitler. Büro des Staatssekretärs: Ungarn, vol. II, Referat 117, Politisches Archiv des AA, Bonn.

8. Statement by Otto Winkelmann, AR 169/61, 19 May 1961.

in Hungary, Eichmann crossed the Hungarian border with his 130-man-strong "Sonderkommando Eichmann," coming directly from the concentration camp at Mauthausen.[9] It is significant that Hitler's 19 March top secret letter of appointment calls for "a higher SS and police leader," whereas the title in other documents is consistently "Higher SS and Police Leader"—that is, intended is not the Higher SS and Police Leader for Hungary, General Winkelmann, but rather Obersturmbannführer Eichmann, with whom the Hungarian Minister of the Interior was negotiating.[10] Not only did Eichmann receive no instructions from Veesenmayer or from Winkelmann, he also never passed his instructions from Himmler on to either of these two functionaries. Instead, he relayed his instructions directly to the Budapest Jewish Council or to the Hungarian Secretaries of State Vites Endré and László Baky in the Hungarian Ministry of the Interior,[11] since these officials were in charge of the Jewish question on the Hungarian side.

A comparison of the above-quoted passage from Hitler's letter of appointment for the Reich Plenipotentiary in Hungary with the following wording regarding the commander of German troops in Hungary further clarifies matters. "The commander is subordinate to the Chief of the Wehrmacht High Command and takes instructions from him." Had it been desired, corresponding provisions for the Higher SS and Police Leader Winkelmann could have been made in this letter of appointment. This was clearly not the

9. Avner Less to author, 30 June 1981.
10. Telegram Budapest No. 2336 of 19 August 1944, Citissime, Grell [very urgent; sent by Grell].
11. Dr. J. Varga, Hungarian National Archives, to author, 9 February 1981; cf. statutory declaration of 10 June 1948 by Wilhelm Waneck: "4. Lastly, I declare that the former Obersturmbannführer Eichmann and his office were attached neither to the Higher SS and Police Leader nor to Plenipotentiary Dr. Veesenmayer, but in fact, so far as I know, took his instructions directly from Himmler via the RSHA" (Israel Police Archives).

intention. What Hitler did want, after his second meeting with Admiral Horthy, was a selection of 100,000 Hungarian Jews from the nearly 400,000 who had been sent to Auschwitz. This selection was made on a running basis at the Birkenau loading platform in the period between 15 May and 30 June, and the 100,000 Jews were employed in the construction of the six underground, bombproof airplane factories that Dr. Hans Kammler had ordered on a top priority basis.[12] The starved and ill-treated men from the Carpathian ghettos were, however, in no condition to increase production in these underground sweatshops by 40 percent, the figure promised to the Hungarian Minister of the Interior Gábor Vajna by the RFSS in his special train "Steiermark" shortly before Christmas 1944. The workers in Mühldorf, Kauffering, and Schwarzheide were dropping like flies, chiefly from stone-dust.[13]

On 15 June, the Jewish community of Budapest had to move into 2,680 designated "Star Houses," not, however, into a declared ghetto. The Budapest City Council had taken seriously the warnings broadcast over the BBC that the establishment of a ghetto would be answered by bomb attacks on the Hungarian capital.

In the meantime, international pressure on Horthy, which persisted until mid-July, was further increased by the Papal Nuntius, the President of the International Committee of the Red Cross, and also by the American Secretary of State, Cordell Hull, who issued repeated warnings. By the end of June, Horthy had sufficient evidence to confirm that

---

12. Albert Speer, *Der Sklavenstaat* (Stuttgart, 1981), 331–32; cf. Reitlinger, *The Final Solution*, 458. Cf. also Albert Speer to author, 25 July 1981: "In any case, it was apparently Hitler's enterprise to make these Jews available to carry out his plan, the construction of six large bombproof factories."
13. Minutes of the Friedrich Jeckeln interrogation (Kammler's report), 21 December 1945, p. 7, Central Historical State Archives, Riga; Statement by Gábor Vajna, Freising, 28 August 1945, NO-1874.

the deported Hungarian Jews who were not sent to Germany under the Jäger-Dorsch Plan were being liquidated at Auschwitz-Birkenau.[14] At this point the Hungarian Regent ordered the withdrawal of the gendarmerie units that had been brought into Budapest to facilitate the deportations. He also sent a train filled with deportees back to its departure point before it could reach the Hungarian border. Even after these two incidents, which needless to say angered Hitler, Admiral Horthy was left in office—but only because the facade of Horthy's freedom of action and the illusion of Hungary's independence had to be maintained before the Germans as well as the Hungarians. However, at the beginning of July Veesenmayer and Winkelmann made it quite clear to the Hungarian Regent that any future interferences in matters regarding the removal of Hungarian Jews would not be tolerated by the German government, as this area was henceforth to be the exclusive domain of the competent Reich authorities.[15] This verbal reprimand was followed up a few days later by a telegram from von Ribbentrop to the Reich Plenipotentiary, as a result of a telephone discussion with Hitler. Von Ribbentrop instructed Ambassador Veesenmayer to disclose immediately to the Hungarian Head of State, in person, the following message in the name of the Führer:

> The Führer was greatly dismayed by a communication from the Reich Plenipotentiary, in which he read that the Regent had announced his intentions to recall . . . the current Sztojay government and to install a military regime. With still greater dismay, the Führer learned in the Reich Plenipotentiary's report that the Regent had issued arrest warrants for individual ministers and state secre-

14. Horthy Interrogation, IMT, Case XI, 4 March 1948, afternoon session.
15. Ibid.

taries of the Sztojay government who recently carried out measures against Jews. . . . Should any member of this clique, whose composition is well known to us in all its particulars . . . , reenter the political arena in Hungary, . . . the Führer will have the person concerned arrested immediately by the SD and prosecuted within twenty-four hours. . . . The Führer expects to see the measures against Budapest Jews carried out by the Hungarian government without any further delays. . . . The Regent should not be intimidated by any ridiculous Jewish-American threats. These are familiar to us, and they should not impress him any more than they do us, since at the end of the war, Germany and its allies, not America, will stand victorious in Europe.[16]

On 5 July 1944, the President of the International Committee of the Red Cross, Max Huber, personally wrote to Regent Horthy: "In the name of the International Committee of the Red Cross I beg Your Highness to give instructions which will enable us to reply to these rumors and accusations. At the same time, in the name of the principles we represent . . . , we implore the Royal Hungarian government to avoid anything that might provide even the slightest cause for such monstrous reports."[17] Huber received a personal response from Horthy on 12 August: "It is unfortunately not in our power to prevent inhuman acts. . . . I have instructed the Hungarian government to take the settlement of the Jewish question in Budapest into its own hands. It is to be hoped that this declaration will not give rise to

16. Diplomgerma Budapest No. 2160, 16 July 1944, author's private archives; "Top priority," "tel. to W[olfs]schanze, 16 July," author's private archives.

17. Die Tätigkeit des IKRK zugunsten der in deutschen Konzentrationslagern inhaftierten Zivilpersonen: 1939 –1945, 3d ed. (Geneva, 1947), 60 – 61. ICRC to author, 16 September 1981: Copy of Max Huber draft of 5 July 1944, from Archives of the International Committee of the Red Cross, in author's possession.

serious complications."[18] The complications were not long in arriving.

On 29 August, after much deliberation, the Hungarian Regent decided to dismiss Prime Minister Sztojay and to install General Géza Lákatos. At the same time Horthy assured the President of the Budapest Jewish Council that there would be no deportations from the capital.[19] On 22 September a Hungarian armistice commission left Budapest to conduct negotiations with Foreign Minister Vyacheslav Molotov in Moscow. On 9 October Hungary was faced with the Russian terms for a truce: an immediate declaration of war on Germany.

Horthy had scarcely announced the cessation of Hungarian hostilities toward Russia when, on 15 October, Veesenmayer informed him, in the presence of the German Plenipotentiary to Mussolini's Italy, Rudolf Rahn, that Horthy's son Miklós was being held hostage, and that Obergruppenführer Bach-Zelewski would shortly shell and storm Horthy's headquarters, the Hofburg, with the forty-two Tiger tanks that had just been unloaded in Budapest.

Already in April 1944 Veesenmayer had secretly met with the leader of the extreme-rightist party, the Arrow Cross, according to the latter's testimony. At this meeting Veesenmayer indicated that "the German Reich saw in him, Szálasi, the only possible man in Hungary for the future."[20] (The official newspaper of the Arrow Cross published this conference after the party had come to power.) Through his reports to von Ribbentrop and the latter's meeting with Hitler, Veesenmayer won the Führer's consent to a German-backed coup that would oust the Horthy government and

18. Ibid.
19. Dr. Reszoe Kasztner, *Bericht des jüdischen Rettungskomitees Budapest: 1942–1945* (Geneva, 1946), 362.
20. Statutory declaration by Dr. Wilhelm Hoettl, 24 April 1947, p. 6, NG-2317.

install the Arrow Cross party. All that remained was to secure Horthy's sanction, which was easily obtained after Veesenmayer and Rahn had driven him into a corner on 15 October. Horthy agreed to legitimize the Szálasi government[21] in return for his son, who had been carried off to Vienna by the SD-Kommando Otto Skorzeny. Thereafter, Horthy and Lákatos were interned in Germany.

For our purposes, it is important to stress once again the key role played by the Reich Plenipotentiary Veesenmayer in the "relocation" of the Hungarian Jews. Although SS-Sturmbannführer Eichmann had been entrusted by Himmler with the actual execution of the action and had negotiated the mechanics of this operation with the two Hungarian representatives—Vites Endré, the Secretary of State appointed expressly for this purpose, and Lászlo Baky, the Secretary for Security—it was Veesenmayer who conducted the decisive political talks with the Hungarian Prime Minister Sztojay. The evacuations were initiated only after agreements had been arrived at during these talks.[22] The Reich Plenipotentiary had had to apply constant pressure on the Hungarian government, doubtless at the prompting of his Minister von Ribbentrop, who was "no less intransigent than Himmler" in his anti-Semitism.[23] For the Hungarian government had repeatedly shown itself a reluctant partner in the policy against the Jews and was afraid of the men from the Reich Main Security Office.

In the inaugural program announced by the Arrow Cross party and the new Head of State Ferenc Szálasi on 17 October, the Jews were declared a Hungarian labor force; but still, they were to be kept in the country. Two days later,

---

21. "During the critical days, Szálasi received a German diplomat's uniform and was driven around in an embassy car, so as to be safe from Hungarian officials who wanted to arrest him" (ibid., p. 8).
22. Dr. Hoettl reports: "Sztojay told me that himself" (ibid., p. 9).
23. Ibid., p. 10; cf. p. 157 above.

the press republished this statement, this time minus the clause, "the Jews will be kept in the country." The "correction" was made thanks to the "energetic intervention by Eichmann."[24] Eichmann's competencies far outstripped those of an ordinary department head in the RSHA; and he was well aware of his organizational talent, which stemmed from fanatical obsession as well as from bureaucratic pedantry, and of his privileged position of power. The Higher SS and Police Leader of Hungary, Otto Winkelmann, described Eichmann as a subaltern character: "By 'subaltern character' I understand someone who pushes his power to its limits, without in the process developing ethical or psychological scruples. He also shows no compunction about exceeding his authority if he believes he is thereby acting as his commander would act."[25]

24. Kasztner, *Bericht des jüdischen Rettungskomitees*, 109–10.
25. Statement by Otto Winkelmann, 19 May 1961, p. 6, AR 169/61.

19

"Kaltenbrunner
Contra Himmler"

The account of Himmler's failed attempt to put the Hungarian Jews up for sale in exchange for trucks and military equipment need not be repeated here; Gerald Reitlinger has given it in his work *The Final Solution*,[1] as has the Hungarian chronicler Eugen Levai.[2] In any case, it is clear that from this point on Himmler increasingly sought—under the growing influence of his physician, Dr. Felix Kersten, and his Chief of Intelligence, Walter Schellenberg—cautiously to dismantle his image as the inhuman and criminal executor of his Führer's liquidation orders (and wishes), an image detrimental to him abroad. This was an illusory hope, which Himmler nourished naively and on which he pinned great personal and political ambitions. It was also a topic that Himmler wisely consigned to silence, except for a few rare conversations with Walter Schellenberg, for he feared his taskmaster practically to the very end, "the way a schoolboy [fears] his strict teacher"—and with good reason.[3] Hitler never revised his position. Where the Jewish ques-

1. Gerald Reitlinger, *The Final Solution*, 3d ed. (London, 1971), 471–79.
2. Eugen Levai, *The Black Book of Martyrdom of Hungarian Jewry* (Zurich, 1948).
3. Albert Speer to author, 20 May 1981.

tion was concerned, he remained the implacable fanatic, sworn and bound to his policy of extermination until his dying breath. Heinrich Himmler, on the other hand, knew what hour had struck and was prepared to assume the consequences of a steadily deteriorating military position.

In a surprise move, taken at the end of November 1944, Himmler called a halt to further gassings and ordered the liquidation machinery at Auschwitz-Birkenau to be destroyed. Himmler's countermanding orders were a direct result of the secret overtures which his confidential aide Kurt Becher had made in Switzerland to representatives of Jewish aide organizations, and of the subsequent meeting on 5 November in Zurich between Becher and Roosevelt's special envoy, Roswell McClelland. Kaltenbrunner's version of these events, as he saw them on 12 April 1946 from the witness stand in Nuremberg, constitutes a not exactly dexterous attempt to divert his prosecutors from the truth and thereby save his own neck:[4]

> Prosecutor: Defendant, we shall now read the document together: "I, the former SS-Standartenführer Kurt Becher hereby declare the following under oath:
> 1. Sometime between the middle of September to the middle of October 1944 I prevailed upon the Reichsführer SS to issue the following order, which I received in two originals, one each for the SS-Obergruppenführers Kaltenbrunner and Pohl, and a duplicate for myself: 'Effective immediately, I forbid all further exterminations of Jews, while on the other hand I am ordering treatment and care for the weak and ill. I am holding you (meant here were he—

---

4. Statement by Ernst Kaltenbrunner before the I.M.C., 12 April 1946, vol. 11, pp. 369–72.

Kaltenbrunner—and Pohl)[5] personally responsible, even in the event that this order is not strictly complied with by subordinate departments.' I handed Pohl his copy personally . . . and left Kaltenbrunner's in an office in Berlin. In my opinion Kaltenbrunner and Pohl therefore bear the responsibility for the subsequent killings of Jewish prisoners.

2. During my visit to the concentration camp Mauthausen on 27 April 1945 at 9:00 A.M., the camp commandant, SS-Standartenführer Ziereis, told me the following, in strictest confidence: 'Kaltenbrunner instructed me that at least a thousand men must still die every day in Mauthausen.'" Is this correct, or is it not, defendant?

Kaltenbrunner: That is partially correct and partially incorrect. Yesterday and today I stated that this order was obtained through Hitler by virtue of my complaints, and evidently this order of Himmler's is based on an order that he received from Hitler. Second, it seems to me perfectly natural that Himmler should have given Pohl such an order, since Pohl was in charge of those concentration camps in which the Jews were located; and third, that he should have informed me as his counterpart in the configuration "Kaltenbrunner contra Himmler." As far as Becher is concerned, I have to go a bit farther back. Himmler did the worst imaginable things through Becher. . . . These consist of the fact that he . . . released Jews first in exchange for war equipment; second, for raw materials; and third, for hard currency. I learned of these actions through intelligence reports and immediately voiced my opposi-

5. Oswald Pohl was Head of the SS Economy Administration Main Office.

tion, not before Himmler—this would have been pointless—but before Hitler.[6]

Kaltenbrunner's allegation that Himmler's order to end the liquidations had not been an initiative of the RFSS, but rather the result of his own objections raised to Hitler, who then issued the order to the RFSS, which Himmler simply passed on, did not impress the Nuremberg judges. They knew that the Gestapo Chief Müller and Adolf Eichmann, Kaltenbrunner's subordinates in the Reich Main Security Office, had sabotaged Himmler's directive, with the result that in October 1944 repeated selections for gassing were made in Auschwitz-Birkenau among Jews transported from the "ghetto for the aged" in Theresienstadt, from Italy, and from the Cracow region. Even in this eleventh hour, Müller and Eichmann, like their superior, Kaltenbrunner, were not prepared to subscribe to Himmler's "soft approach." To all three of them, the radical about-face of the RFSS, who now found it expedient to create for himself the image of a realistic, even magnanimous, politician of moderation, was distasteful. Along with Hitler and his *éminence grise* Martin Bormann, Kaltenbrunner and company persevered in the extermination policies. They stood, to the bitter end, faithfully by the originator and architect of the massively scaled liquidation measures, the Führer of the nation, Adolf Hitler—whom Kaltenbrunner sought out with increasing frequency beginning in March of 1944.[7]

6. After Hitler heard that on 6 February 1945 Himmler had allowed twelve hundred Jews coming from Theresienstadt to enter into Switzerland—the news was published in two Swiss papers on 8 February—he made such a violent scene in front of the RFSS that Himmler again revoked all relief measures for the Jews and instructed Hermann Pister, the commander of the Buchenwald concentration camp, not to allow any concentration camp prisoners in southern Germany to pass into enemy hands alive (Affidavit Becher, Case XI, IMT, NG 2675).

7. "I saw Kaltenbrunner frequently during these months" (Nicolaus von Below to author, 21 July 1981).

Equally familiar to the judges at Nuremberg was the ominous letter from Kaltenbrunner to his friend Blaschke, then Mayor of Vienna, in which Kaltenbrunner maintained that of the 12,000 Jews who had been evacuated from Hungary and relocated to the Strasshof camp in Vienna, only 3,600 were fit for work. Among these Jews "the women and children not fit for work, all of whom will be kept in readiness for a special action, must also stay in the guarded camp in the daytime.[8] For further details, will you please consult with the State Police Headquarters in Vienna . . . and SS-Obersturmbannführer Krumey from the special Einsatzkommando of Hungary, who is currently in Vienna."

8. Case XI, IMT, PS 3803, 313/express letter, secret, 30 June 1944.

20

"Duty at Auschwitz
Is Frontline Duty"

We have repeatedly called attention to Hitler's practice of translating his hatred for the Jews into unambiguous threats, which he broadcast to the public at seemingly opportune moments.[1] With these outbursts Hitler sought to present himself not only as the steadfast enlightener, but also as the bold and righteous Volksführer fearlessly and openly battling for existence against his nation's mortal enemy.[2]

These ice-cold threats of annihilation, after years of verbal and pictorial propaganda, were intended to stir the fears and hatred in the German masses until at last the desired pitch of fanaticism and unity had been reached and the fighting morale of the nation bolstered. The symbol of an identifiable, common enemy, "Jewish Bolshevism" and "Jewish High Finance," was essential as a unifying factor in this ideologically medieval campaign against the devil, which paralleled the national military campaign both in intensity and duration.

Despite the many threats Hitler issued against the Jews, both in public and in private,[3] he painstakingly avoided being in any way associated personally with the implementation of the liquidation orders he himself had

1. Cf. p. 19 n. 5.
2. Cf. p. 30 n. 28.
3. *Hitler's Monologe im Führerhauptquartier: 1941–1944*, ed. Werner Jochmann (Hamburg, 1980), contains no less than fifty references to Jews.

originated. As a result, a constant game of deception, concealment, and cover-up was played on many different levels—a game that afforded not a few of its participants cynical satisfaction and joy. The highest officers reveled in their supreme power and successful cunning; those on the lowest executive level, in the unbridled life force of the animal in man.

The German people were to be given no opportunity, no proof, to make the correlation between the originator of the liquidation orders and the gas-masked SS "disinfector" who stood in perfect ease on the flat roof of the gas chamber in Auschwitz-Birkenau while emptying a box of Zyklon-B crystals down the duct. The immaculate image of the Führer had to be preserved, for Hitler and his court had every reason to suspect that the German people would not submit for very long to a regime that had elevated the cold-blooded murder of millions to a *raison d'état*.

We can now understand the historical significance of a directive signed by Bormann and received in the Ministry for the Eastern Occupied Territories late in autumn 1941,[4] which stated that "only written Führer-orders" could be referred to for authority. Naturally, verbal Führer-orders concerning the Final Solution were also subject to strict secrecy,[5] as former Unterscharführer Josef Houstek, who served at the end of February 1942 in the Auschwitz political department, confirms.[6] When he sought to be transferred from Auschwitz, he was "verbally informed" in August of 1942 by his "immediate superior" and head of the political department of the camp Gestapo, Untersturmführer Maximilian Grabner, that duty at Auschwitz was, "in accordance with a Führer-order," to be regarded as front-

4. Per Dr. G. Leibbrandt to author, 8 April 1981; and Dr. O. Bräutigam to author, 9 March 1981.

5. Cf. on this p. 22.

6. Personnel File Josef Erber, note of name-change from Houstek to Erber, 14 May 1943, Berlin Document Center.

line duty. "I myself never saw the actual Führer-order in written form; it obviously was top secret."[7]

Reference to this same directive—that duty at Auschwitz is frontline duty—is made in the document that Franke-Gricksch dictated to his wife shortly after his return from British captivity,[8] and which she submitted as evidence in the Treblinka trial[9] on 19 January 1965. Here Himmler explicitly draws the connection we seek: "You are of course familiar with the Führer-order." The efforts of certain participants in the Final Solution to be transferred from the death factory at Auschwitz, preferably to the front, posed a potential risk to the cover-up of the mass murder.[10] This risk was in all likelihood the incentive behind Himmler's orders to his Chief of the Personnel Main Office and the latter's aide, Franke-Gricksch, that they immediately thwart all such attempts. That the Führer-order regarding duty at Auschwitz "was top secret" goes without saying. The precise count of those murdered at the Auschwitz-Birkenau camp alone cannot be given with complete, attestable certainty, for the Jews "cleared" [abgeschafft][11] from occupied Europe and deported to Auschwitz for liquidation were brought immediately "into the gas," without any prior registration in the camp index files.[12] Reitlinger's figure for Auschwitz—700,000 gassed—is undoubtedly too low.[13]

7. Statement by prisoner Josef Erber to author, 25 August and 2 September 1981.

8. Cf. pp. 145 and 154.

9. Franke-Gricksch Interrogation, London, August to September 1947 (Franke-Gricksch was released from British captivity [as prisoner of war] in August 1948). Cf. p. 145.

10. Albert Speer, Der Sklavenstaat (Stuttgart, 1981), 356: "During the Stalingrad days and thereafter, Hitler spoke with somber and ambiguous undertones . . . 'We can only go forward. We've burned all our bridges behind us. There is, gentlemen, no going back any longer.' All of us suspected that monstrosities were occurring. . . ."

11. Cf. p. 140 n. 2.

12. Czeslaw Pilichowski, No Time-Limit for These Crimes (Warsaw, 1980), 113.

13. Gerald Reitlinger, The Final Solution, 3d ed. (London, 1971), 501.

21

"They Shall Go Under with Us!"

When in February 1945 two Swiss papers published news of the rescue operation that had been initiated under the joint auspices of the former President of the Swiss Confederation, Jean-Marie Musy, and Himmler, Hitler recoiled with a harsh denunciation of the action, forbidding its continuation and threatening heavy punishment.[1] Nevertheless, that same month the Swedish Red Cross seized the initiative: its Vice President, Count Folke Bernadotte, met for the first time with Heinrich Himmler on 19 February to negotiate the fate of the Scandinavian concentration camp prisoners, including the release of a number of Danish and Norwegian prisoners.[2] The meeting had been arranged with the help of Walter Schellenberg.

A second mediator in Himmler's privy court was Felix Kersten, Himmler's Finnish masseur of German extraction. Kersten increasingly exercised a salutary influence over his patient, chiefly by virtue of his ability to keep the Reichsführer's serious stomach disorder in check and to massage away the associated pains. On 25 February, Kersten and the director of the Stockholm branch office of the

---

1. Cf. p. 170 n. 6; and statement by Dr. Jean-Marie Musy, 8 May 1948, Schellenberg Document No. 44, U.S. National Archives.
2. Bernadotte met with Himmler on four separate occasions: 19 February and 2, 21, and 24 April 1945.

Jewish World Congress, Hilel Storch, drew up a rescue plan. In spite of a personal risk, Kersten wanted to exhort Himmler to underwrite the plan, which comprised four steps: (1) Kersten was to negotiate as the representative of the Jewish World Congress and seek to obtain permission from the RFSS for deliveries of foodstuffs and medical supplies into the concentration camps; (2) the concentration camps were to be monitored by observers from the International Committee of the Red Cross; (3) certain prisoners were to be released; (4) Jews were to be transported to Sweden and Switzerland.[3] With this objective in mind, Kersten flew back from Stockholm to Germany on 3 March 1945, determined, "in the name of humanity," to negotiate maximal concessions from Himmler. His mission was all the more critical because every attempt by the International Red Cross to secure civilian internee status and tolerable living conditions for Jewish concentration camp prisoners had conspicuously failed.[4] The risk that Kersten ran in his personal interventions with Himmler—interventions pursued with great tact, determination, and courage—was a ruthless attempt at sabotaging these efforts on the part of Kaltenbrunner. Reacting to the Swedish Count's proposal on 5 March in Berlin, Kaltenbrunner declared: "I have no intention of supporting you in your plans," by which he meant that he would prevent Bernadotte and his Red Cross workers from setting foot in the camps. "And I shall not stand for a subordinate of Himmler's trying to sabotage an agreement concluded between the two of us," was Bernadotte's reply, referring to his first conference with Himmler on 19 February.[5]

3. Cf. Gerald Fleming, "Die Herkunft des 'Bernadotte-Briefs' an Himmler," *Vierteljahrshefte für Zeitgeschichte* 26 (1978): 582.
4. In the absence of such a status, internees under protective custody, viz, civilian prisoners held in custody on political or racial grounds, were not deemed to be under the protection of the Red Cross (CIRC to author, 1 April 1976).
5. Folke Bernadotte, *The Fall of the Curtain* (London, 1945), 33.

While Sipo-Chief Kaltenbrunner was denying the Swedish Count access to the Neuengamme and Ravensbrück concentration camps, Felix Kersten was holding a still more critical, and stormy, session with Himmler. For Kersten had decided on that morning of 5 March to persuade Himmler to reverse Hitler's order that the concentration camps be blown up on the approach of the Allies. Kersten's awareness that the Swedish Red Cross and Hilel Storch looked to him as their only hope in reaching Himmler gave his arguments added intensity and determination, but he still did not achieve the results he had hoped for. He had overestimated Himmler's readiness to play his last trump card and to make the final breach with his Führer. "If National Socialist Germany should collapse, then our enemies, those betrayers of our Greater Germanic aspirations who are now sitting in the concentration camps, shall not know the triumph of departing as victors. They shall not know that day; they shall go under with us! That is the clear and logical order of the Führer, and I will see that it is carried out thoroughly and meticulously."[6]

It took Kersten a week to demonstrate to Himmler the senselessness of this Führer-order. They struck a verbal agreement not to allow the concentration camps to be blown up on the approach of the Allies, but instead to surrender the camps with all their inmates intact. Himmler further promised to prohibit any further killing of Jews.[7]

"I am of the conviction," a contrite Himmler wrote on 21 March to his physician-masseur, who had by now all but assumed the role of father confessor, "that with the elimination of demagogy and superficiality against all odds

6. Quoted in Achim Besgen, *Der stille Befehl* (Munich, 1960), 48–49. Cf. also n. 13 below.
7. Hilel Storch to author, 6 September 1976; Felix Kersten to Swedish Foreign Minister Christian Günther, 23 April 1945 (Archive Kersten, Stockholm, and Archive of Swedish Ministry of Foreign Affairs; copy in author's private archives).

and not withstanding the bloody wounds inflicted on all sides, wisdom and reason must prevail, and with these the humane heart and the willingness to help."[8] These carefully chosen words have a hollow and grotesque ring to them in view of the enormous guilt which the executor of the Führer-wishes had accumulated for himself—a guilt that he now, at the last minute, sought to reduce to "comprehensible" proportions, in the belief that such humanitarian measures could still improve the chances of his own survival.[9]

On 7 April two reliable German informants in Stockholm warned Hilel Storch that Kaltenbrunner had ordered that the Bergen-Belsen camp be blown up the next day at 6:00 A.M.,[10] a camp in which at least forty thousand typhus- and famine-stricken prisoners were slowly dying. In Storch's presence Kersten contacted Himmler's assistant, Dr. Rudolf Brandt, from Stockholm and succeeded, through this dead-of-night telephone conversation, in frustrating Kaltenbrunner's plans.

Faced with the very real fears, however, that Kaltenbrunner would expose and denounce him to Hitler as a traitor and a saboteur of Führer-orders, Himmler wavered once again. On 14 April, he dispatched a telegram to the camp commanders of Dachau and Flossenbürg with instructions that a surrender "was out of the question." "The camp must be evacuated immediately. No prisoner may fall into enemy hands alive."[11]

8. Archive Kersten, Stockholm; photocopy of original letter in author's private archives.
9. Count Folke Bernadotte to H. Storch, Stockholm, 17 April 1945: "I wish to inform you that in the course of my negotiations with Reichsführer Himmler it was pointed out to me that the concentration camps for Jews in Germany would not be evacuated, but instead would be surrendered intact to the allied military officials concerned. Particular mention was made of the camps in Theresienstadt, Bergen-Belsen, and Buchenwald" (Archive Storch, Stockholm; photocopy of original letter in author's possession).
10. Hilel Storch to author, 6 September and 10 December 1976.
11. U.S. National Archives; photocopy in author's possession.

As the frontlines in both the east and west were driven progressively deeper into German territory, the RSHA began to evacuate concentration camps closest to the fronts, marching the prisoners to camps in the rear. The decision to evacuate proved a disaster. The lines of transportation and provision increasingly broke down, and maintenance of the great crowds became impossible. In their miserable physical condition, hundreds of prisoners perished daily. In the march toward the camps of the shrinking Reich, those who could simply go no farther were on a number of occasions summarily shot down at the side of the road by the SS guards.[12]

Walter Schellenberg's confidant, Obersturmführer Franz Göring from the RSHA, describes what he experienced when he drove into the Ravensbrück concentration camp on 22 April 1945 with orders from Himmler, via Schellenberg, to release "all women":

> On 22 April 1945, at about 12:00 P.M., I arrived in the Ravensbrück camp. I immediately conducted an extended interview with the commandant of the concentration camp, Sturmbannführer Suhren. Through a detailed inquiry, I established that 9,000 Polish women and 1,500 women of French, Belgian, Dutch, and other nationalities, in addition to approximately 3,000 Jewish women, were presently in the camp. . . . Here as well, the uncooperative attitude of the camp commandant and his staff toward the release of the prisoners was in evidence. Suhren attempted to evade precise questions with unclear answers. His excuse in every instance was that, following orders from the Führer, he had already destroyed all the documents, files, and other remaining materials. . . . In connection with the evacuation of the women, I told Suhren that I had halted . . . the columns of the

12. *Die Tätigkeit des IKRK zugunsten der in den deutschen Konzentrationslagern inhaftierten Zivilpersonen: 1939–1945*, 3d ed. (Geneva, 1947), 104, 121–22, 146.

Swedish Red Cross, so that it was advisable to begin marching the women by foot to Malchow in order to expedite their release. I would then signal the transport columns to receive the women in Malchow. Suhren gave me his firm promise to start the women on their march to Malchow that same day. . . . A column of seventeen buses of the Swedish, Danish, and International Red Cross was held ready for the evacuation of the women, who ought in the meantime to have reached Malchow, according to my agreement with Suhren. When we arrived in Malchow, we learned from the camp commandant that he knew nothing about the arrival of the prisoners from Ravensbrück. We then drove back to Ravensbrück and confirmed for ourselves that Suhren had in fact not sent the women on their march as agreed. When I asked him why he had failed to keep his end of the agreement, he answered . . . that in accordance with the Führer's orders, the prisoners had to remain in the camp. I then telephoned the special train Steiermark from Suhren's office, in his presence, and was connected with Standartenführer Dr. Brandt, Himmler's personal assistant. I described the situation to Dr. Brandt and requested an immediate decision from Himmler. Not long afterward, Dr. Brandt called back and ordered Suhren to release the prisoners for evacuation as agreed. Suhren then declared to me in private that he was now completely at a loss, since he had explicit Führer-orders to liquidate the women upon the approach of the enemy troops. Suhren now became very uncertain and confided to me that he had a group of women in the camp whom he had likewise been explicitly ordered to eliminate: fifty-four Polish and seventeen French women, on whom experiments had been conducted. When I asked him what sort of experiments, he explained that the women in question had been inoculated with bacilli, which had developed into a disease, which in turn had been cured through surgery, partly through muscle surgery, partly through bone surgery. Thereupon I had two of the women brought before me and was convinced of what Suhren had told me. I immediately pointed out to Suhren that he could not, under any circumstances, carry out the order Kaltenbrunner had given until he had received a decision from Himmler. In Lübeck, I contacted Dr. Brandt once again and apprised him of this matter, requesting that he obtain a decision from Himmler as soon as possible, and further indicating that these women ought not to be eliminated under any circumstances, especially since the women who were about to be released knew of the experiments. The experiments were known in the camp under the code name "Kaninchen" [rabbit]. About two hours later I received word from Dr. Brandt that Himmler had ordered the release of the so-called "Versuchskaninchen" [guinea pigs]. Dr. Arnoldson of the Swedish Red Cross, whom I briefed on the whole affair, personally supervised the evacuation of these women.[13]

Fifteen thousand women were rescued by the Swedish, Danish, and International Red Cross on that 23 April.

13. Statutory declaration by Franz Göring, 24 February 1948; Schellenberg Defense Exhibit No. 36, U.S. National Archives.

22

The Beginning of the End

Himmler was afflicted with a continuous vacillation during the final, decisive weeks of the war. In his desperate search for a way out of a hopeless position, he found himself caught between antithetical motives and pressures. His blind devotion to Hitler and to the system was challenged by the growing desire to make concessions through which both he and Schellenberg ultimately hoped to negotiate a separate peace with the Western Allies, and furthermore to enable the new statesman Himmler to take over a key position after Hitler. The divided state of Himmler's mind was never more evident than in the contrast between his order of 14 April 1945 to the camp commandants in Dachau and Flossenbürg, and his secret parley on 22 April at 3:00 A.M. with the representative of the Jewish World Congress in Stockholm, Norbert Masur. The RFSS met with Masur on Kersten's estate, "Hartzwalde," near Berlin, in the presence of Schellenberg and Kersten. At this truly unique meeting Masur wanted to confirm personally Himmler's verbal assurances to Kersten and Bernadotte: no further executions of Jews; no more deadly evacuation marches for Jewish concentration camp prisoners. Swayed by Kersten's private and assiduous entreaties, Himmler reiterated his previous consent, and the result was the release of the thousands of women from the Ravensbrück camp on the following day.

But three hours after his talk with Masur, when the RFSS returned with Schellenberg to the SS sanatorium Hohenlychen and met with Bernadotte once again as agreed, his resolution faltered. Bernadotte had come to urge the RFSS to evacuate the remaining Danish and Norwegian internees in the Neuengamme camp near Hamburg; Red Cross buses would be available to convey them to Sweden. Himmler hesitated; he felt that he lacked the real power to grant the Count his wish. Following this rebuff, Schellenberg once again put Himmler's request to Bernadotte that the Count fly to General Eisenhower and try to arrange a meeting between the General and Himmler. "The Reichsführer no longer grasps the reality of his own situation," Bernadotte answered. "I cannot help him any more. He should have taken the destiny of Germany into his own hands after my first visit."[1]

The RFSS and the Vice President of the Swedish Red Cross met for the last time on the night of 23–24 April, by candlelight, in the Swedish consulate in Lübeck. In the course of their discussion (which was interrupted at one point by an air raid on a nearby airfield), Himmler put his significant principal wish to the Swedish Count: "We Germans must declare ourselves defeated by the Western powers; and I beg you to have the Swedish government convey this to General Eisenhower, so that further bloodshed may be avoided. To capitulate to the Russians, however, is impossible for us Germans, and particularly for me. We shall continue fighting them until the front of the Western powers has replaced the German front."[2] Bernadotte agreed

---

1. Walter Schellenberg, *Aufzeichnungen* (Munich, 1979), 360.
2. Report on the Case of Walter Schellenberg, 1980, p. 104, U.S. National Archives; see also Chiefs of Staff to A.F.H.Q. War Dept. Classified Message Center, Nr. OZ 2642, 25 April 1945, pp. 1–3. RG 218, Records of the United States Joint Chiefs of Staff, Leahy file, U.S. National Archives.

to pass Himmler's qualified declaration of surrender on to the Swedish government, for examination by the Western Allies (who rejected it on 27 April). Himmler sent along with it a personal covering letter requesting the Foreign Minister's support. The letter, written in dim candlelight, reads as follows:

> Your Excellency,
>
> I have asked Count Bernadotte to inform you of a number of problems which I had the opportunity of discussing with him today. Please accept in advance my genuine appreciation for your kind attention to these matters.
>
>
> With the expression
> of my highest respects
> I remain Your Excellency's
> very devoted,
> H. Himmler[3]
>

Himmler now also declared himself willing to allow the evacuation of the Danish and Norwegian prisoners from Neuengamme camp to Sweden. The demolition of the camps was averted; hundreds of thousands of prisoners lived through the end of the war,[4] and through the last, furious surge of Adolf Hitler's fundamental nihilism, which in the end was directed at his own people.

Hitler was not to be spared the knowledge of Himmler's betrayal. On 28 April at 9:00 P.M., as the Russians drew critically near to the Reich Chancellery, Hitler's press aide, Heinrich Lorenz, descended into the Führer's bunker with a report from the Ministry of Propaganda. The report

---

3.   1945 Ars Svenska Hjälpexpedition till Tyskland, Swedish Foreign Ministry, Stockholm, 1956, p. 39.
4.   Hans Marsalek, *Die Geschichte des Konzentrationslagers Mauthausen*, (Vienna, 1974), 103: According to a statistic from 15 January 1945, 487,290 male and 156,000 female prisoners were interned in German concentration camps. Eugen Kogon gives 53,000 as the number of surviving internees (*Der SS-Staat* [Munich, 1946], 45).

was handed directly to Hitler. Since 16 February 1945, the dictator had remained in virtual confinement, ruling, and now fatally beleaguered, in his underground bunker. And now came the news of Himmler's negotiations with Folke Bernadotte, recounted in the foreign press. Of all the setbacks and personal disappointments Hitler had to endure in these final weeks (events that Hugh Trevor-Roper has so masterfully described),[5] this experience surely stunned him most deeply.

After all, Hitler had given his most loyal follower Himmler the ultimate token of confidence by entrusting him with the execution of the Final Solution of the European Jewish question. "The Führer has laid upon my shoulders the execution of this very difficult order. Moreover no one can relieve me of this responsibility."[6] Such was the stoic pronouncement of the RFSS in a single-copy top secret paper dated 28 July 1942 and addressed to his Chief of the SS Main Office, Gottlob Berger. And had not the obedient soldier Himmler furnished this singular proof of fidelity to his Führer by executing the orders "thoroughly and meticulously," even if reluctantly so? And now this humiliating offer to capitulate, from the once most faithful of faithfuls! Such thoughts may have raced through Hitler's tortured mind when he received the news of Himmler's negotiations. The end was obviously at hand.

5. Hugh Trevor-Roper, *The Last Days of Hitler* (London, 1972).
6. RFSS to Gottlob Berger, geheime Reichssache, one copy, 28 July 1942, RG 238, No. 626, U.S. National Archives.

23   The End of an Obsession

On the night of 28 to 29 April, after Hitler had finally granted his faithful mistress, Eva Braun, her long-cherished wish for marriage, he called in his secretary to dictate his personal and political testament, to be typed in three copies.

This testament is the last venomous word of the demagogic orator, the obsessed zealot, the battling, and now fallen, prophet. Beyond the collapse of the Third Reich, Hitler sought once again to bind the German nation to an eternal, wretched hatred for the Jews: "Centuries may lapse, but from the ruins of our cities and monuments will rise anew the hatred for that people to whom we owe all this, they who are ultimately responsible: international Jewry and its acolytes!"[1]

What, after all, had Hitler announced before members of the press on 10 November 1938? "Circumstances have forced me to talk for decades practically only of peace. . . . This constraint was the reason why I only talked peace over the years. Then it became necessary to realign

---

1. Adolf Hitler, "Mein politisches Testament," p. 2. Johannmeier original in Imperial War Museum, London; photocopy in author's possession (see plates). (Major Willi Johannmeier, Wehrmacht adjutant under General Wilhelm Burgdorf in the Führer bunker, left the bunker on 29 April with a copy of Hitler's political testament that was addressed to Field Marshal Ferdinand Schörner and never reached its destination.)

gradually the psychological bearings of the German people and to make it slowly clear to them that there are things which must be accomplished by means of violence if they cannot be accomplished by peaceful means."[2] Hitler's meaning was clearer still on 25 January 1939, when he addressed the officer training class of 1938: "Only the most recent periods have managed to show a dichotomy, so to speak, between war and politics; of course, such irreconcilability could not objectively and actually exist. . . . During the great periods that shape history, that is, in the formation of the state, politics is in effect the art of the possible; which is to say, attaining an objective by using every conceivable means: persuasion, obligation, intelligence, determination, kindness, shrewdness, even brutality—that is, even the sword, when other means fail."[3]

He had not left "a shred of doubt," Hitler resumed in his political testament some six years later, that "the real culprit in this murderous contest," Judaism, would be "called to account." "Further, I have made it quite clear that this time, . . . the real culprit must expiate his guilt, though by more humane means."[4]

The precise mechanics involved in the implementation of the "more humane means"—read: Zyklon B—as described by a competent and reliable source, are still little known to the public. "The can opener was placed on the lid of the canister [of Zyklon B] and forcefully struck with a hammer weighing from two to five pounds. Then the canis-

---

2. C 1136 Deutsches Rundfunkarchiv 1'28". This speech by Hitler was known only to the heads of the party and the representatives of the German press. The Reichsrundfunkgesellschaft was commissioned to make a record of the Führer's address. This circumstance made possible the preservation of this important recording for posterity.
3. C 1386 Deutsches Rundfunkarchiv 0'40".
4. Hitler, "Testament," p. 3.

ter was open."[5] "In each of these gassing areas [of the crematoria 1 and 2 in Birkenau] were two ducts: in each duct, four iron pipes ran from the floor to the roof. These were encased with steel mesh wire and inside there was a tin canister with a low rim. Attached to this tin was a wire by which it could be pulled up to the roof. Each of the ducts was covered over with an iron lid on the roof. When the lids were lifted, one could pull up the tin canister and shake the gas crystals into it. Then the canister was lowered, and the lid closed."[6]

Hitler's self-justifying remarks about the expiation of Jewish guilt through "more humane means" wore this face in sordid practice, stripped of their incidental components of opportunism, servility, weakness, and petty-bourgeois obsequiousness of a following whose idealism he abused. Shortly before 4:00 A.M. on 29 April 1945, Hitler dictated the final sentence of his political testament: "Above all, I obligate the leaders of the nation and their following to a strict observance of the racial laws, and to a merciless resistance to the poisoners of all peoples, international Jewry."

As he had done earlier in the pages of *Mein Kampf*, Hitler again attributed to the Jews "a unificatory devil-function,"[7] to justify this hatred.

Adolf Hitler's Final Solution ideology represented in stark reality a cult of the irrational bordering on lunacy yet advanced under the guise of ice-cold reason, a cult whose founder saw himself as the benefactor and savior of his Greater German Reich.

Now that the huge surge of power had ebbed away and the great gamble had failed, the only remaining course

5. Prisoner Josef Erber to author, 2 September 1981.
6. Prisoner Josef Erber to author, 14 September 1981. Cf. pp. 173, n. 6 and 174, n. 7.
7. Kenneth Burke, *Die Rhetorik in Hitlers "Mein Kampf" und andere Essays zur Strategie der Überredung* (Frankfurt, 1967), 12.

for Hitler, given his painful realization of all that had happened, was suicide. On 30 April 1945, between 2:00 and 3:00 P.M., Adolf Hitler, the most notorious anti-Semite of all time, put his Walther pistol against his right temple, bit into a cyanide capsule, and pulled the trigger.

Epilogue

What lesson does this account clearly have to offer us? The German writer Erich Kästner already anticipated it in 1932:

> You love hatred and want to measure the world against it.
> You throw food to the beast in man,
> That it may grow, the beast deep within you!
> Let the beast in man devour man.[1]

"The beast," however, which claimed over 39 million human lives in the last war—30 million on the side of the Allies and 9.26 million on the side of the Third Reich and its allies—this beast inhabits us all!

1. Erich Kästner, "Marschliedchen," from *Gesang zwischen den Stühlen* (Zurich, 1932).

Jewish Casualties Due to the Final Solution

German Reich (boundaries of 1938)	130,000
Austria	58,000
Belgium	26,000
Bulgaria	7,000
Czechoslovakia (boundaries of 1938)	245,000
France	64,000
Greece	58,000
Hungary and Carpatho-Ukraine	300,000
Italy	8,000
Latvia, Lithuania, Estonia	200,000
Luxembourg	3,000
Netherlands	101,800
Norway	677
Poland (boundaries of 1939)	2,700,000
Romania (boundaries prior to 1940)	220,000
USSR (boundaries prior to 1939)	800,000
Yugoslavia	54,000
	4,975,477 *

* It is impossible to establish a definitive, absolutely accurate total of victims. One can only say with certainty that the figure reaches the five million mark.

Select Bibliography

Adler, H. G. *Der verwaltete Mensch: Studien zur Deportation der Juden aus Deutschland.* Tübingen, 1974.

Arndt, Ino, and Wolfgang Scheffler. "Massenmord an Juden in NS-Vernichtungslagern." *Vierteljahrshefte für Zeitgeschichte* 24 (1976):112-60.

Below, Nicolaus von. *Hitlers Adjutant.* Mainz, 1980.

Besgen, Achim. *Der stille Befehl.* Munich, 1960.

Best, Werner. *Die deutsche Polizei.* Darmstadt, 1941.

_____. "Betr. Adolf Hitler." Unpublished; written in Copenhagen, 1949.

Binder, Gerhart. *Geschichte im Zeitalter der Weltkriege.* 2 vols. Stuttgart, 1977.

Binion, Rudolph. *Hitler among the Germans.* New York, 1976.

Bräutigam, Otto. *So hat es sich zugetragen: Ein Leben als Soldat und Diplomat.* Würzburg, 1968.

Broszat, Martin. *Studie zur Geschichte der Konzentrationslager.* Stuttgart, 1970.

Buchbender, Ortwin. *Das Tönende Erz: Deutsche Propaganda gegen die Rote Armee im zweiten Weltkrieg.* Stuttgart, 1978.

Buchheim, Hans, Martin Broszat, H.-A. Jacobsen, and Helmut Krausnick. *Anatomie des SS-Staates.* New ed. 2 vols. Munich, 1979. Trans. Richard Barry, Marian Jackson, and Dorothy Long as *Anatomy of the SS State.* London and New York, 1968.

Cohn, Norman. *Warrant for Genocide: The Myth of Jewish World-Conspiracy and the Protocols of the Elders of Zion.* New York, 1967.

Datner, Szymon. *Biuletyn Glownej Komisja Badania Zbrodni Hitlerowskich w. Polsce.* Vol. 13. War Crimes Commission, Polish Ministry of Justice. Warsaw, 1960.

Dawidowicz, Lucy S. *The War Against the Jews: 1933–1945.* New York, 1975. Reprint. London, 1977.

Diederich, Reiner, Richard Grübling, and Max Bartholl. *Die rote Gefahr.* Berlin, 1976.

Eckart, Dietrich. *Der Bolschewismus von Moses bis Lenin: Zwiegespräch zwischen Adolf Hitler und mir.* Munich, 1924.

Eichmann, Adolf. *Eichmann Interrogated: Transcripts from the Archives of the Israeli Police.* Ed. Jochen von Lang. New York, 1983.

Eichmann Trial. Uncorrected and unpublished notes, Minutes of Session 42. 16 May 1961. Israel State Archives, Jerusalem.

Euthanasia Trial. Vorberg Prosecution. Allers, Js 20/61 and 1968. Generalstaatsanwalt Frankfurt am Main.

Fest, Joachim. *Hitler.* Frankfurt am Main, 1973.

Fleming, Gerald. "Die Herkunft des Bernadotte-Briefs an Himmler vom 10. März 1945." In Walter Schellenberg, *Aufzeichnungen.* Munich, 1979.

Friedländer, Saul. *Kurt Gerstein: The Ambiguity of Good.* New York, 1969.

Gersdorff, Rudolph-Christoph von. *Soldat im Untergang.* Berlin, 1977.

Goebbels, Josef. *Tagebücher aus den Jahren 1941–1943.* Zurich, 1945.

Görlitz, Walter. *Generalfeldmarschall Keitel: Verbrecher oder Offizier.* Göttingen, 1961.

Gordon, Sarah. *Hitler, Germans, and the Jewish Question.* Princeton, 1984.

Haffner, Sebastian. *Anmerkungen zu Hitler.* Munich, 1978.

Halder, Franz. *Kriegstagebuch 1939–1942.* Ed. Hans-Adolf Jacobsen. 3 vols. Stuttgart, 1962–1964.

Hammerstein, Kunrat von. *Spähtrupp.* Stuttgart, 1963.

Heiber, Helmut, ed. *Reichsführer . . . Briefe an und von Himmler.* Stuttgart, 1968.

Heydecker, J. J., and Johannes Leeb. *Der Nürnberger Prozess.* Cologne, 1979.

Hilberg, Raul. *The Destruction of the European Jews.* Chicago, 1967.

———. *Documents of Destruction.* London, 1972.

Hillgruber, Andreas. *Die "Endlösung" und das deutsche Ostimperium als Kernstück des rassenideologischen Programms des Nationalsozialismus.* Munich, 1972.

Hitler, Adolf. *Adolf Hitler, Monologe im Führerhauptquartier: 1941 – 1944.* Ed. Werner Jochmann. Hamburg, 1980.

———. *Mein Kampf.* 3d ed. Munich, 1943. Trans. Ralph Manheim as *Mein Kampf.* London, 1974.

———. *Hitlers Zweites Buch: Ein Dokument aus dem Jahr 1928.* Ed. Gerhard L. Weinberg. Stuttgart, 1961.

Hoffmann, Peter. *Widerstand gegen Hitler.* Munich, 1979.

Höhne, Heinz. *Der Orden unter dem Totenkopf.* 2d ed. Munich, 1976. Trans. Richard Barry as *The Order of the Death's Head.* New York, 1969.

Höss, Rudolf. Typescript Report from Rudolf Höss. Archives of the Polish Ministry of Justice, Warsaw.

Irving, David. *Hitler's War.* London and New York, 1977.

Jäckel, Eberhard. *Hitlers Weltanschauung.* 2d ed. Stuttgart, 1981.

Joffroy, Pierre. *Eichmann par Eichmann.* Paris, 1970.

Kaufmann, Max. *Die Vernichtung der Juden Lettlands.* Munich, 1947.

Keitel, Wilhelm. "Aufzeichnungen." Archive of Major in the General Staff Ernst-Wilhelm Keitel (retd.).

Kersten, Felix. *Totenkopf und Treue: Himmler ohne Uniform.* Hamburg, 1952.

Kogon, Eugen. *Der SS-Staat.* Munich, 1946.

Krausnick, Helmut, et al. *Anatomy of the SS State.* See Buchheim.

Krausnick, Helmut, and Hans-Heinrich Wilhelm. *Die Truppe des Weltanschauungskrieges.* Stuttgart, 1981.

Kubizek, August. *Adolf Hitler, mein Jugendfreund.* Graz, 1975.

Langer, Walter. *The Mind of Adolf Hitler: the Secret Wartime Report.* New York, 1972.

Laqueur, Walter. *Le Terrifiant Secret.* Paris, 1981.

———. *Weimar.* London, 1974.

Leeb, Wilhelm Ritter von. *Tagebuchaufzeichnungen und Lagebeurteilungen aus zwei Weltkriegen.* Stuttgart, 1976.

Löwenstein, Karl. "Minsk: im Lager der Deutschen Juden." Supplement to the weekly newspaper *Das Parlament,* 7 November 1956.

Lübbe, Hermann. *Spengler heute.* Munich, 1980.

Lukacs, John. *Der letzte europäische Krieg: 1939 –1941.* Stuttgart, 1980.

Madajczyk, Czeslaw. *Die deutsche Besatzungspolitik in Polen: 1939 – 1945.* Wiesbaden, 1967.

Maser, Werner. *Die Frühgeschichte der NSDAP*. Frankfurt, 1965.

Mollo, Andrew. *A Pictorial History of the SS*. London, 1980.

Mommsen, Hans. *Hitlers Stellung im nationalsozialistischen Herrschaftssystem*. Stuttgart, 1981.

Morse, Arthur D. *While Six Million Died*. New York, 1967.

Müller, Filip. *Sonderbehandlung*. Munich, 1979.

Nellessen, Bernd. *Der Prozess von Jerusalem*. Düsseldorf, 1964.

Oppitz, Ulrich-Dieter. *Strafverfahren und Strafvollstreckung bei NS-Gewaltverbrechen*. Ulm, 1979.

Pilichowski, Czeslaw. *No Time-Limit for These Crimes*. Warsaw, 1980.

Poliakov, Léon, and Josef Wulf. *Das Dritte Reich und die Juden*. Berlin, 1956.

Reitlinger, Gerald. *The Final Solution*. 3d ed. London, 1971.

Riga Trial. Sentence against Jahnke. (50) 9/72. 23 February 1973. Staatsanwaltschaft Hamburg.

Ringelblum, Emanuel. *Notes from the Warsaw Ghetto*. New York, 1958.

_____. *Polish-Jewish Relations during the Second World War*. Jerusalem, 1974.

Rückerl, Adalbert. *NS-Vernichtungslager*. Munich, 1977.

Scheffler, Wolfgang. "Zur Entstehungsgeschichte der Endlösung." Supplement to the weekly newspaper *Das Parlament*, 30 October 1982.

Schellenberg, Walter. Report on the Case of Walter Schellenberg. Unpublished. U.S. National Archives, Washington, D.C. (declassified 1980), and Cabinet Office, Historical Section, London.

Schneider, Gertrude. *Journey into Terror*. New York, 1979.

Schulze-Kossens, Richard. *Die Junkerschulen*. Osnabrück, 1982.

Semler, Rudolf. *Saadan var Goebbels*. Ed. Helge Knudsen. Copenhagen, 1947.

Sereny, Gitta. *Into that Darkness*. London, 1974.

Seubert, Franz, ed. *Die Nachhut*. (Internal information organ for former members of the German Intelligence Service only.) 18 issues. Munich, 1967–1975.

Speer, Albert. *Der Sklavenstaat*. Stuttgart, 1981.

Stern, Fritz. *The Politics of Cultural Despair*. London, 1974.

Streit, Christian. *Keine Kameraden: Die Wehrmacht und die sowjetischen Kriegsgefangenen, 1941–1945*. Stuttgart, 1978.

Sydnor, Charles W. *Soldiers of Destruction*. Princeton, 1977.

Szasz, Thomas S. *Die Fabrikation des Wahnsinns*. Olten, 1974.

Thies, Jochen. *Architekt der Weltherrschaft: "Endziele" Hitlers*. Düsseldorf, 1976.

Waite, Robert. *The Psychopathic God, Adolf Hitler*. New York, 1977.

Wiedemann, Fritz. *Der Mann der Feldherr werden wollte*. Göttingen, 1964.

Wolff, Jeanette. *Mit Bibel und Bebel*. Bonn, 1980.

Wolff, Karl. Criminal Proceedings. 10 Js 39/60. 17 May 1963. Landgericht Munich.

Acknowledgments

I wish to thank all the foundations that have made this undertaking possible: the British Academy, the Deutsche Forschungsgemeinschaft, the Memorial Foundation for Jewish Culture, the Simon-Wiesenthal Foundation, and the Research Committee of the University of Surrey.

I would like to give special thanks to the following institutions and individuals that have repeatedly provided clarifying information during my research of nearly four years: Archivoberrat Dr. Josef Henke, of the Bundesarchiv, Koblenz; Mr. Loos, of the Bundesarchiv-Militärarchiv, Freiburg; Oberst Dr. H. Wieseotte and Wissenschaftlicher Oberrat Dr. Georg Meyer, of the Militärgeschichtlicher Forschungsamt, Freiburg; Mr. W. Finkelnburg, of the Deutsche Dienststelle, Berlin; and Chief Prosecutor and the Deputy Chief Prosecutor of the Office of the District Attorney for the Oberlandesgericht Frankfurt; the Deputy Chief Prosecutor of the Office of the District Attorney for the Bavarian Oberste Landesgericht; the Chief Prosecutor of the Office of the District Attorney for the Landgericht Hamburg; the former Director of the Kulturcller Tonbanddienst Inter Nationes in Bonn–Bad Godesberg, Karl-August Adrian; Dr. Maria Keipert, of the Political Archives of the Foreign Office; Dr. Anton Hoch and Dr. Hermann Weiss, of the Institut für Zeitgeschichte; Dr. Adalbert Rückerl, the First

Deputy Chief Prosecutor of the Zentrale Stelle für Landes-justizverwaltungen; Dr. Harry Slapnicka, of the Oberöster-reichisches Landesarchiv, Linz; Dr. Rudolf Heilinger, of the Österreichische Nationalbibliothek; Prof. Othmar Pickl, of the Historisches Institut of the University of Graz; Mr. Simon Wiesenthal, of the Dokumentationszentrum, Vienna; Dr. O. Gauye, of the Schweizer Bundesarchiv; Mr. Vibert and Dr. Jacques Moreillon, of the archives of the Comité International de la Croix-Rouge, Geneva; Dr. Janos Varga, of the Hungarian National Archives; Mr. Nikolaijs Rizous, of the Historical State Archives of Latvian SSR, Riga; Dr. Wilhelm Carlgren, of the Archives of the Swedish Foreign Office; Mr. Sven Lundkvist, of the Swedish National Archives; Mr. Helge Paulsen, of the Norwegian National Archives; Mrs. Birgit Logstrup, of the Danish National Archives; Prof. Louis de Jong, of the Rijksinstituut voor Oorlogsdocumentatie; Mr. J. Vanwelkenhuyzen, of the Centre de Recherches et d'Etudes Historiques de la Seconde Guerre Mondiale; General Guinard and General Porret, of the Historical Archives of the French Ministry of Defense; Mrs. Claudine Cohen-Naar, of the Centre de Documentation Juive Contemporaine; Dr. N. Cox, of the Public Record Office, Kew; Mr. J. G. Morgan-Owen, Judge Advocate General; the Departmental Records Officer (Review) for the Ministry of Defence, London; Mr. R. R. A. Wheatley, of the Library and Records Department Foreign and Common-wealth Office, and his archivist, Mr. N. Hiscock; Mr. F. H. Dean, Judge Advocate General; Mr. R. Wolfe, Chief of the Modern Military Branch, Military Archives Division, U.S. National Archives, and the archivists T. P. Mulligan and D. E. Spencer; Mr. D. P. Simon, Director of the Berlin Document Center; Dr. P. A. Alsberg, of the Israel State Archives; Mgr. K. Smolen, of the Państwowe Muzeum, Oswiecim; Prof. Czeslaw Pilichowski, of the Archives of the Polish Ministry of Justice; Prof. Helmut Krausnick; Prof. Eberhard Jäckel; Prof. Gerhart Binder; Dr. Ortwin Buchbender; Prof. Peter Hoffmann; Prof. Charles Sydnor; Mr. Joachim Fest; Mr. Richard Schulze-Kossens; Dr. Werner Best; Mr. Werner Grothmann; Mr. Jochen v. Lang; Dr. Robert Kempner; Colonel Otto Wagner (retd.); Lt. Colonel Franz Seubert (retd.); Mr. W. A. Less; Dr. Otto Bräutigam; Major in the General Staff E. W. Keitel (retd.); Dr. Ulrich Oppitz; Mr. Fritz Tobias; Mr. Lennart Westberg; Prof. Gertrude Schneider; Prof. Janis Dzintars; Dr. P. Züger; Prof. Hugh Trevor-Roper; Prof. Andreas Hillgruber; Prof. Hans Mommsen; Mr. Werner Isensee; Prof. Joseph Parnas; Dr. Hans Holzamer; Mrs. Erika-Ilse Schulz-Du Bois; Major General Erich Abberger (retd.).

I also gratefully remember the assistance of Albert Speer and Rudolph-Christoph Freiherr von Gersdorff.

Index

Designer: Steve Renick
Compositor: Innovative Media Inc.
Text: VIP Palatino
Display: Optima Medium
Printer: Vail-Ballou Press
Binder: Vail-Ballou Press